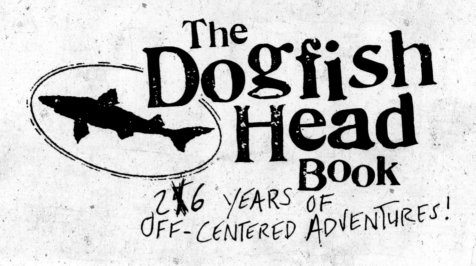

The Dogfish Head Book

2~~5~~6 YEARS OF OFF-CENTERED ADVENTURES!

SAM CALAGIONE
MARIAH CALAGIONE
ANDREW C. GREELEY

WILEY

Published by John Wiley & Sons, Inc., Hoboken, New Jersey.

Published simultaneously in Canada.

Library of Congress Cataloging-in-Publication Data is Available:
ISBN 9781119649571 (Hardcover)
ISBN 9781119649649 (ePDF)
ISBN 9781119799436 (ePub)
ISBN 9781119799511 (print replica)

Cover image and design: Dogfish Head Craft Brewery
Interior design: Tara Arjona, Jaimie Muehlhausen
Interior photos: Dogfish Head Craft Brewery

SKY10028549_090921

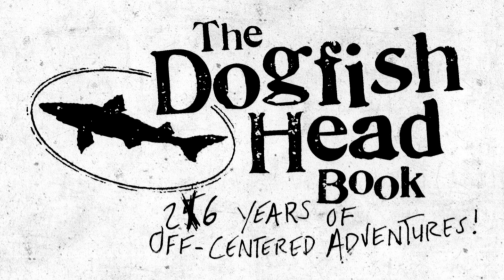

The Dogfish Head Book

26 YEARS OF OFF-CENTERED ADVENTURES!

"This book is dedicated to you."

To all the loyal fans, OGs, and recently converted. All the coworkers, past, present, and future contributing to our off-centered journey. The ones who come out to support and work the events, who truly experience the brand in all its depths, who travel to the brewery, brewpub, and the Inn, who buy a beer, not just because of the flavor, but because Dogfish Head is bigger than beer. Without YOU, we wouldn't have an audience or material for a book like this. Together we are all a thriving tribe of disruptors, misfits, and romantics.

Together we are HEAVY.

Thank you ALL.

Like perfecting a new beer, this book took time. An extra year, in fact. What started as 25 years of photos, stories, and memories became 26 years of off-centered adventures. There was so much good stuff to choose from, we had to change the title of the book to fit it all!

Thanks for joining us on the first 26, and cheers to the next 26.

-Sam, Mariah, and Andrew

Contents

Contents cont.

Thanks

Mariah, Andrew, and Sam would like to share a special shout-out of eternal thanks to Dogfish Creative Director Paul Thens, who shepherded the look, layout, art, color, and other aesthetic wonders woven into all of these pages. At every step of the way, Paul went above and beyond the call of duty …
and THENS some.

Preface

When we decided to start Dogfish Head over 26 years ago, we never would have imagined the journey that decision would take us on. We were considered heretics and weirdos for screwing with the century-long tradition of making beer with just water, yeast, hops, and barley. We were one of the first modern breweries in the world to brew beers with exotic culinary ingredients. Those early efforts played a meaningful part in establishing today's craft beer marketplace, which is much more exotic and intensely flavorful. We're proud that Dogfish Head has staked our little claim and made a true and enduring impact on the world of adventurous beers.

As we've grown, we've become more experimental, more creative, and we've embraced more risk on the production and research and development (R&D) side than when we were smaller. Of course, we do still—to some limited degree—face a perception issue, where maybe for those at the epicenter of the beer community—the super-hard-core, dyed-in-the-wool beer geeks, as we call ourselves—Dogfish itself as a brewery isn't a new thing. There are always new, exciting little breweries, and everyone always wants to talk about what's new. But what has kept our company very relevant over the years is the consistency with which we pushed the boundaries of not just what beer can be, but what a brand can be.

We recognize that we aren't brewing for the status quo—that the average beer drinker will probably never try our beers, even if we were to have a significant five or ten percent market share in the United States. We are "off-centered," meaning that we're not going to appeal to the majority. That said, we've been able to carve out a niche, growing by catering to a small but increasing and engaged segment of the beer drinking population—those who want more flavor, more diversity, more complexity, and more food compatibility in their beer. Those are the folks our brand has grown up with; and there are a lot more of them today than there were when we were the smallest craft brewery in the country.

Passion, dedication, and commitment are the foundation of Dogfish Head. Our passion for what we do, our determination and dedication to our brand, has given us an opportunity to make a mark in the craft beer world and to create and serve a community of like-minded people like no other. To see where independent craft beer is today with 26 years in our rear-view mirror is staggering to say the least, and to know that we are a major force in the revolution keeps us motivated every day to keep making an impact as we look toward the next 26 years.

In that time, we have shared our stories and what we have learned along the way in earlier books, including *Brewing Up a Business* and *Off-Centered Leadership*.

But this book is a bit different.

This book chronicles the complete 25-year history of Dogfish Head beer. It highlights and celebrates the different beers and brewing innovations we've created over the past 25 years. It includes insider stories from coworkers who have helped us create the brand we are today. It includes never-before-seen photos, documents, and details from the history of Dogfish Head. The strength of our company has always been driven by the people who are a part of it and the people in the community that our brand serves. This book is for them. This book is for you. Thank you for the support you've given Dogfish Head over the years. Thank you for buying our beers, spirits, and cocktails. Thank you for trying new brews. Thank you for bringing our beers to your events. Thank you for visiting our brewpub, our restaurant, and our Inn. But most of all, thank you for being some of the most loyal fans in the world.

—Sam

Twenty-six years. It feels like forever, and at the same time, it feels like a blip in time.

If you are at all familiar with Dogfish Head, you know we love a good story! Whether it's telling you how we came up with the idea for a new beer, a new brewing process invention, or the most recent piece of art created for one of our hospitality properties, you can bet there's a backstory. In 26 years, we have lots of backstories to share with you. That's what this book is: a collection of stories, snippets, photos, thoughts, and other off-centered goodness that fits on a page.

Sam often calls himself Dogfish Head's analog storyteller and often refers to me as our digital storyteller. He's that extroverted storyteller in front of the audience or at the event. I've been the introverted storyteller, behind the screen and the camera lens. It works! We have different approaches, but the end result is the same—we both get the chance to connect with Dogfish drinkers, listen to them, answer their questions, watch them interact with our beers, ask them questions, and learn from them.

For this project, I had the opportunity to dig through boxes of photos, clippings, and memorabilia. I scrolled through thousands (more likely tens of thousands) of photos and went back in time via our social media feeds. I relived so many moments of beer creation (that first time we brewed Tweason'ale, our strawberry gluten-free beer) and so many contraptions (do you remember that sweet Randall Jr. "infomercial"?), but the most enjoyable rabbit holes I dove into drew me in with familiar faces. Long-lost regulars, long-time coworkers, industry friends, current guests, and those I still get to work with every day.

As you'll see in this book of stories, snippets, photos, and thoughts, Dogfish Head is first and foremost a collection of off-centered people who make off-centered beer. If you've ever enjoyed one of our beers, visited our brewpub, toured the brewery, or stayed at the Inn, you are part of the story.

Thank you for being on this off-centered journey with us. Now, grab a beer and settle in; we have stories to share. Cheers!

—Mariah

Growing up on Lookout Mountain in the foothills above Golden, Colorado, had its benefits, and having access to great craft beer was one of many. It was a special place indeed. The time outside was vital to me as a person. I grew up exploring my backyard of Clear Creek Canyon with my two older brothers, Ted and Bob, and younger sister Penny. With friends, we would snag what micro (or macro) beers we could from our parents' fridges and ride down the hill on single-track trails to sneak into whatever show might be going on at Red Rocks Amphitheatre.

The activity and time spent with friends and loved ones took precedence over anything else. The beers were just fringe benefits. We were learning quickly what was really important in life but we didn't know it at the time. If we were going skiing or snowboarding, we would go where the lift ended ... and then keep going. There were always better tracks the harder we had to work for them. If we were riding our bikes bombing down Apex Trail to Golden, we'd wear a helmet, but whoever used their brakes the most was having the least amount of fun. Without a little blood spilled, we were not doing it right. If we were rock climbing to the top of North Table Mountain or bouldering above the town of Morrison, we knew the best way to get down to the car at the end of the day was to race.

As I moved on to college in Chestertown, Maryland, and fell in love with Chesapeake Bay and the Delmarva Peninsula, I found the same tribe of people living at the same pace. Whether it be on the lacrosse field, in the classroom (yes, it is cool to be smart), or in a goose blind, the name of the game was to push the envelope and always drive it until it broke. At least that is what I did with the '87 VW Fox I shared with my big brother. It was like Henry Rollins was speaking to us directly when he yelled at the top of his lungs, "GET SOME! GET SOME! GET SOME! GET SOME! GO AGAIN!" All these lessons translated to life.

The first time I had Dogfish Head, in the early 2000s, I was pretty sure it was not going to live up to my expectations. There was no beer out East that was going to stand up to what I had been drinking my whole life in Colorado. I was WRONG. I went to Dogfish Head in Rehoboth Beach and I knew the moment I walked through the front door that I had once again found my tribe of people. Yes, the beer was awesome, and the food was killer, but it was the vibe—the feeling I got walking into the place for the first time—that struck me to the core. I have heard coworkers describe Dogfish Head as home, but where does that come from? It was surely what I felt that day and the main reason I kept coming back, and what led to me filling my fridge with Shelter, 60, IBA, and any other Dogfish I could get my hands on. The same feeling pushed me to apply for jobs at Dogfish Head in 2010, 2011, and 2012. I never got a callback until the third try, but I knew if I got my foot in the door it was all I needed. What was it that was pulling me in so hard? I came to realize it very quickly once I got my time card and started clocking in as a seasonal tour guide for the summer.

That feeling I speak of came from the people of Dogfish Head and still does today. With the ever-changing landscape of beer and there being more than 8,000 breweries in the U.S. today, what sets one apart from the other? For us, it is the people. Plain and simple. The people who show up to work and populate Dogfish Head spaces create, cultivate, and feed that elusive feeling that keeps us all coming back for more. This culture started with Sam and Mariah in '95. It is a spirit of fellowship, family, competition, laughter, lifelong learning, inclusivity, relationships, community, and a relentless pursuit of creation and evolution. All of the same aspects of life that fed my soul growing up in Colorado I found again on the Delmarva Peninsula. The Dogfish Head community is truly inspiring. In speaking with coworkers, some still with us and others who have moved on, and listening to their stories, it is clear that the relationships that have been cultivated at Dogfish Head will surely stand the test of time. I know mine will. When I was asked by Sam and Mariah to be part of this book project, I could not have been more honored. As we went through the process, it became clearer and clearer that there are so many people who have been inspired by Dogfish Head: fans and coworkers alike. There is no possible way to encapsulate it all in one book. This book is really the next installment in the journey of Dogfish Head and all our coworkers: past, present, and future. While we take some time to look back on the past 26 years and all we have accomplished together, and we look to the future and ask ourselves what we will do next, let us not forget our true moment of power: the present. This is where we have always thrived at Dogfish Head. I think of Robert Hastings's essay "The Station," where he says, "Life must be lived as we go along." There is no end point for us at Dogfish Head and no destination. I believe the best by-product of our products will always be the relationships and memories created surrounding what we make and the communities built because of them.

"In a world that always wants to label, we march to the beat of a different drum. Disrupting the status quo and subverting the dominant paradigm brings light into our eyes and a fire into our bellies."

There are so many amazing people who are a part of Dogfish Head and the accomplishments are too vast to ever list. It reminds me of something B. H. Liddell Hart, a British soldier and military strategist, said: "In war, the chief incalculable is the human will." This is a concept I often spoke to in my former life as an English teacher and a coach for over 15 years. As individuals, when we believe in ourselves, we are more capable than we can possibly imagine. If we take our individual capabilities and combine them with others, we can do absolutely anything. At Dogfish Head, we are motivated when people say we "can't" do something or, "that is not possible." This human will to push the boundaries started with Sam and Mariah and continues to grow today. We know we can do anything we put our minds to. You just need to drink a 60 Minute to tap into it. Well, maybe the 60 is not required, but anything is possible if you believe it. This is part of our "off-centered" way (Go ahead and have that 60!).

For years, people have always wanted to define "off-centered." This book will not answer that question. Alan Watts once said, "Trying to define yourself is like trying to bite your own teeth." One of the greatest aspects of Dogfish Head and who we are is that we cannot be defined. In a world that always wants to label, we march to the beat of a different drum. Disrupting the status quo and subverting the dominant paradigm brings light into our eyes and a fire into our bellies. This book, in many ways, reveals the spirit of "off-centered" but it will never define it.

What inspired me about life growing up in the mountains is the same thing that inspires me today in Costal Delaware and at Dogfish Head. Taking risks always brings us into the present and when we are present, we are most alive and in touch with our true selves. I am deeply grateful Sam and Mariah took a risk on me.

Now I invite you to go digging into that cellar of yours and pull out that 120 you have been sitting on for a few years now and crack it open, or mix up a Milton Mule, and start making your way through the stories contained here. I thank you for being part of this exploration of goodness, and—do not stop supporting Independent craft beer! Come on, here we go ...

—Andrew

The City Lights Library at the Dogfish Inn

Throughout the text of this book you will see quotes selected by our coworkers from our City Lights Library, located in the cottage at the Dogfish Inn. This library was curated by the staff of the famed City Lights bookstore in San Francisco, and Lawrence Ferlinghetti was in on the process. Guests have open access to this library when they stay with us and can also purchase any of the books.

In its previous life, Dogfish Inn was called the Vesuvio Motel. The landmark bar next to City Lights bookstore—The Vesuvio Café—is where everyone from Jack Kerouac to Dylan Thomas to Allen Ginsberg has gathered over poetry, beers, benevolence, and brotherhood. This is the same café Mike Myers delivered his poetry readings at in *So I Married an Ax Murderer*. The co-existence of these bi-coastal Vesuvios is not a coincidence, in our minds. City Lights and Dogfish Head are both fiercely independent and focused on celebrating the creativity of artistic production. So, we asked our friends at City Lights to curate the library of 50 American literature classics, especially for the Dogfish Inn.

In the fall of 2019, the University of Delaware opened the "Beat Visions and the Counterculture" exhibit, which Dogfish Head supported. Sam Calagione and Andrew Greeley, both recovering English majors, traveled with coworker Mark Carter to get a behind-the-scenes look at the Special Collections exhibition and to hold much of the original work produced from this movement, including a dime bag with some of Ginsberg's beard hair in it.

At the Dogfish Inn, you will not find a Bible in the desk drawer. In our first floor rooms, you will find a copy of *Howl* by Allen Ginsberg and on the second floor you will find *A Coney Island of the Mind* by Lawrence Ferlinghetti. Thank you all for supporting indie art in all its forms.

Because of you, we are us.
And together, we are heavy.

Dogfish Head

Chapter 1

Brewing Up...a Love of Beer

It was March, 1988. My dad backed his red pickup truck beneath the second-story window of my dormitory bedroom. My schoolmates in the next dorm room were orchestrating a grand send-off by blasting Frank Sinatra's "That's Life" out their windows as we threw green garbage bags filled with clothes, cassette tapes, and books into the back of the truck below.

I received this rousing tribute partly in acknowledgment of my proud Italian-American heritage, but mostly because I had just been kicked out of my college preparatory school a mere two months before graduation.

We drove home in silence. When we reached the driveway of our house, my dad said simply, "Sammy, sometimes you're a tough kid to love." I was so disappointed in myself at that moment. Yes, I was disappointed because I had let my father, my biggest supporter in the world, down to a cosmic degree. But I was mostly disappointed in myself because I had just lost the connection to the place where I had learned who I was and who I wanted to be—the place where, I would later realize, I decided I wanted to be an entrepreneur.

I figured out who I was and who I wanted to be while attending Northfield Mt. Hermon School (NMH)—the high school started by the world-renowned evangelist D. L. Moody—the school I never graduated from.

Not that I didn't deserve to be kicked out. The administrators there finally sealed my fate under the vague and all-encompassing "Accumulation of Offenses" category in the student handbook.

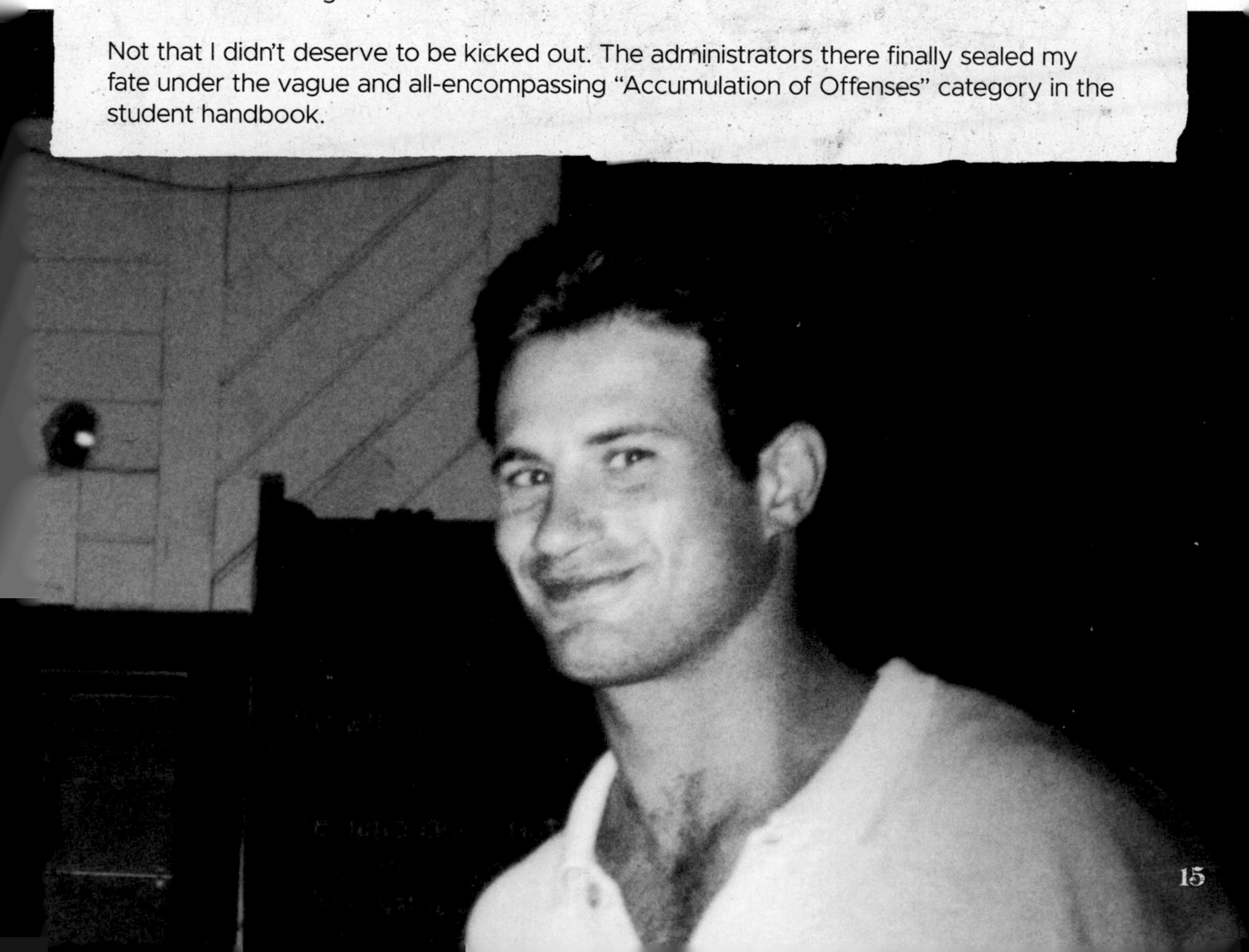

Looking back, I believe these offenses were indicative of the entrepreneurial fire I had burning within me.

I had a willingness to embrace risk. I had an innovative spirit. I even set a record for the earliest point in the school year when a student was placed on disciplinary probation.

I had grown up in the town next to the school, and I wanted to show my two best friends the beauty of my new school as well as the beauty of the girls at my new school. We snuck out of our houses, climbed into my parents' station wagon in the middle of the night, and headed to campus—just three sophisticated 16-year-olds, smoking cigars and listening to Journey. We approached the school in a covert fashion that we thought would surely allow us to elude campus security. Instead of using the road, we drove up the football field, through the quad, and straight into a motion-detecting light. Not into the shaft of light, mind you, but into the pole that was holding the light itself. It detected our motion. We were greeted by a dorm parent who soon invited campus security to the party, and the rest was history.

My next year marked the second phase of my delinquent entrepreneurial development in which I exhibited ambition and an ability to organize coworkers toward a common objective. Our objective at this juncture was not getting kicked out. In my junior year, I was not permitted to attend the prom. So another junior classmate and I designed a foolproof plan. We would act as chaperones for a bunch of senior friends who would be attending the prom. We decided to do this in style: A Winnebago was rented, beers were procured, bow ties were straightened. We headed off to the prom but never reached our destination, as much beer drinking, pool hopping, and roof surfing ensued. Though going down the highway at 60 miles per hour sitting Indian style on top of a Winnebago seemed like a good idea at the time, I can now see that it probably was not. The local authorities felt similarly, and we received a two-cruiser escort back to campus.

"You're not going to get out of this one."

"You're not going to get out of this one." I believe those were the actual words used by the teacher whom the authorities handed us over to. We were all separated into different rooms so as not to be able to corroborate each other's stories as we awaited our morning tribunal. The Winnebago was locked safely on campus, nearly overflowing with the various and sundry contraband. But this is where it turns into a story of uncommon valor and the creation of a united front committed to reaching a shared goal: beating the man. Walkie-talkies were employed, as were bicycles and door-opening coat hangers. We even used the sheets-tied-together-to-rappel-out-the-window motif celebrated in nearly every prison-break movie. The following morning we were called to meet outside the Winnebago. There was a short, self-congratulatory speech by the teacher that mostly revolved around our foolishness for actually thinking we could get away with it. The door swung open and revealed ... nothing but a very clean and contraband-free recreation vehicle. We were set free for lack of evidence. In the middle of the night we had successfully executed Project-Break-Back-In-and-Throw-It-All-Out. We had even made sure there was a vase of fresh-cut flowers on the dining table in the camper.

By senior year my entrepreneurial spirit knew no bounds. After the Winnebago incident, the powers that be decided to keep an eye on me. They said I could come back for my senior year but only on the grounds that I live on campus in a dormitory. They didn't realize that my friends had formed a juvenile delinquent all-star team by signing up to live in the same dorm. We had diverse talents but shared a common love of partying and rule breaking. This would be the setting of my first endeavor into the beer business. I would visit my parents on the weekends, borrow the car, and cruise liquor stores for sympathetic western Massachusetts libertarian hippies willing to buy me beer as I waited in the shadows. I would return to school with an inordinately heavy hockey bag and parse out the booty. There would always be an extra six-pack in it for me—the businessman. This proceeded throughout the year without a hitch. Yes, our beer-addled behavior sometimes raised suspicion—like when a faculty member opened the door to the recreation room only to find me and some buddies playing two-on-two Ping-Pong wearing nothing but tube socks and ski goggles. But my luck couldn't last, and I tempted fate. The businessman got caught and was put out of business.

How Sam Met Mariah

There are a number of reasons why my time at Northfield Mt. Hermon was so crucial to my development as a creative person. The most important is that it was the place where I met and began to date my future wife, Mariah. At that time, aside from reading and writing, being with Mariah was one of the few things I was good at. I actually met Mariah's mom, Rachel, first. She was friends with my favorite teacher, Bill Batty, and was at his house visiting his family for the weekend. Some friends and I were there that evening hanging out with Bill and his son John, who was a classmate of ours. Mariah's mom made brownies for us that I was sure were the best I had ever tasted. She told me her daughter had just started her first term at NMH, and I told her that if her daughter could cook anything like her mom I was

going to marry her someday. Within a couple of months, I was dating Mariah, and we've been together ever since. We began dating when we were all of 16 years old, so we've pretty much grown up together. Our personalities evolved to complement one another's strengths and weaknesses. We attended different colleges in different parts of the country but still worked hard to see each other every chance we got. So much time and distance apart is not easy on a relationship, but through it all I got my first taste of how, if you want something bad enough and are willing to do anything necessary to make it happen, you can make it happen. This lesson has served me well in love and in life. I sensed that the first time I met her at NMH, and even more so after I was kindly asked to leave the school.

In those first few weeks apart, our relationship became more difficult but also more rewarding as I saw she was willing to stand by me.

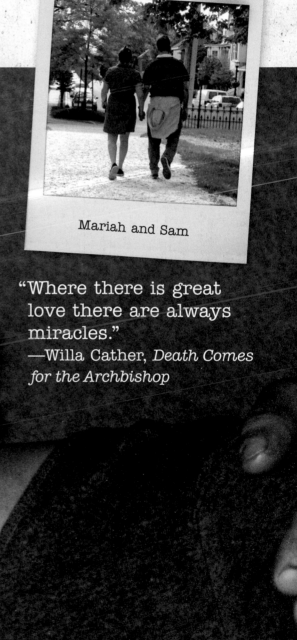

Mariah and Sam

"Where there is great love there are always miracles."
—Willa Cather, *Death Comes for the Archbishop*

How Mariah Met Sam

It was 1985, and my friend and I were high school freshmen at NMH, walking out of the dining hall and heading down the hill to our first afternoon class. We were most likely talking about who had been sitting with whom at lunch or what was happening on campus that coming weekend. I looked up and stopped listening. The cutest boy was coming up the hill toward the dining hall. He sort of reminded me of Jake from *Sixteen Candles* (swoon).

That was the first time I saw Sam.

The next semester Sam and I were assigned to work in the dining hall kitchen on the same shift. I was supershy and he was supergoofy. He made me laugh. The flirting commenced.

The next fall, we had art class together. Sam says it was pottery class, and usually makes a *Ghost* reference ... but I think it was a drawing class.

Regardless, it was during that semester that we finally became official.

1997 Mug Club prototypes

Sam and Mariah host a group at the Lewes Historical Society exhibit honoring 20 off-centered years of brewing in Delaware.

Learn from those who came before you

I learned a lot about the kind of person I wanted to be while at Northfield Mt. Hermon. In opening the Northfield and Mt. Hermon schools (the two combined in the 1970s), D. L. Moody successfully created a community that nurtured the heads, hands, and hearts of its members.

D. L. Moody's name is essentially synonymous with evangelism. An evangelist is someone who believes in something so strongly that he becomes consumed with a passion for convincing everyone around him to share in his belief. Isn't this pretty much the definition of an entrepreneur? Of somebody committed to bringing a vision to fruition even (or especially) when that vision does not reflect the consensus of the day? In his essay on self-reliance, Emerson wrote, "To believe in your own thought, to believe that what is true for you in your private heart is true for all men—that is genius. Speak your latent conviction and it shall be the universal sense; for always the inmost becomes the outmost, and our first thought is rendered back to us by the trumpets of the Last Judgments."

By the time I got to NMH there was no longer a course specifically on D. L. Moody and the history of the school, but a number of teachers incorporated that history into their lessons. In addition to what I learned about Moody while I was there, I have read books about him, and have read about him in other books. President Woodrow Wilson once described a memorable encounter he had in a barbershop:

While sitting on the chair I became aware that a personality entered the room. A man had come quietly upon the same errand as myself and sat in the chair next to me. Every word he uttered showed a personal and vital interest in the man who was serving him. I was aware that I had attended an evangelistic service because Mr. Moody was in the next chair. I purposely lingered in the room after he left and noted the singular effect his visit had upon the barbers in that shop. They talked in undertones. They did not know his name, but they knew that something elevated their thought. And I felt that I left that place as I should have left a place of worship.

Woodrow Wilson was no slouch in the charisma department himself, but he recognized a passion for life in the man next to him in the barbershop that was singular and infectious. Before becoming a preacher, Moody had been a shoe salesman in Boston and Chicago. He was so good at it that a year before he quit to do the Lord's work he was earning a salary over 100 times the average of his day. Moody was a gifted salesman because he was able to concentrate, distill, and direct his passion to the people around him. This is a skill that every person needs, and it comes only with an honest and wholehearted belief in what you put out into the world. As evidenced in his encounter with Woodrow Wilson, Moody took his house of worship with him wherever he went.

RE
PAT OFF

The first seeds of beer inspiration

What sounds like a sad ending to a high school career was actually a pretty revelatory beginning. While getting kicked out of high school was one of the worst things to happen to me because it was at that school where I learned who I was, the day I got kicked out, I also came to realize the person I wanted to be. I wanted to create. I wanted to make something that was a reflection of who I was. I decided I wanted to be a writer so I attended Muhlenberg College in Allenton, Pennsylvania, as an English major with hopes of being just that. Yes, I'm one of the elite fraternity of people in the country who graduated from college without ever actually receiving a high school degree .... We aren't exactly Mensa.

While in college my passion for anything beer only grew. I continued to hone my skills identifying ways to incorporate beer into my life and the lives of my friends. One of my many inventions involved modifying a thrift-store recliner to have a covert compartment that could house a beer keg. When campus security would show up to bust a party, we could sit in the chair and ask, "Keg, what keg?" I also proudly contributed to the development of a new drinking game called Biff that involved squeegees, milk crates, a Ping-Pong ball, and four contestants dressed only in tube socks and ski goggles. By the time I graduated Muhlenberg College 1992, I realized I was more passionate about beer than I was about writing.

Because English was the only subject I had excelled in during college, I had a vague notion that I could either teach or write while pursuing my greater passion. I also had a pretty strong desire to move to the biggest city in the United States, go out all night, and revel in my youth, so I moved to New York City and enrolled in some writing courses at Columbia University.

To pay the bills I took a job as a waiter at a restaurant called Nacho Mama's Burritos. There, I quickly became friends with one of the owners, Joshua Mandel. While the decor and the fare bespoke Mexican fare, Joshua was so passionate about beer that serving a wide variety of unique and high-quality beers became one of the offerings the restaurant was known for. Joshua was not only one of the first restaurateurs in New York City to serve obscure import beers, but also to serve beers made by small, first-generation American microbreweries that were just starting to gain favor in a few corners of the world. The restaurant was serving beers like Sierra Nevada Bigfoot, Anchor Liberty, and Chimay Red.

While working in the restaurant I quickly realized that selecting, recommending, and serving beers felt very rewarding. There was a pivotal moment when I realized that I had developed somewhat of a customer base at Nacho Mama's who actually asked for and trusted my recommendations on which unusual, exotic beers they should try next. These were people I admired simply for taking the risk of trying something new. Like me, they were ready and willing to experiment, so I was encouraged to educate myself further about the world of good beer. Joshua and I decided to take our love of beer to the next level, so we began the work of brewing our own. We located the one shop in all of New York City that sold beer-making equipment and ingredients and began what would be my first of many batches of beer.

Mariah Catherine Draper

Mo

Such a rich chapter it had been when one came to look back on it all. LUV U 3 Stooges, Sam, wdrl, M+D 4

Samuel A. Calagione III

More

WORD
Thanks Dad and Mom
Love you Mia

Cherry Pale Ale

The first beer I ever brewed happened while I was living in New York City working at Nacho Mama's. I had started writing a business plan for a craft beer brewery while living in New York City in 1993, and while there, I brewed my first batch of home-brewed beer. I bought a homebrewing kit and the ingredients for a pale ale style of beer at the only homebrew supply store that existed in Manhattan in the early '90s. It was a shop called Little Shop of Hops. As I walked home with that kit and the ingredients for the pale ale back to my apartment in Chelsea, I passed a bodega that had piles of fruit outside. They were having a sale on cherries. As I looked closer, I noticed above the cherries was a swarm of fruit flies. No wonder they were having a sale on cherries. They were obviously overly ripe and not really edible. But they smelled so good that I couldn't help myself. I thought, "You know what? I think I'll buy these supercheap cherries and add them to this batch of pale ale." So I brought a giant bag of the well-aged cherries home.

Back then, it was common practice for home brewers to sanitize the bottles used for home brewing by dipping them in a sanitation solution, or you could just sterilize bottles by placing them in an oven for 15–20 minutes. I chose the latter path and I put these big old empty recyclable bottles in my NYC apartment oven. I heated the crap out of them until they were almost red hot. I took them out with kitchen tongs and placed them on the floor to cool. The floor of our apartment was carpeted with a supercheap, really ugly, wall-to-wall, green, acrylic carpet. I didn't anticipate what happened next: after letting the bottles cool for an hour, I went to fill the empties with the brew from my home brew system, but the heated bottles had melted and fused to the carpet. I knew I couldn't afford the expense of buying new bottles and I also knew the security deposit for the apartment wasn't in my name—it was in my roommate's. So I promptly grabbed an X-Acto knife and cut the carpet around the base of every bottle to free them, leaving a swath of carpet that looked more like Swiss cheese than actual carpet. That first batch of home brew was all of five gallons, which is about the equivalent of two and a half cases of beer—so that's also two and a half cases of holes in the carpet. As a result, every single one of our bottles had a built-in coaster fused to the bottom of it. I filled each of those bottles with my home brew, which again was just an off-the-shelf pale ale recipe kit, but while the wort was boiling I squished the overly ripe cherries into the beer at the end of the boil. The batch turned out absolutely beautiful. It was so great that I shared it with my roommates and hosted a party on the night of the inaugural release.

The party where I first hosted friends and shared the Cherry Virgin Brew included a motley crew of assorted characters, some of whom went on to achieve celebrity status—my current and former roommates, as well as other friends including folks like actor, director, comedian, and my future best man, Ken Marino. You might recognize that name. He's been in many films, including *Wanderlust* and *Wet Hot American Summer*. Actor, comedian, and writer, Joe Lo Truglio, was also in attendance, who since then is known for his role in the comedy series, *Brooklyn Nine-Nine*, and has been in numerous television shows and films including *Super Bad*. Actress and talk show host, Ricki Lake, was also there. At the time, I was trying to earn some money on the side by doing some modeling. A week before the party, I appeared as a guest on the Ricki Lake Show. The title of the episode was, "Why Good Girls Fall for Bad Boys." I played a bad boy in that episode, and I think Ricki kind of took a liking to me. After the show, she gave me her card. I invited her to that party, but my girlfriend, Mariah, was there too. It was a little awkward when Ricki Lake pulled up in our then-shitty neighborhood of Chelsea in a limousine and made the trek up the stairs to our shitty fourth-floor walk-up for the party. She was very gracious as she hung out and had a few beers with us. I remember distinctly that she really liked the cherry brew as well.

It was during that party that I stood up on the coffee table in my New York City apartment and shouted, "This is what I want to do with my life. I want to open a brewery and call it Dogfish Head." I was only 24 or so, 23 maybe, when I brewed that Cherry Pale Ale, so I had the immature idea, since it was my virgin brew, of calling it Dogfish Head Virgin Brew and that it took a lot of cherries to make that beer.

As I watched my friends kick back and enjoy the beer I had made, I experienced a sense of pride and accomplishment on a level I had never felt before. The beer was the hit of the party. More than that, I had created something unique that people enjoyed. I had given people something that, at that moment, they really needed. That evening I spent as much time as my friends could stand talking about all the different types of beers in the world, the ingredients used in making them, and all of the small breweries that were popping up around the country. My buddy Joe listened, sipped, and said, "Dude, you're obsessed." He was right, and, instead of being embarrassed by his comment, I was actually quite proud. As we sat there drinking, I could not help but begin planning the next batch to brew. I began considering new ingredients and different methods, but I decided to keep my signature rug-bottomed bottles for the time being. I also started thinking that, while maybe I would never actually write the Great American Novel, I might be able to make the great American beer. That evening I stood up and, with Ricki Lake as my witness, told everyone in the room that I was going to be a professional brewer. They laughed at my bold and unlikely statement, and I laughed at myself, but I woke up the next morning, left the apartment with a fuzzy head, and camped out in the public library to research just what it would take to open a brewery.

I continued brewing beers and adding unique ingredients. Unfortunately, the next two batches of home brew I brewed in our New York City apartment tasted like shit, but I'd already publicly committed to my plan, so I wasn't going to back out now. The next successful batch of beer that I brewed with the Dogfish Head name was a year or so later.

I'm still great friends with Ken Marino and Joe Lo Truglio, and they've even done ads and little TV vignettes for films that Dogfish has made for our YouTube channel. And, of course, I ended up marrying Mariah.

"And, of course, I ended up marrying Mariah."

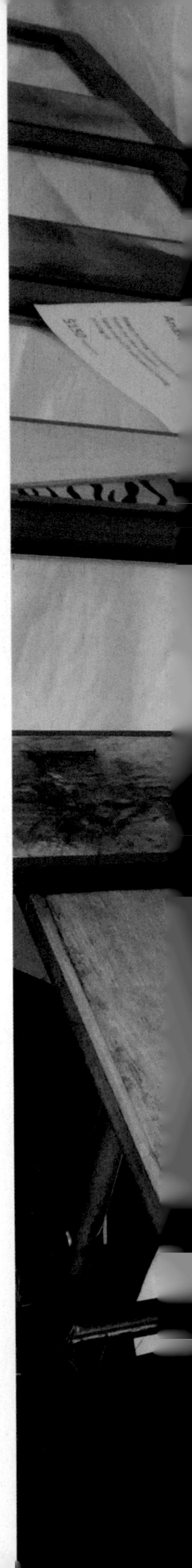

Sam Calagione's
ANALOG
HIGH 5
MACHINE

Olivia Dickinson

Brewings and Eats Server
Start Date: 1999

A Delaware native, Olivia has been serving at Dogfish Head Brewings and Eats for almost as long as we have been around. Today, Oliva is still on the floor as a sever at the pub bringing people wood-fired pizza, teaching them about why 60 Minute is called 60 Minute, and keeping the Dogfish Head culture alive and well. Olivia knows where all the bodies are buried, so getting her going on some of the stories is one hell of a trip.

Olivia has some items from Dogfish's early days in her archives, like one of the very first Punkin Ale T-shirts and old block and tackle hooks that hung at the OG pub for many years. Punkin Ale was actually made before we opened in 1995. Since it was one of our first beers, it was also one of our first T-shirts.

Olivia grabbed the block and tackle hooks one of the last nights she was working at the pub. These were part of the pub decorations, but likely came from an old ship. We often speak to one of our shared values: "Together We are Heavy." At one point, when people were hired at DFH, they were given a Klean Kanteen stainless steel pint that also had a block and tackle lifting a shark and shield with "Together We are Heavy" written on it. We find it fitting that Olivia is the keeper of these old block and tackle hooks. With her dedication, open heart, and genuine love for people, Olivia has truly lifted us beyond anywhere we could have possibly imagined.

Olivia never applied to Dogfish. Her ex-husband had started working there in the late 90s, and he would help Sam out at the original brewpub in Rehoboth. It was New Years Eve '98, and they didn't have enough people working. She filled in for the night and knew all the folks who worked there. The rest was history.

Olivia's favorite beer of all time is Festina Peche. She got a chance to brew it one summer with Bryan Selders and fellow coworker Ashlee Brown. She leans toward the sours these days, and has been drinking more Super 8. Her least favorite beer was Black and Red. It was TERR-I-BLE. The worst thing ever. It was almost like a Fort that went bad with mouthwash in it. Nobody liked it, but then two people came in and LOVED it. We ended up selling them two sixtels of it!

There was another one called Hot Thoup. That one was made with carrots and ginger. We would garnish the beer with a carrot and serve it warm. That was a fail! We even had shirts and stuff made for it.

Then there was the Flip—it was done in conjunction with Eataly and Mario Batali. We would take custom-made cast-iron rods, heat them on the wood-fired grill, carry them tableside, and then drop them into the beer! We called that, "let's table-side burn people."

Thinking back over her time at Dogfish, Olivia remembers the early days at the pub and some of the beer dinners we did there. There was something so intimate about them. Sam and Mariah were always there working, and it was something that grew organically. One time, there was a Grandma's Italian Dinner. Eric Mihaly was working in the kitchen and Sam and Eric's grandmothers provided recipes. They came and

Coworker Profile

If you were on a deserted island and could have one album to listen to and an unlimited supply of one beer, what would it be?

Beer: Super 8

Album: *An Innocent Man* by Billy Joel. It was the first record she ever bought as a child, and she would play it on her Fisher Price brown record player.

were honored at the dinner. The whole thing was heartfelt and special.

Olivia has a whole crew of folks that have been coming to the pub for years and years that will almost always request to be seated in her section. Many of them are original mug club members from back in the day, and she doesn't pull any punches with them. Olivia may be one of the toughest people you will ever meet, and she isn't going to take any flack form anyone. This speaks volumes of who she is as a person. She lives to take care of people while at the same time asking that they bring their best selves to the table (literally and figuratively). If you don't, she will let you know. The next time you end up in the pub, ask to be seated in her section. It will likely already be full, but if you are lucky enough to be seated in it, you will come to understand how lucky we are to have had her as a friend and coworker for 20 years.

Chapter 2

What's in a Name?

By 1994, I had traded my fourth-floor New York City walk-up, for an apartment in Rehoboth, Delaware, where I could develop my business plan and look for locations to open a business. I decided to open shop in Mariah's hometown of Rehoboth Beach, Delaware, where we had spent a few summers together. The coastal towns of Delaware are absolutely beautiful, with wide beaches, pretty harbors, and a thriving commercial community. For a small, seasonal

town, Rehoboth has lots of restaurants and a sophisticated, varied clientele that includes locals, transplants, and vacationers from the surrounding cities.

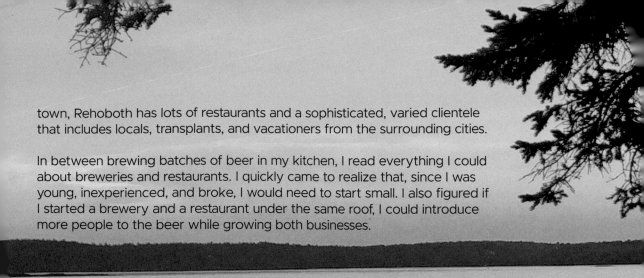

In between brewing batches of beer in my kitchen, I read everything I could about breweries and restaurants. I quickly came to realize that, since I was young, inexperienced, and broke, I would need to start small. I also figured if I started a brewery and a restaurant under the same roof, I could introduce more people to the beer while growing both businesses.

I took a job as a brewer's assistant as I completed my business plan to learn more about larger-scale brewing. I took a break from New York City and signed up to take a short brewing class at a small commercial brewery in Maine. While there, I decided the name of the brewery I imagined I would someday build. It would be Dogfish Head, named after a small peninsula off Southport Island, Maine. As a child, my parents had a small cabin on Dogfish Head, so that's where we spent summers. The name was very nostalgic for me. I also thought the name had very rustic connotations, and would bring to mind the simple, natural beauty of the capes and bluffs common in rural coastal areas. That would be the name of the beer and that would influence the look, feel, and menu of the brewpub.

I returned from my trip to Maine ready to make the leap.

“Whoso would be a man
be a non-conform

The Motto

In his essay, *Self-Reliance,* Ralph Waldo Emerson wrote, “Whoso would be a man, must be a non-conformist. He who would gather immortal palms must not be hindered by the name of goodness, but must explore if it be goodness. Nothing at last is sacred but the integrity of your own mind.”

These lines became the mission statement of Dogfish Head, and the standard by which we measure our offerings. We would make off-centered beer and food for off-centered people.

I believed the most critical line in that quote paramount to our company's identity was: “Whoso would be a man must be a non-conformist.” “Non-conformist” was the word I focused on when I decided to frame the short version of our mission around the ideal of off-centeredness. However, in the last five years I have matured as a leader and Dogfish has matured as a business, and I've come to realize that the true key to our ongoing success is revealed in a different line of Emerson's quote: “Must explore if it be goodness for himself.”

I have learned that the whole notion of goodness must be at the heart of everything you do. Goodness can be hard to define but I liken it to a non-secular version of the golden rule—the idea that you should treat people as you yourself would want to be treated. Confucius preached it as well as the Bible, and it has roots and references in many cultures around the world. As a company, we have worked really hard to surround ourselves with good people and businesses that are successful, because they care more about people than they do about money.

“Whoso would be a man, must be a non-conformist. He who would gather immortal palms must not be hindered by the name of goodness, but must explore if it be goodness. Nothing at last is sacred but the integrity of your own mind.”

"Nothing at last is sacred but the integrity of your own mind."

'Must explore if it be goodness for himself."

Whoso would be a man must be a nonconformist. He w
ould gather immortal palms must not be hindered by
name of goodness, but must explore if it be goodnes
sacred but the integrity of your own m
NIKE

"Off-centered beers for off-centered people."

Non-conformist."

The Shark & Shield

"Everything may be labeled—but everybody is not."
—Edith Wharton,
The Age of Innocence

I began work designing the Dogfish Head logo. I knew the nautical reference of the name needed to be represented graphically as well. I also knew I wanted to incorporate a sort of broken border around the shield to represent the rustic, comfortable, and casual elements that I hoped would be contained in the company I would one day build. As I drew numerous drafts of the shark and shield, I knew I wanted it to look like a handmade stamp. I actually did make an ink stamp of the logo before we opened the business and used it everywhere I could: on stationery, on the borders of the framed pictures in our pub, on our menu, and in the print advertisements I'd draw by hand.

I would try to put the logo anywhere I could. We created stamps to stamp stationery, small metal sharks and shields, and even created an electric branding iron that allowed us to burn our logo into paper, leather, you name it. We often branded items by hand, using the hand-operated branding iron. It gave the items a very authentic feel. Of course, later we designed three-foot-wide metal shields that we would hang in restaurants and liquor stores where we sold our beers.

Dogfish Head
Dogfish Head
Craft Brewed Ales
Dogfish Head
Shelter Pale Ale
Dogfish Head
Small Batch Spirits
Dogfish Head
Dogfish Head
Dogfish Head
Craft Brewed Ales
Tortugas Bitter
available here
Dogfish Head
90 Minute IPA
Dogfish Head
Craft Brewery

The Plan

It was time to seek out a location and financing. I knew I wanted the restaurant to have an open kitchen so guests could watch the action in the kitchen from their vantage point at the dining tables or bar stools. The concept was to be fully transparent, to give every guest complete access into the workings of the restaurant and pub, and to celebrate the ingredients and the process of brewing and making great food directly with the consumer. We wanted everyone in the restaurant to see the ingredients for everything we served, the artistry behind making it, whether it was food or beer, coming out of one commercial kitchen—either going out to tables in the form of food on their plates, or coming out of that same kitchen in buckets or baking pans and walking those pans and buckets out of that commercial kitchen in the other direction from the dining hall and into the little brewery. I envisioned bringing pans of pumpkin meat or buckets of brown sugar or raisins or coffee or licorice root out, walking by the customers and hopefully sparking their curiosity about what the heck we were doing with these massive piles of culinary ingredients in a brewery, and then of course we would put those beers we were making on tap in that very same room and talk to every customer about the intention behind the recipe. It would be thoughtfully designed to not just include culinary ingredients in the beer, but to be awesome, diverse partners for great food as well, and away we went on that culinary mission in the brewing world.

The building I chose had a room attached to the main bar that used to be a take-out kiosk. I realized that if we put a picture window into this wall, which overlooked the main dining area, this room would be the perfect spot to install the brewing equipment. Now all I needed was a brewery to install.

I created a menu and tested different pizza-grilling techniques on my backyard barbeque. I made pilot batches of beer and developed recipes, homemade labels, and names for the different beers I brewed.

I began to understand the place Dogfish Head would fit in the market. The big breweries were so focused on maximizing efficiency, marketing, and distribution that although their beers were simple, mass-produced, and all very similar, they got pulled through the marketplace every step of the way. They created mass demand for their brands, and their pricing structure was such that they were guaranteed a high volume of sales. To find my niche I basically had to create a product and brand that were the absolute opposite of the giant beer brands.

"As for me, I am tormented with an everlasting itch for things remote. I love to sail forbidden seas, and land on barbarous coasts."
—Herman Melville, *Moby-Dick*

In my vision for Dogfish Head, it would stand out in a crowded field of brewing companies by being the first commercial brewery in America that was committed to brewing the majority of our recipes using culinary ingredients instead of just the traditional beer ingredients of water, yeast, hops, and barley. Knowing that was going to be our mission and knowing that we wouldn't have a lot of money to advertise, opening the brewery inside the walls of a restaurant was integral to that plan. I wrote the following statement in my business plan long before we opened:

> Dogfish Head will focus on producing a wide range of beer styles using a wide range of ingredients. While we will make the standard, more accessible styles like Pale Ale and Golden Ale, we'll focus on stronger beers made with fruits, sugars, and even pumpkins in an effort to establish a unique identity in the brewing community.

The bar in the pub would serve as a barometer to measure customer response to new beers, and our customers would serve as our de facto research and development (R&D) lab, getting exclusive access to new beers in return for their feedback. They would provide real-time feedback on the new beers we would brew, while enjoying a level of access and input into what we brewed that is unheard of in the world of large-scale commercial brewing. I also liked the idea of a brewery being within a restaurant because the stronger, more complex, and more wine-like beers that we always focused on were designed to go well with food.

I knew that if I tried to bring our beer to a wide market immediately my business would fail. To succeed, we had to build demand at the individual customer level, which would lead to demand at the retail level, which would lead to demand at the distributor level. Since it was still an unknown entity, Dogfish Head beer had to be pushed through distribution as opposed to being pulled through like the beer of the larger corporations. Since I wanted to make full-flavored, stronger beers—something that contradicted all of the marketing by the big three—I knew our beers needed to be sold directly by people who understood them, me, and the Dogfish Head coworkers.

The best way to build an audience for our beer was to brew it ourselves, sell it ourselves, and pour it ourselves. In other words, I decided to open the brewpub—a restaurant with an onsite brewery, as opposed to a microbrewery, which bottles and kegs beer solely for distribution to outside retailers. Starting with a brewpub instead of a microbrewery presented a number of advantages. One was that we would have a built-in market. Our restaurant patrons would help us build demand for our beers every time they told a friend about us or came back for another pint. They could see us brewing; smell the barley juice as it boiled; watch us shovel out the grain by hand; and understand everything that goes into producing top-quality, adjunct-free, fresh beer. Customers would receive an education while we served them their meals, and we would receive critical feedback.

I began presenting my business plan to bankers and investors to pitch my idea for Dogfish Head and raised the capital to open the business. It outlined how Dogfish Head would be the first brewery in Delaware, and that we would brew our beers by incorporating culinary ingredients, along with the four traditional brewing ingredients of water, yeast, hops, and barley.

MUG CLUB!
SPUSTA

And we're still making it!

I thought it would help potential investors better understand the brand if they could sample one of the beers while they reviewed the business plan during our meetings. So I started brewing batches of an ale using pumpkin meat from the local farms, and fermenting that in a brown ale base along with some brown sugar and fresh cinnamon, nutmeg, and allspice that I was hand grating in a cheese grater. So in 1994, I bottled the first beer under the Dogfish Head brand. I named it Punkin Ale.

Punkin Ale

For the batch of Punkin Ale I'd serve to investors, I made special DIY labels for the bottles. I used an X-Acto knife to cut the shape of a pumpkin into a slice of potato and I used that potato as a stamp to make labels for the two and a half cases of Punkin Ale from that batch.

First batch of Punkin Ale

The bottling date of one of those first batches of home-brewed pumpkin ale coincided with a famous event based in Coastal Delaware called Punkin Chunkin. In its early days, the Punkin Chunkin was an event held on a farm in rural Delaware where a bunch of locals would get together after having some beers on Thanksgiving and have a contest to see who could throw a pumpkin the farthest. As the years went on, people began building and bringing contraptions to make the pumpkins go farther. One year, someone came with a big sling shot to make it go even farther; another year, someone built a trebuchet connected to a bicycle. Eventually these devices became so elaborate that they included pneumatic cannons that could shoot a pumpkin over a mile.

Well, by 1994, the Punkin Chunkin had amassed thousands of spectators and a recipe contest was added. The participants were mostly grandmothers with their secret family recipes, experienced home cooks, and professionally trained chefs. The contest called on participants to submit their best recipes that included pumpkin as the main ingredient. The table was lined with mostly baked goods—stuff like pumpkin pies, pumpkin spice cakes, pumpkin cupcakes, and whatnot.

"Life starts all over again when it gets crisp in the fall."
—F. Scott Fitzgerald, *The Great Gatsby*

I rolled in there as a newbie and plopped down my bottles of home-brewed Punkin Ale amidst rows of baked goods. Behold, when the winners were announced, all the grandmothers and professional chefs were pretty surprised when a beer brewed by a 24-year-old home brewer won the competition.

Our Punkin Ale winning the Punkin Chunkin contest was written about in the local papers. The article included the first mention in print of what was to come: "Brewed by Sam Calagione, who is going to be starting Dogfish Head Brewery. This is the first time he's ever entered a beer in a competition, and it got first place." So that was a pretty wonderful way to get the word out in Coastal Delaware that Dogfish Head Brew and Eats was about to open.

The Punkin Chunkin event

Punkin Ale comes in all shapes and sizes.

Punkin Ale®
12 FL. OZ.

The first brewing system

By the time I'd finished renovating the building, upgrading kitchen equipment, and installing a wood grill for the restaurant, I had very little left in my budget. I still had to buy the food, the ingredients for the beer, and actual brewing equipment. So I began contacting every manufacturer and broker of new and used small-scale brewing equipment in North America. I knew even the smallest, prefabricated commercial system would cost at least $100,000 to buy and install, but at this point I had exhausted much of my capital. When I inquired about buying a commercial brewing system for about $20,000, the equipment manufacturers laughed at me.

I was forced to be creative. I recalled seeing an ad for a small rack system used by home brewers that might fit within my budget. It was essentially three kegs propped on a welded steel frame. I bought this little system, and then I bought a bunch of used kegs at a scrap yard. Some would be used to ferment the beer, and some to carbonate and serve the beer in. We ripped the tops off the kegs and made lids so those could be the fermenting vessels and installed sanitary ball valves at their bases. If we left room for the yeast head in every 15-gallon keg, we could get 10 gallons of beer per batch as opposed to the industry average of 310 gallons per batch big breweries produce.

Ten gallons at a time!

There are essentially two kinds of beer in the world: ale and lager. While lager is what the big, mainstream breweries make (lager accounts for over 90 percent of the beer made in the world), our equipment could only make ales. Brewers calibrate their world in barrels, which is also how the federal government taxes us. For every barrel brewed (31 gallons), small brewers are taxed $7. Therefore brewing equipment is built in barrel increments. The average microbrewery system produces 30-barrel (930-gallon) batches. The average brewpub system in a restaurant produces 10-barrel (310-gallon) batches. The original brewing system produced 10 gallons or 0.3 barrels per batch. We would be completely inefficient, have no economies of scale, and have no way of filtering or pasteurizing our beer, but with everything in place, the brewing system was perfectly designed to experiment with the different beers I wanted to brew.

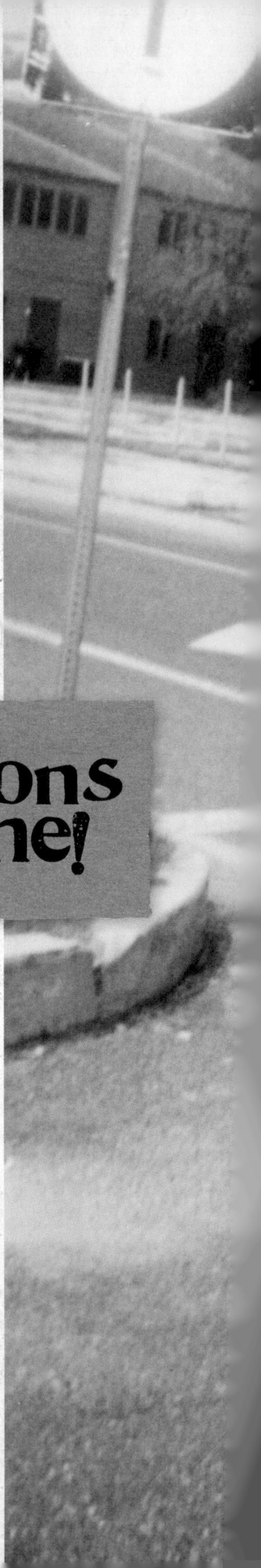

Let the brewing begin

The little home-brewing system finally arrived one chilly spring day. In addition to a few other packages we received from UPS that day, there was a big box containing a little brewery in the back of the truck. I unwrapped it, rolled it into place, plugged it in, and began making test batches in the weeks before the restaurant opened. We were officially the smallest commercial brewery in the world, and we couldn't have been happier. We got to work creating demand for Dogfish Head beer 10 gallons at a time. Thinking globally and drinking locally.

While it would be a challenge to brew enough beer for the restaurant on such a small system, I figured I could just brew a lot more often than I would on a true, full-scale commercial system. Of course, I would need somewhere to store and ferment all of the little batches that would come out of the brewery. So we built an air-conditioned room full of racks where I could store my homemade fermenting vessels. And although brewing on such a small system really sucked from a labor perspective (it takes pretty much the same amount of time to brew a five-barrel batch of beer as it does to brew a 50-barrel batch), it was great from an experimental perspective.

To make enough beer for the restaurant, I would have to brew two or three batches a day five or six days a week. I quickly got bored brewing the same few beers over and over again, so I started to wander into the kitchen of the restaurant for new ideas. I would grab some apricots or maple syrup or raisins and toss them into the beer. I trusted my palate more than the recipes I'd come across in brewing books. I would change one variable each time I brewed and track the progress and evolution of that batch through fermentation and into the keg. By brewing on such a small scale, we could take wonderful risks: I would brew two or three beers a day, and tweak one ingredient every time I brewed. When the beers were done, I could taste all three batches to compare the balance of ingredients. For the beers I thought nailed the brand's promise, I kept notes, and three weeks later I would brew three of the better batches of the earlier three-trial batches, and that was how Dogfish Head got on the road to obsessing about continual improvement and aspiring to world-class quality and consistency, not just world-class well-differentiated recipes.

From the beginning, I knew I wanted to experiment.

From the beginning, I knew I wanted to experiment and find my own way. I was unaware of it at the time, but Dogfish Head's reputation for experimentation and quality was born from the humble beginnings of that 10-gallon system.

Signs

Even before the brewpub opened, people began driving into the lot to get an inside glimpse of the first restaurant in the state to brew its own beer. I hired a great crew of co-workers, all of them restaurant veterans from the area and trusted friends from college and home. We worked night and day painting and decorating the restaurant, hoping to open before the summer rush. I was furiously pumping out little 10-gallon batches of beer to stock up for opening day.

So many emotions went through me as we counted down the days to our opening. While I can look back and laugh at it now, there was a monumental moment that gave me great anxiety. Our big, spiffy Dogfish Head Brewings & Eats sign arrived a week before our planned opening. I drove my piece-of-junk pickup truck onto the sidewalk alongside the façade of our building to hang the sign. Mariah stood across the road ready to capture a historic moment with a disposable camera. However, as we removed the old sign from the previous business from the building, behind that sign was yet another, older sign from the business that occupied the space before the last business. As I pried it off the building, a flood of emotion came over me: Oh, my God! What am I doing? I remember thinking, They are not you, Sam. Their ideas were not your ideas. If your ideas are as potent as you think they are, and you work your ass off to see them to fruition, nobody will tear your sign off the front of this building. Execute your ideas well, and you will achieve your goals.

After I finally got off all the layers of restaurant signs, I proudly hung our sign, "Dogfish Head Brewings & Eats." As I was admiring the sign, a guy came by and read it, "Brewings and Eats? Do you mean beer brewing?"

I said, "Yeah."

He explained, "Well, it's illegal to make beer in Delaware."

It turns out he had a friend who was also thinking about opening a brewery in Delaware, and told him he couldn't open one because it was illegal. I thought to myself, "Oh, shit. I don't have a choice. I've got to open, because I've sunk all of my investors' money into this endeavor." My parents, my uncle, the guy I built stone walls for, my orthodontist. I couldn't turn back.

I knew that the federal government had changed the laws to make it legal for home brewers to brew beer in their homes. The bill, making home brewing legal without federal taxation was passed under President Jimmy Carter on October 14, 1978. What I didn't realize was that when prohibition ended, the federal government passed a law making it legal to drink beer and alcohol in America again, but the law did not include the brewing or selling of beer. That was left up to each individual state to determine when to make it legal for alcohol to be produced and sold on their own schedule.

As it turned out, Delaware was one of the last states left to change state laws about producing alcohol post-prohibition. I hadn't realized that I would have to first address the fact that it was illegal to make beer in Delaware, and it had been since prohibition. Before I could sell Dogfish Head to customers I had to sell it to legislators. I would need to rewrite state laws in order to open Dogfish Head Brew & Eats.

CRAB POT
REMBERT
CRAB POT RESTAURANT
REHOBOTH BEACH
DELAWARE
05038

"It's illegal to make beer in Delaware."

Prohibition and

Dogfish Head

After Prohibition was repealed in 1933, it was up to each individual state to establish and regulate its own brewing laws, so Delaware still had laws on the books prohibiting the operation of breweries in the state. One of the main reasons I decided to open the brewpub in Delaware was that, in 1995, there were only a handful of states that didn't have breweries yet. I recognized the marketing opportunity and curiosity factor that would come with being the first brewpub to open in the state. What I didn't realize was that I'd have to change the laws to operate in the state. Thanks to leaders like then-governor Carper.

Opening day arrived, and we put the finishing touches on the restaurant as we unlocked the door. I remember standing by the front door with my mother and staring at the throng of people who crowded the bar and tables before me. Mariah, my parents, sisters, grandparents, investors, old friends, and new friends were there to celebrate with me. It was a bittersweet moment since we opened our doors before being able to serve the beer we brewed. Instead, we had to lean on the kindness of strangers and reach out to other small craft breweries in other states who let us serve their beer while we worked to rewrite laws to make serving ours legal.

In the weeks that followed, I drove to the capital of Dover to attempt to change the laws dictating whether Dogfish Head Brewing & Eats could sell the beer we brewed. As I made my way through the center of the city, I asked passers-by, "Which building is the House? Which one is the Senate?" I went to the door and they let me in. I explained the mess I was in and it's a testament to how welcoming and entrepreneurial-minded our state's legislators are that they didn't shut the door on my nose.

"All these weirdos, and me getting a little better every day right in the midst of them. I had never known, never even imagined for a heartbeat, that there might be a place for people like us."

—Denis Johnson, *Jesus' Son*

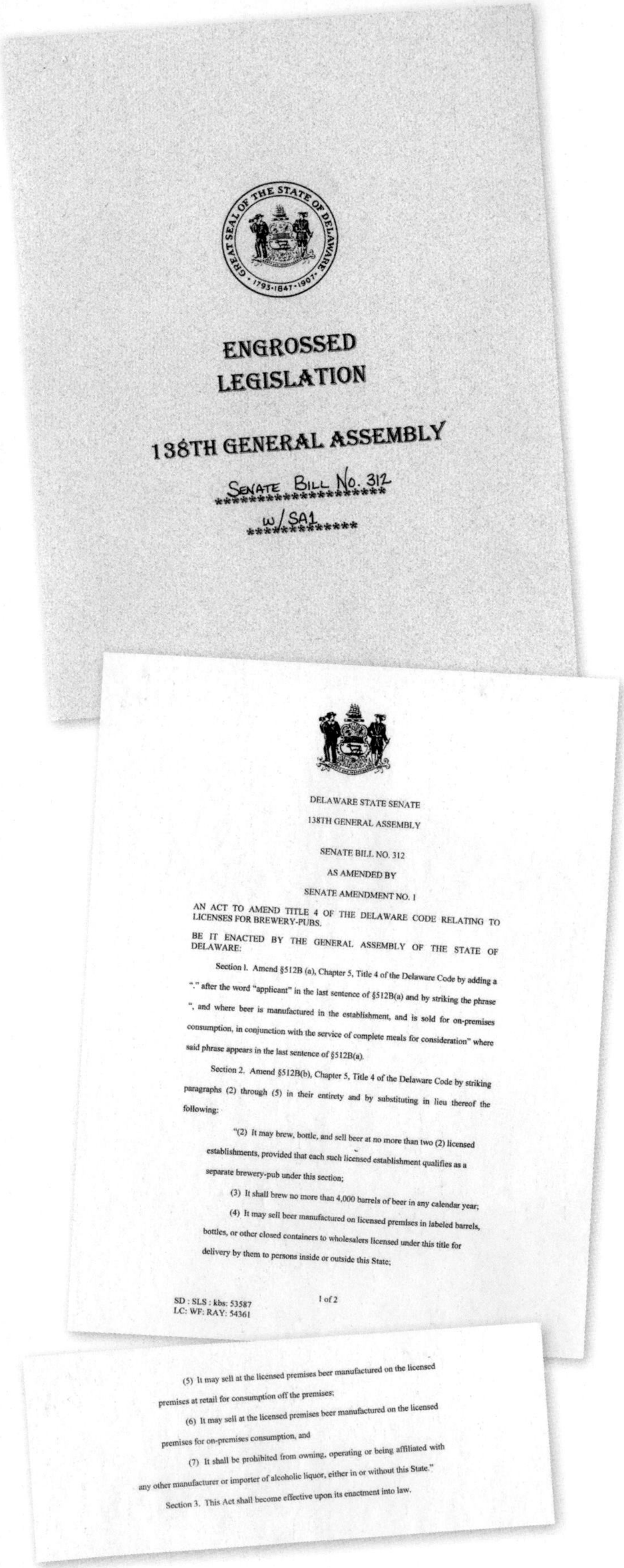

GREAT SEAL OF THE STATE OF DELAWARE
1793 · 1847 · 1907

ENGROSSED
LEGISLATION

138TH GENERAL ASSEMBLY

SENATE BILL NO. 312
****
w/ SA1
****

DELAWARE STATE SENATE

138TH GENERAL ASSEMBLY

SENATE BILL NO. 312

AS AMENDED BY

SENATE AMENDMENT NO. 1

AN ACT TO AMEND TITLE 4 OF THE DELAWARE CODE RELATING TO LICENSES FOR BREWERY-PUBS.

BE IT ENACTED BY THE GENERAL ASSEMBLY OF THE STATE OF DELAWARE:

Section 1. Amend §512B (a), Chapter 5, Title 4 of the Delaware Code by adding a "." after the word "applicant" in the last sentence of §512B(a) and by striking the phrase ", and where beer is manufactured in the establishment, and is sold for on-premises consumption, in conjunction with the service of complete meals for consideration" where said phrase appears in the last sentence of §512B(a).

Section 2. Amend §512B(b), Chapter 5, Title 4 of the Delaware Code by striking paragraphs (2) through (5) in their entirety and by substituting in lieu thereof the following:

"(2) It may brew, bottle, and sell beer at no more than two (2) licensed establishments, provided that each such licensed establishment qualifies as a separate brewery-pub under this section;

(3) It shall brew no more than 4,000 barrels of beer in any calendar year;

(4) It may sell beer manufactured on licensed premises in labeled barrels, bottles, or other closed containers to wholesalers licensed under this title for delivery by them to persons inside or outside this State;

SD : SLS : kbs: 53587
LC: WF: RAY: 54361

1 of 2

(5) It may sell at the licensed premises beer manufactured on the licensed premises at retail for consumption off the premises;

(6) It may sell at the licensed premises beer manufactured on the licensed premises for on-premises consumption, and

(7) It shall be prohibited from owning, operating or being affiliated with any other manufacturer or importer of alcoholic liquor, either in or without this State."

Section 3. This Act shall become effective upon its enactment into law.

I literally knocked on the doors of a few different state senators and members of the house as well. They were helpful from the very first day and sympathetic to my situation. They explained that there had been attempts to change the laws in previous years but the legislation had never made it to the floor. The sponsors of the proposed bills had just given up.

Traditionally one would hire a lawyer and hand off the responsibility of navigating the bureaucratic process. However, unless I was able to help local legislators buy in to our vision, our proposed bill might not be voted on in the upcoming spring session. It was imperative that this be resolved quickly enough to allow me to open for the critical summer season.

I found an ally in a lawyer named Dick Kirk who was affiliated with a Wilmington-based law firm. Dick and I went to work drafting a bill and then spoke for it on the floor of the state senate and house of representatives. While I worked with a great lawyer, I also did a lot of legwork and lobbying myself. We met with some resistance in the senate, but our bill passed with an overwhelming majority, as they all got behind our company and saw us for what we were—a David in a brewing world full of Goliaths. They moved quickly to help the first brewpub open in the state. The story of that victory and the brewpub's opening made the pages of the state and local newspapers. In our first few years, we ended up making multiple legislative changes.

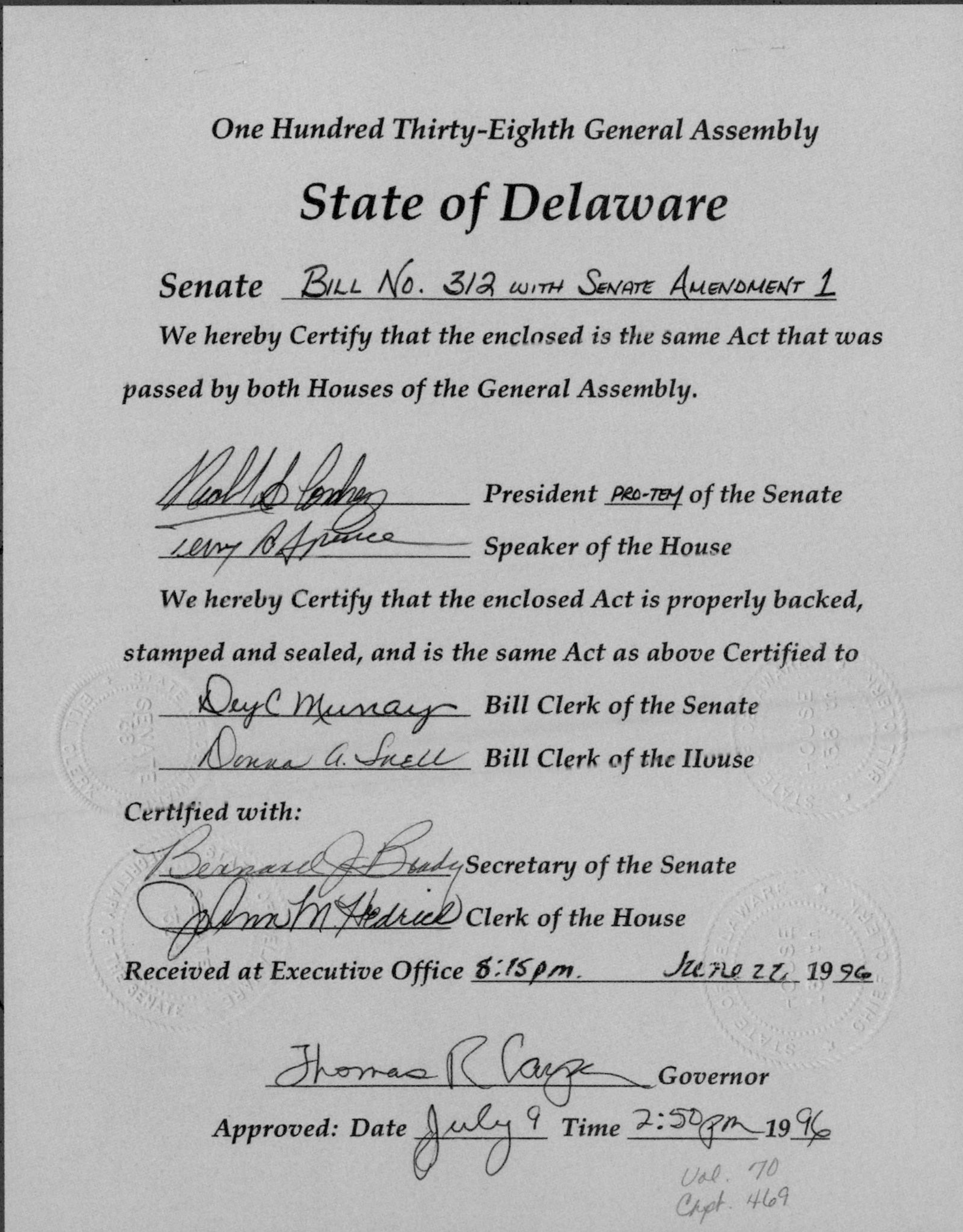

One Hundred Thirty-Eighth General Assembly

State of Delaware

Senate BILL NO. 312 WITH SENATE AMENDMENT 1

We hereby Certify that the enclosed is the same Act that was passed by both Houses of the General Assembly.

_______________ President PRO-TEM of the Senate

_______________ Speaker of the House

We hereby Certify that the enclosed Act is properly backed, stamped and sealed, and is the same Act as above Certified to

_______________ Bill Clerk of the Senate

Donna A. Snell Bill Clerk of the House

Certified with:

Bernard J. Brady Secretary of the Senate

John M. Hedrick Clerk of the House

Received at Executive Office 8:15pm. June 22, 1996

Thomas R. Carper Governor

Approved: Date July 9 Time 2:50pm 1996

Vol. 70
Chpt. 469

One of the many bills we were involved with in the first years.

Off-centered ales & spirits
For off-centered people
www.dogfish.com or 1-888-8dogfish
available throughout the midAtlantic & more
Dogfish Head
Craft Brewed Ales
visit our
Rehoboth Beach, DE
brewpub/distillery
Fine, woodgrilled food
& homemade beers

When we opened our brewery-restaurant in spring 1995, the first print ad we ran in the local paper showed our logo, address, and three simple sentence fragments in our proprietary Doggie font: Original beer. Original food. Original music. Another one of our earliest ads showed a group of asymmetric cartoon people all leaning in different directions while sitting on a couch.

Beneath the drawing was the slogan "Off-centered ales for off-centered people."

"Off-centered ales for off-centered people."

Over time we have even broadened the slogan to include other things. As we kept using this filter to make decisions, we realized that we create so much more than just "Ales." Today, internally, you will find this language to say "Off-centered goodness for off-centered people." From our Inn to our two restaurants in Rehoboth Beach and our production facility in Milton, our off-centered filter is alive and well.

"Off-centered ales for off-centered people" influences every aspect of Dogfish Head and what we do. We trademarked the slogan and began incorporating it into the design of T-shirts, glassware, and other unique merchandise. But we use it in an even more fundamental way than that. We strive to make this off-centered ideal synonymous with everything we do. Since expanding the product line to include everything from maple syrup to soap, we now use the slogan as a lie detector. We simply swap the word "ales" and fill in the blank with whatever product or service we are considering bringing to market: "Off-centered soda for off-centered people." That's true because we sweetened our birch beer soda with natural brown sugar and real vanilla beans, unlike the large soda companies that rely on cheaper, less-flavorful corn syrup. "Off-centered rum for off-centered people." That's true because we originally aged our rum on wildflower honey and toasted French oak instead of the ordinary methods used by big distilleries. "Off-centered steak sauce for off-centered people." That's false. We were approached by a company that made sauces and asked if we wanted to do a custom Dogfish Head steak sauce. It wouldn't use our beer in the sauce, so the association between the product and Dogfish Head would be inauthentic and we felt we knew our customers well enough to know that this hollow approach would disappoint them and us.

OFF-CENTERED
ales for
OFF-CENTERED
people.
DOGFISH HEAD
MILTON, DE

Off-centered ales
for off-centered people.

Dogfish
Head
OFF-CENTERED
ALES FOR OFF-CENTERED
PEOPLE.

OFF-CENTERED
OFF-CENTERED
people.

OFF-CENTERED
ales for
OFF-CENTERED
people.

OFF-CENTERED
ales for
OFF-CENTERED
people.

Shelter Pale Ale (5.0% ABV) and Chicory Stout (5.2% ABV)

The first ales we brewed on that cobbled-together, 15-gallon system were our Shelter Pale Ale and Chicory Stout. For the Shelter Pale Ale we used some Delaware-grown barley along with the traditional English style pale ale barley. I figured I needed to brew at least one beer that adhered to traditional brewing styles and techniques, because I knew that many customers coming in our doors at first were going to be looking for styles of beer they were familiar with and would not be super-hard-core beer geeks looking to challenge their taste buds. That brew was sort of our nod to early customers who just wanted to try fresh, local beer but not have it be superchallenging. Every now and then it still makes an appearance at the pub and some of our oldest fans come out for it when it lands on the tap lineup.

Our Chicory Stout, which was one of if not the first distributed beer-coffee hybrid. For that beer, we worked with Amy, the owner of Nottinghill Coffee at the Lewes Bake Shoppe, a beautiful little coffee roastery located in Lewes, Delaware. They designed and roasted a special blend of coffee for that brew.

I added roasted oatmeal grains, black patent malt, chocolate malt, St. John's Wort, licorice, and roasted chicory to make it sort of a New Orleans style coffee stout. We not only use that coffee in our beer but we also served that roast as the coffee within the walls of our restaurant as well.

A rich, dark beer made with a touch of roasted chicory, organic coffee, St. John's Wort, and licorice root. We brew ou stout with Cascade and Fuggles hops. The grains include Pale, Wheat, Roasted, Oatmeal and smoked barley. We use coffee from the Oby Lee Coffee Roastery in Lewes, DE!
5.2% abv.
22 ibu
1.888.8dogfish
www.dogfish.com
Dogfish Head
Craft Brewed Ales
Chicory Stout
available here
COFFEE BEANS
CHICORY STOUT
Dogfish Head Shelter Pale Ale
On tap here.
"Dogfish Head is America's most extraordinary and interesting small brewery." - MICHEAL JACKSON
Order a pint to find out what the buzz is about.
Dogfish Head Shelter Pale Ale
On tap here.
An English-style pale ale that you'll find refreshing and addicting. The best selling beer from Delaware's *only* microbrewery.

Sugar

Traditionally the process of fermentation is about introducing yeast, a single-cell fungi, into a sugar-rich environment, because sugar is what yeast eats and converts into alcohol, and the by-product of that process is CO_2. Almost all traditional beer includes crushed barley as a sugar source. When the barley is ramped through different heat temperatures in the mashing process it changes the starches in the barley into fermentable sugar. For Dogfish Head, knowing we wanted to look at all culinary ingredients meant that it wasn't just about herbs and spices to add flavors and aroma, it was about seeking out exotic and interesting sugar sources in addition to the traditional brewing sugar source of barley. From our earliest years we were incorporating fermentable sugars from fruits. The beers would also have a higher alcohol by volume (ABV) because of the ingredients and amount of sugars used.

For context, the average American light lager, that's the biggest volume beer style sold in America, is roughly 4.5 percent alcohol. I knew I wanted to brew these big, strong, flavorful, culinary inspired beers and I knew to make the distinction really stand out I wanted them to stand up to flavorful foods. I wanted to brew some beers that were more wine-like in their complexity, food compatibility, and alcohol content than beer.

Stirring things up

This style of beer calls for an inordinate amount of hops to be added to a brew.

Aprihop (7.0% ABV)

In the case of Aprihop, we used fruit sugars. In 1996, we brewed our first batches of Aprihop, which was the first fruit-fermented, fruit IPA, sold in America. Our desire to brew culinary ingredients would dovetail really well with the recent resurgence of the English beer style, IPA, which stands for India Pale Ale. This style of beer calls for an inordinate amount of hops to be added to a brew. The American varieties of hops grown for these types of ales, like Centennial and Cascade, give off a lot of citrusy, fruity aroma qualities inherent to those varieties of hops, so I thought adding a fruit to that brew would amplify the fruitiness of those hop varieties. We trialed a bunch of different fruits with the different hop varieties and landed on the best combination. The Aprihop brew was a blend of Centennial (Cascade) hops along with Apricot. For the brew, I'd buy apricots, hand cut them, add them to a Robot Coupe food processor with hot wort, puree the shit out of it, and add that syrup back to the beer as it was fermenting. The yeast in the fermenter was not just eating the sugars from the barley and wheat in the basic recipe, it was also eating the sugars from the apricots as well, which meant that the apricot character of the beer was woven into the taste of the beer, not just in the aroma, but in the flavor. The tartness of the apricot complemented the aromatic, citrusy hops really well.

Dogfish Head
APRIHOP

Immort Ale (11% ABV)

In 1996, we'd started combining our desire to use alternative sugar sources to not only impact the flavors in our beers but to also function as a source for fermenting to achieve beers higher in alcohol content.

For our next beer, we added honeys and grape musts (grape juice that contains the skins and seeds), to add even more fermentable sugars and bring even more complexity to the styles of beers than what was found on the shelves in America at that time. This beer was the first one we brewed based on the recipe of an ancient ale. The recipe itself was a feast of culinary ingredients: It was based on an ancient Scandinavian brew called Sahti that uses a lot of rye and juniper. I used dark grains so this beer would be fairly dark, reddish, ruby red, dark red, in its color, and I brewed it to 11 percent alcohol originally using a champagne yeast. To even further give this ale the characteristics of wine, I added oak chips that we toasted in our oven to the stainless-steel fermentation tank, much as you would oak a Chardonnay wine. During the fermentation process, I also added the maple syrup from my family's farm, juniper berries that I would crush with a rolling pin in the kitchen, and Madagascar vanilla beans that I would slice open with a razor blade vertically. In addition to the traditional brewing barley that we made the beer with, we also got peat-smoked barley from a whiskey distillery in Scotland that gave this beer its smoky, earthy hue that complemented so well the woodsy quality of the maple syrup and the oak chips.

The beer we ended up bringing out commercially was first brewed in 1997 and name Immort Ale. The name itself was a play on the fact that it was a beer designed to stand the test of time.

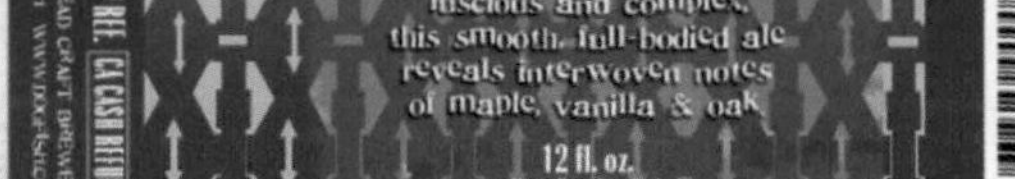

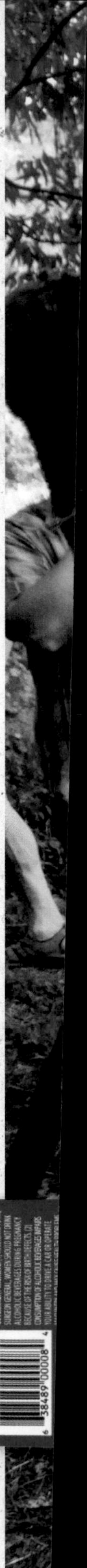

Other Music
NYC

Holding true to the mission, 20 years later

Raison D'Etre (8.0% ABV)

With our Immort Ale in 1997 we had success by incorporating alternative fermentation sources and flavors with techniques that would result in wine-like characteristics and alcohol levels. The success of our Immort Ale got me wondering, "What else can we do creatively to make a beer that's wine-like in its pairing with a steak?" By the mid-90s, the wine industry had done a really good job of making it easy for consumers to understand certain wines paired well with certain foods. The most renowned and simplest concepts are that red wines pair great with red meats while white wines pair better with fish and vegetable dishes. Along with that basic knowledge, I did some research to identify what was considered the quintessential wine to pair with a flavorful steak, and found that big, robust Bordeaux. I set out to build a beer that had the same complexity and age-ability as a Bordeaux, and went one step further by even incorporating the quintessential ingredient in Bordeaux into this beer.

And thus, in 1998, Raison D'Etre was born. Closer to wine in its alcohol content at eight percent, the beer is brewed with dark grains to give it great ageability. Being a Dogfish Head product, we were uninterested in brewing to authentic style, so our beer was fermented with a Belgian yeast, Belgian beet sugar, and raisins to give it some of the flavor of a Belgian beer.

From there we added both green raisins, which are raisins at a point in their maturity that are between a grape and a raisin connecting them to the wine world, and beet sugar. The beet sugar contributed not only additional fermentable sugar, but also contributed to the ruby red hue of that beer creating a red wine-like color.

The name Raison D'Etre is a play on words. Raison d'etre in French means "reason to be." This beer was designed for a very specific "reason to be" the ultimate partner for a delicious steak. It's a reverse-engineered beer, I think the first of its kind as we described it at that time. I'd never heard of someone saying, "I'm going to start with a culinary dish and build a beer recipe around that culinary dish," and that was the goal behind Raison D'Etre, for the concept of raison d'etre. Also, the French word, raison, is close in spelling to the main ingredient that makes the recipe so distinct—raisins.

Alison Ruark

Distillery Operations Coordinator
Start Date: 2001

"Hey, we are short staffed, can you help, Alison?" Alison first started at Dogfish Head in 2001, but this was under the table. Her "official" start day was May 7, 2002 but who's counting? Her first job was getting it done on the floor as a busser. They asked her if she could help and she asked, "You mean, today?" "Yup." And she never left. At the time, she was most excited about the extra side money to help pay for her tattoos.

Alison is a complete and total badass and has been with Dogfish Head through a tremendous amount of growth. She has had her hands, literally and figuratively, on some of our more innovative moments. If you ever visited the old pub and were lucky enough to partake in some of our Brown Honey Rum or Analog Vodka, the odds are extremely high that she is the one who distilled it and bottled it for you. Today, we still have a few bottles of our first lines of spirits in the archives ... and a few in our closets and basements. Pretty much all of them were bottled by Alison. In the true spirit of Dogfish Head, Alison became our distiller by learning on her feet. With no training or deep background, she just said, "Okay, I'll help with this project." Jumping into totally new activities is stressful, but this willingness to jump right in without hesitation, fail, and get up again is one of the keys to our success at Dogfish. Without people like Alison who have the willingness to learn, the patience to work through problems, and a deep soul strength to suck it up and keep going when shit gets hard, we would not be where we are today.

In her time at Dogfish Head, she has been a busser, a server, a distiller, and today she is the Distillery Operations Coordinator. She started working with our pal Mike Gerhart who was the head brewer at the time down in Rehoboth. How did she get the foot in the door upstairs in the Distillery? It was déjà vu all over again when she was asked yet another time. "Hey, we are short staffed, can you help, Alison?" Her answer, as it has always been when we need her help, "Yes. Yes, I can."

Alison knew zero about distilling but was there the very first time they fired ol' Frank up. Now that she has spent time on some real deal stills in Milton, she has come to realize that Frankenstill was aptly named. That thing was weird! There were some bumps between Frank and Alison along the way. Like the day he almost blew up.

The door on the front of Frank was removable. It had bolts around it that would hold it in place and maintain the seal through a run. While she was tightening it with a rachet, one of the bolts sheared off right at the start of the run. The vapors were leaking out and filling the room. There were people in the dining room; it was filling with vapors and Alison was getting a full dose of it. She was stuffing rags in the hole and at one point was wetting corn starch and trying to get it to seal the leak. There were ratchet straps wrapped around Frank covering the hole as well. The good news is, just below Frankenstill was the kitchen and the wood fire grill was in full swing. At the end, the run was preserved, Alison almost had a heart attack, we were a little lighter on cornstarch, but the gin was just right. And nobody died.

Today when she comes into work, Alison walks by her old friend Frankenstill. It is set up outside of the new Distillery in Milton as a homage to our roots. Not just an icon

Coworker Profile

to what we have done in the past, but an old friend of Alison's. We couldn't bring her up without having Frank there to greet her every morning. A reminder of not only how far we have come, but that it didn't and often doesn't come easy. It is Alison's grit that has helped make the distillery what it is today.

Dogfish is home. This comes up time and time again with coworkers and it rings true with Alison. The people she has met, worked with, laughed with, and cried with over the past 18 years has been staggering and created a real family and home.

If you were on a deserted island and could have one album to listen to and an unlimited supply of one beer, what would it be?

Beer: Noble Rot (and smoky Laphroaig, since she's a distiller)
Album: Bob Marley, *Kaya*

Noble Rot stands out as her favorite beer, but what about the Spirits world? Of all the runs Alison pulled of Frankenstill down in Rehoboth, the White Lite Rum was the cleanest and the purest. Now most folks who had been to the OG pub would likely remember the Brown Honey Rum. A house favorite for sure, but not for Alison. Alison's favorite today coming out of our distillery in Milton—Alternate Takes Volume 2: Whiskey finished in Palo Santo Marron Barrels. It is first aged in American oak and then moved to casks used for aging our Palo Santo Marron. While this one is going to be harder to find, Alison also loves our Compelling Gin even though she is not a huge gin drinker. She was on the ground floor running Frankito, a 500 ml glass still named after Frankenstill, helping learn what different botanical profiles might work in exploring possible options for what would become Compelling Gin. Mix this gin with a Seaquench Ale and you will be pleased with the results.

The 5-Barrel System

When Dogfish opened its doors, we were the smallest commercial brewery. Brewing beer in a 15-gallon system and yielding 10 gallons per batch, there was not enough beer for us to bottle and distribute, so every ounce of beer that we brewed in 1995 was sold and served within the building's walls from kegs through our tap system.

In 1996, a local canning company in Delaware went out of business. There was an auction announced to sell off the contents of the cannery. The equipment for sale included tanks that were used in the cannery to hold cleaning chemicals, but they were built out of food-grade stainless steel and had the geometry that would allow us to repurpose them into brewing vessels that were 10 times as big as our original 15-gallon system. On the day of the auction, I filled a bunch of jugs with beer off the draft system and brought them to that auction. While the auctioneer was in full swing selling items, I began pouring beer for all the farmers and construction workers that were bidding on the remnants of that cannery.

I made sure each of them had a couple rounds of Chicory Stout and Shelter Pale Ale. As we were drinking, I made them a proposition I hoped they couldn't refuse, "Hey, guys, I'll keep you in beer all day long if you promise just not to bid on those three old, dusty tanks in the corner." Sure enough, when those tanks went to bid, the room went quiet. The auctioneer's gavel went down and for $900 I got three 150-gallon stainless steel tanks. The farmers and construction workers clapped and threw their hats in the air and high-fived each other. The auctioneer shot us a confused glance, but he didn't question it and allowed me to take the tanks I bid on. The farmers helped me load the tanks into my pickup truck and away I drove with our next-generation brewing system—essentially a 5-barrel brewery, or 150-gallon brewing system

> "The story is not in the words; it's in the struggle."
> —Paul Auster, *The New York Trilogy*

I called on my friend Doug Griffith who was the owner of Delmarva Home Brewing Supplies, the first home brew equipment store in Southern Delaware, to help turn those tanks into Dogfish Head's next brewing system. Besides being knowledgeable about how brewing systems worked, Doug was very talented and handy with tools. He and I stayed up staring at these tanks and sketching out in pencil drawings, over a few beers, how we could modify, tweak, and MacGyver equipment together to turn these tanks into a functional brewery.

In 1996 we installed this Frankensteined 5-barrel brewery in place of the 15-gallon system. We contacted a local fabricator and shared with him the dimensions and drawing for two ten-barrel double-batch fermenters to go with the homemade 5-barrel brewing system. Now we were brewing at a much bigger scale with a 10-barrel (150 gallon) batch or a double 5-barrel batch that equals 10 barrels in a fermenter. This was the yield size of about 120 cases of beer. We were producing a volume of beer that we could not only sell in the kegs in the restaurant but also to outside customers.

End of the 15-gallon era

Bottling

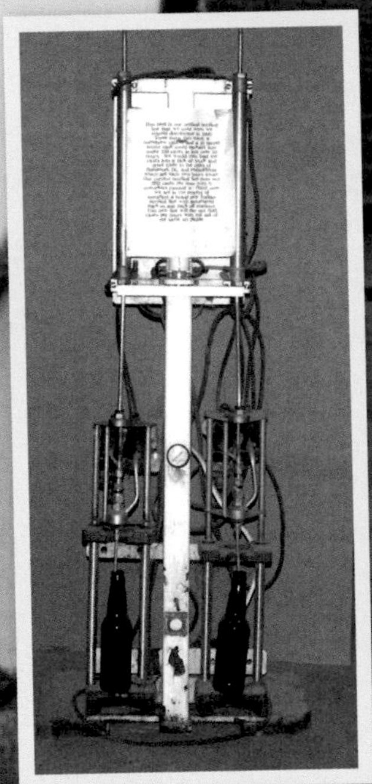

In 1996 we also cobbled together our first small-scale bottling line.

As I developed designs for our bottle labels, it would have been very easy to look at what other brewers were doing and assimilate those ideas into my design, but I knew such an approach would do very little to differentiate my brand. I also knew that the kinds of beers we intended to bottle would be very different in composition, alcohol content, and price from the other beers on the shelf.

Because there were more similarities between the wine world and Dogfish Head than there was between the beer world and Dogfish Head, I looked to the bottles on the shelves of high-end wine stores and read publications like *Wine Enthusiast* and *Wine Spectator* for inspiration for our packaging. We bought rich and rough estate paper to print our labels on rather than smooth, thin beer paper. We paid a premium to design a metallic bottle cap that mirrored the foil wraps you see on some wines. We put a lot of descriptive language on our bottles as opposed to a giant logo. All of the research I have done on wine informed the development of our brewery.

To fill the bottles, we bought a used, two-head tabletop bottle filler previously owned by a winery, and then we hand-capped every bottle. Three of us were able to bottle 100 cases in 10 hours before we'd load up my pickup truck so I could deliver the beer to the surrounding cities of Philly, Baltimore, and D.C. We were finally distributing Dogfish Head beer outside of the restaurant. It was hard work, but it felt great. We were now able to brew two batches of five barrels each to yield 300 gallons to the bottling tank. This allowed us to experiment with the beers without having to worry about costs, and without having to brew beer every single day. The new cobbled-together brewery looked more like the bride of Frankenstein than a traditional brewing system, but it made damn good beer.

The first beer we bottled for distribution was Shelter Pale Ale. Along with Shelter Pale Ale, we distributed Chicory Stout and Immort in kegs. For our inaugural batch of bottled beer, we hand-filled 22-ounce bottles with Shelter Pale Ale, I put 100 cases in my pickup, and drove them to Philadelphia.

The Six Packs

Here is the poem I wrote that appears on the bottom of every six-pack that leaves our brewery. I think it summarizes the Dogfish Head definition of craft:

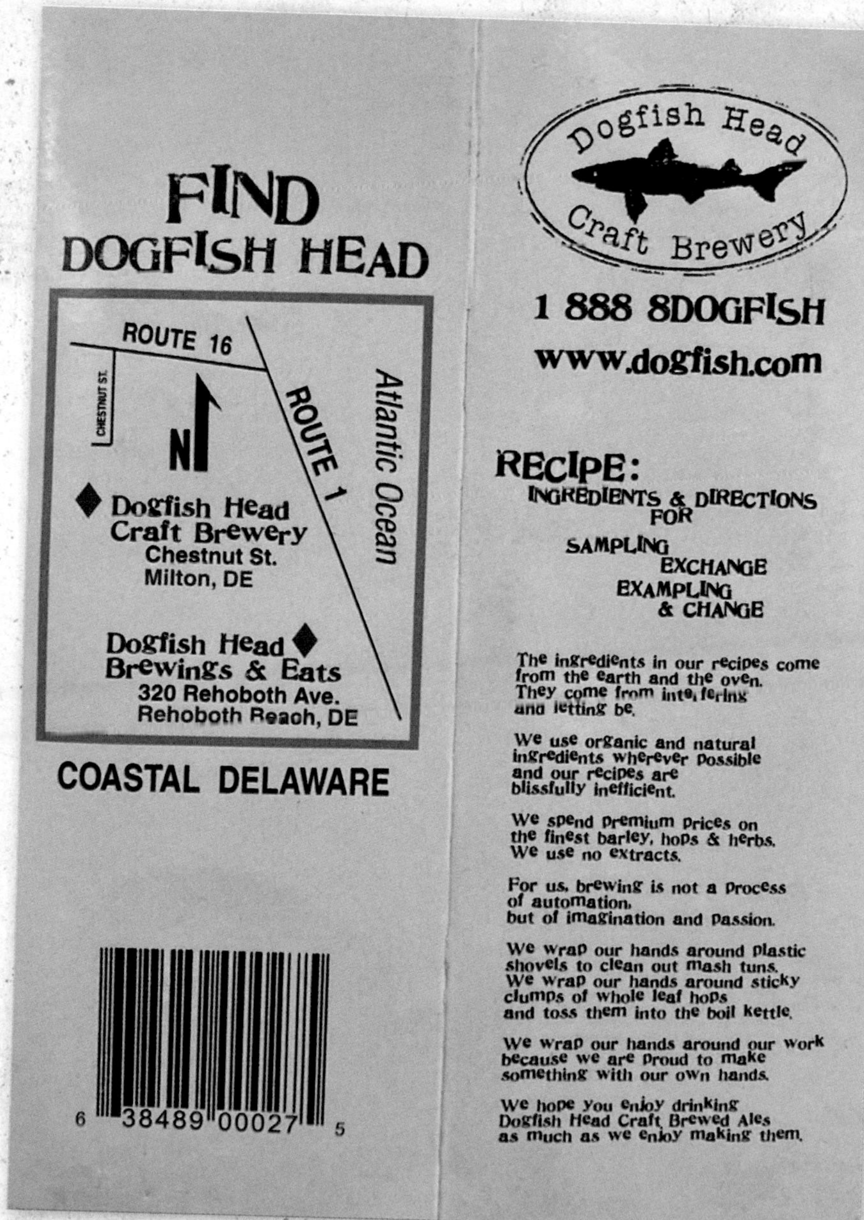

We want people to know we make our beer by hand—that real people add the hops to our boil kettle, take the bottles off our bottling line, and load the pallets onto trucks. We make our beer in small batches using the finest ingredients and you know it when you taste it. The fact that we use expensive, hard-to-find ingredients speaks to our obsession with quality.

Building a Bigger Brewery

In 1997 we built and opened a brewery in Lewes, Delaware—about six miles from our original location in Rehoboth, and moved our production brewery there. There, we cobbled together, out of used dairy and cannery equipment, a 30-barrel direct fire piece of shit Frankenstein brew house. It had a bunch of horizontal dairy tanks and a piece of shit East German soda bottle filler that really sucked and would throw bottles at your face while you filled on it. You could tell who worked on the bottling line because they were very jittery, nervous people who stood out wearing ski goggles and motorcycle helmets to work because the equipment threw shit at you while you tried to fill bottles. In hindsight, the ski goggles were still haunting me from my high school and college drinking game days even without the tube socks to complete the outfit.

Our grain silo at the Lewes Brewery

I wanted to kick off the opening of our new brewery with a big publicity event, but I also knew that every cent we had was tied up in the build-out of our new brewery. Although the brewery and restaurant were three hours away from the New Jersey border by car, they were only 20 nautical miles away from the New Jersey border. Knowing we planned to sell our beers in New Jersey, I decided to build a rowboat in which to hand deliver the first Dogfish Head export of our handmade beer from Lewes, Delaware, to Cape May, New Jersey. This publicity event was loosely based on George Washington's crossing of the Delaware. I bought a kit out of the back of *Wooden Boat* magazine and began assembling my ocean-going rowing skiff in the upstairs dining room of our pub. This seemed to be a better use for the underutilized space than throwing late-night DJ parties.

I did some research on the New Jersey shore and found a bar that was located right on the beach in Cape May. I contacted the owner and sent him some promotional posters, and he said he would help me get the word out about the event. We also made 10-inch replicas of the boat into which we stuffed samples of our new location's first bottled beers and sent them out with press kits to a bunch of newspapers and beer periodicals. Once the real boat was completed I did a few practice rowing sessions in the canal, where I learned firsthand just how top-heavy a keg of beer can be in a rowboat. After almost drowning and losing a full keg of really good beer to an outgoing tide, I downgraded my cargo to a six-pack of beer. The date arrived, and I loaded my boat with the six-pack, some grapes, and some Gatorade. A local reporter and my father-in-law sent me off with a push and a prayer. It was a little disorienting once I was in the middle of the bay and couldn't see land on either side, but my compass and a guide boat kept me headed in the right direction. Soon, the Jersey shore was before me and I looked for the landmark water tower that the bar owner had described. I arrived on the beach five and a half hours after shoving off from Delaware. I was probably hallucinating with delusions of grandeur on my trip over, because I expected a welcoming committee of at least a couple dozen boating and brewing enthusiasts.

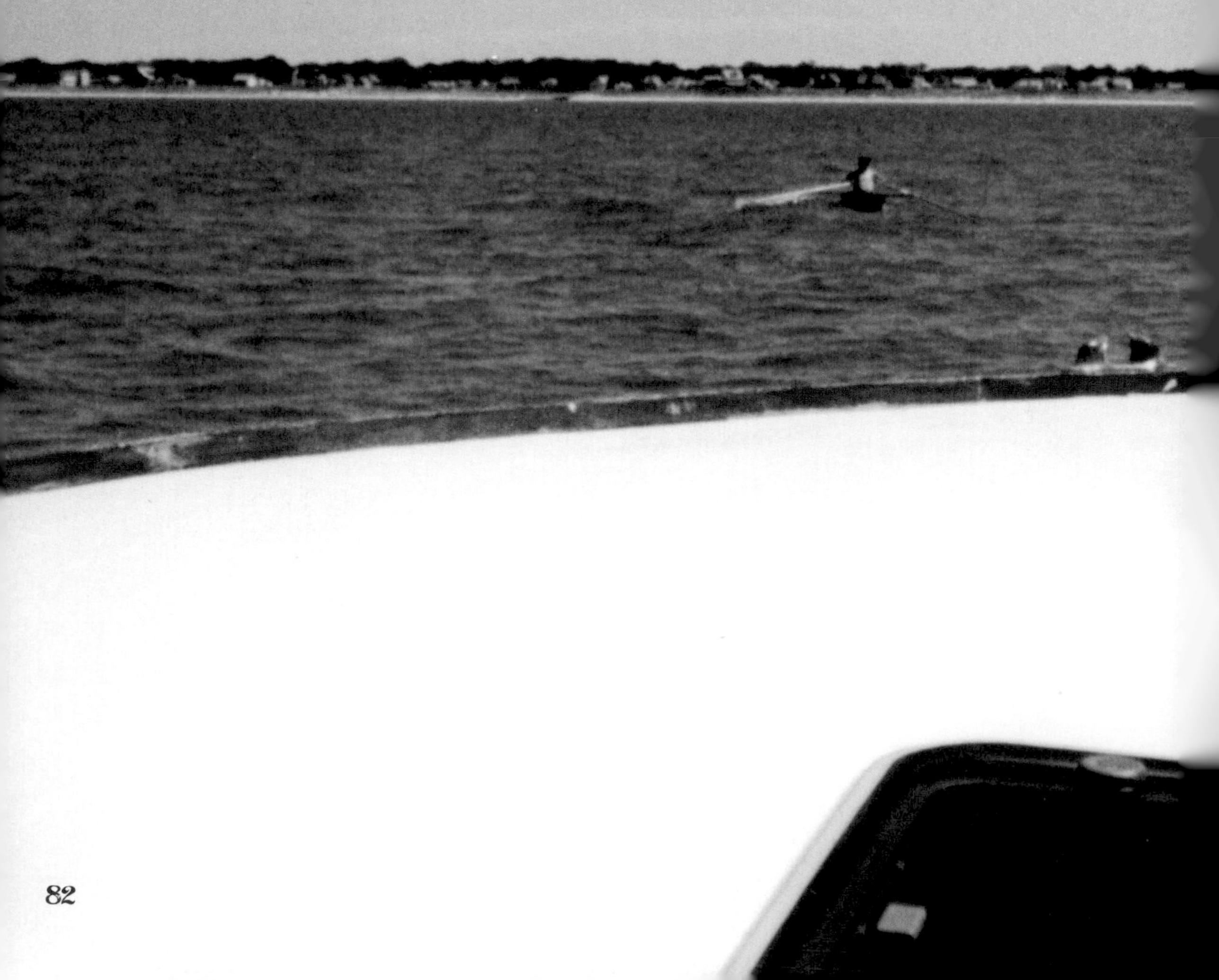

Three people walked down from the seaside bar: the owner, my New Jersey distributor, and George Hummel, a writer with a beer newspaper called *BarleyCorn*. I hid my disappointment as George snapped a few photos of me and my six-pack next to the boat. My wife and a friend had come over from Delaware on a motorboat and joined me on the outside deck of the bar. Nobody else showed up for the event. I saw my posters, still rolled up, gathering dust by the cash register behind the bar.

Things went from bad to worse when my distributor asked me where the keg was. I told him that I had left a message explaining that he needed to bring a keg from his warehouse, as I would be rowing only a six-pack across the canal. So we sat there, eating jalapeño poppers and nursing the six warm beers that I rowed over as I wondered what went wrong. I was exhausted, but I talked with George about the brewery, our beers, and our plans for distribution before throwing my rowing scull onto a guide boat for the ride back to Delaware. I tried to forget about it when I returned to work. I told my coworkers that everything had worked out fine. Obviously, it hadn't. I thought about all of the things that I had done wrong. I didn't check in with the bar to make sure it was promoting the event. I didn't follow up on the press releases to make sure people would

attend. I didn't make sure there would actually be any beer present at my brewery event. I called it a learning lesson and went on with the chores of selling and making beer at the newly opened brewery.

A few weeks later a number of interesting coincidences came to light. George's article came out in *BarleyCorn* with a very positive review of our warm beer. Also, the reporter we sent the story to at *USA Today* ran it without ever contacting us. We received a flurry of calls as a result of both of these stories from people looking to buy our beer. We then received a call from someone in the marketing department at Levi's. They had seen the picture of me and my six-pack after rowing across the bay and asked me to send them more information on the press release and our company. Within weeks Levi's had decided to use me and five other young entrepreneurs to launch Slates, its line of casual business clothes.

Two months after rowing across the bay I found myself in a fancy photography studio in Manhattan. There must have been 10 people running around getting everything ready for the photo shoot. I was kind of nervous, so, to break the ice, I asked the photographer if he had been doing this for a while. Everyone looked at me with shock and disgust. The guy with the camera was the world-renowned photographer Richard Avedon. As we spoke, he said he owed his longevity to the glass of beer he had before going to bed each evening. The Slates ad ran in major publications like *Rolling Stone*, *GQ*, and *Sports Illustrated* and led to stories in *Forbes* and *BusinessWeek*.

Sore arms and a six-pack

Opening our production brewery coincided with an era in the brewing industry where demand for local craft beer was exceeded by too many small breweries opening. Having to compete with so many craft beers, getting distribution and sales those years were tough. We did well as a restaurant right out of the gates, located three blocks from the Boardwalk in downtown Rehoboth, but during the early years of our production brewery, we fought to find our place in the market. Dogfish Head had some lean years in 1997, 1998, and 1999.

In 1999 we came up with some new, off-centered, and innovative recipes that brought attention for our brand beyond the mid-Atlantic region and into publications like *People* and *Food and Wine* and television shows like the *Today Show*. One of the beers that was the catalyst for that moment was World Wide Stout.

"Life is not a matter of holding good cards, but sometimes playing a poor hand well."
—Jack London, *The Call of the Wild*, *White Fang*, and *To Build a Fire*

World Wide Stout

(18%-20% ABV)

The winter of 1999 was slow so we decided, "Wouldn't it be fun to take some time now that it's slow here at the beach and try to brew the strongest beer known to mankind?" The holy grail of strong beers that year was the Sam Adams Triple Bock brewed by Boston Beer Company. The beer came in a beautiful little ten ounce cobalt blue bottle and it poured like A1 Steak Sauce. It was superdark and rich and viscous and it had sort of a soy, umami, salty character to it. The beer was superintense, sherry like, and beautiful.

We enjoyed the characteristics of that beer, but we wanted to brew a beer that was more recognizable as a beer style, but one that was also superstrong. We wanted to brew a beer that was the strongest beer in the whole wide world. Back then, the World Wide Web was just coming out and I recall David Letterman also had a production company called Worldwide Pants. We decided to name this beer World Wide Stout. The name was an homage to both Worldwide Pants, because I was a big Letterman fan, and the World Wide Web that was just kind of coming into people's homes.

We'd learned a lot about how to make beers that were inordinately strong in alcohol. The reason you'll never have a beer or a wine as strong as a vodka or a gin or a rum is that natural fermentation relies on the yeast to make the alcohol, not on the distilling process. The irony—and the limitation—to brewing beer is that the same by-product that the yeast makes—the alcohol produced when yeast eats sugar—actually becomes toxic to the yeast and it breaks down the cell wall and kills the yeast. Because of this, you rarely find beers that are over 10 or 11 percent alcohol.

The first step was finding a yeast that could survive high-alcohol environments. We were able to isolate some sadomasochist yeast strains that could tolerate inordinately high alcohol environments, and by process of elimination we got the right combination of these hearty yeast strains into our fermentation tank and added additional sugar to the brew incrementally during fermentation. The result was a beer that was 18 percent alcohol in that first batch.

Dogfish got national attention in our tiny little rural Delaware brewery for brewing what was then the strongest beer in the world.

That first year we made our World Wide Stout we made only 100 cases. This media attention resulted in the 100 cases being sold in a matter of weeks. Our distributors went from freak-out mode for having to pay $100 per case to freak-out mode for not being able to buy more than their initial 10-case allotment in the same amount of weeks.

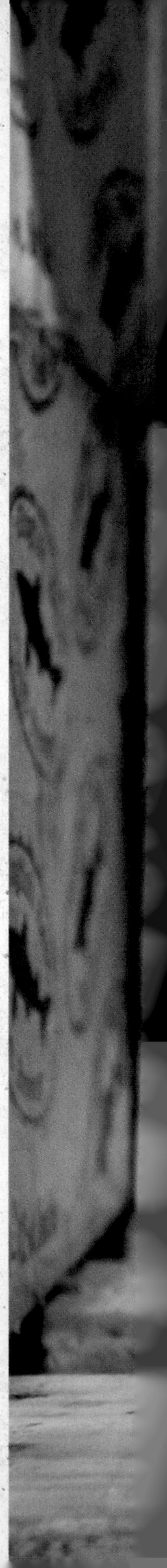

We were able to isolate sadomasochist yeast strains that could tolerate inordinately high alcohol environments.

"A true freak cannot be made. A true freak must be born."
—Katherine Dunn, *Geek Love*

The next year we made 300 cases, and the year after that we made 1,000. Our goal is to always produce just a little bit less than we can sell. If the beer isn't worth the price, we will have a harder time selling it each year even if we do get great initial press coverage.

But I'm proud to say this hasn't been the case with our beers, particularly as the craft brewing renaissance was blossoming. It sent a powerful message to our retailers, distributors, and customers when, for over a decade, we could say we had never introduced a beer that had shrunk in sales from one year to the next. We very rarely discontinue a beer, and only do so to allocate more of our finite capacity toward styles we feel better represent us. The fact that we make so many different styles of beer wreaks havoc on our production schedule, inventory control, tank utilization, and brewers' peace of mind. But if we say we are all about off-centered ales for off-centered people, we need to put our money where the pint glass is.

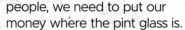

Dogfish and Boston Beer went on to compete for the title of who could brew the strongest beer over a number of years. Dogfish Head took the title from Triple Bock with World Wide Stout. Boston Beer took it back from us with their Sam Adams Millennium. Then Dogfish Head took it back in 2003 with Raison D'Extra—a version of Raison D'Etra with a 20.5 percent ABV. Sam Adams took the title back—and still holds it—with Utopias, which rings in at 28 percent ABV.

modern brewery age

50 Day Street, P.O. Box 5550, Norwalk, CT 06856 (203) 853-6015 Fax: (203) 852-8175

January 26, 1998

Dear Brewmaster:

Since 1938, Modern Brewery Age has compiled an annual brewery ranking, a sequential listing of all U.S. brewers based on their barrelage. This year, we are compiling the listing once more, and would like to include your brewery.

To be listed, simply note your 1996 and 1997 barrelage on the enclosed form, and mail it back to us with the self-addressed, stamped envelope provided. Alternatively, you can fax the sheet to us at (203)852-8175.

If your company does not have a final barrelage number yet, please provide an estimate. To include your company in the ranking, we will need the information by February 12.

If you have any questions, you can reach me at (203)853-6015, ext. 131. Thank you very much for taking the time to respond.

Sincerely,

Peter V.K. Reid

Peter V.K. Reid
Editor

PVKR/dba
Enclosure

1998 *MODERN BREWERY AGE*

BARRELAGE RANKING REPORT

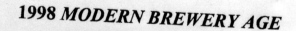

Please complete this form and return it to us in the postpaid envelope provided, or fax by February 12, 1998.
(*Modern Brewery Age*, P.O. Box 5550, Norwalk, CT 06856-5550)
Fax: 203-852-8175; Phone: 203-853-6015, ext. 131

Microbrewery

Brewery Name/Address:
Dogfish Head Craft Brewery
22 Nassau Commons
Lewes DE 19958

Enter address corrections here:

Year Founded: 1997

1997 Taxable Production: 2000

1996 Taxable Production: N/A - opened July 1997

Volume expressed in 31-Gallon Barrels

Note: Please provide an estimate if a firm number is not yet available.
Contract Brewers should distinguish between in-house and contract production.

Thanks for your help!

Midas Touch (9.0% ABV)

In 1999 we also brewed a British version of fruited gruit based on an ancient recipe for British beer I uncovered at a local beer festival, the Roasting and Toasting Festival. It was kismet that this festival was held at the Museum of Archeology and Anthropology at the University of Pennsylvania in Philadelphia. Michael Jackson, the famous beer writer, was speaking at the event. After his session, he met Dr. Pat McGovern, a molecular archeologist based at the University of Pennsylvania. Dr. Pat, as he's known, had recently made some scientific advancements that allowed him to analyze the residue found on shards of pottery in the University of Pennsylvania's collection of artifacts, and identify on a molecular level what these ancient people were drinking. The result was a modern-day grocery list of ingredients that came from that research, that could be used to re-create those drinks. He explained all this to Michael Jackson who responded, "Well, there's a guy in this room who makes all kinds of weird beers with coffee and licorice and pumpkin—this sounds like it would be right up his alley."

Michael Jackson introduced me to Dr. Pat, who is now recognized as the world's foremost expert on ancient fermented beverages. The first project of many that we worked on together was Midas Touch, whose recipe was based on the residue that was found in the shards

of crockery in the dig site of the tomb that's believed to have belonged to King Midas in modern day Turkey. The tomb was so well sealed and well preserved that when the excavators and archeologists first opened the tomb, they could see all the color of the room drain before their eyes. As the air went into that room, it instantly oxidized the color from all of the objects in the tomb, the tapestries on the walls, and even the skeletal remains of the King, which were laid out. The tomb also stunk. While the legend, of course, is that King Midas was buried with all this gold, there was, in fact, no gold in the tomb. The only gold that he was buried with was the liquid that was in the vessels in this tomb—a golden colored liquid that Dr. Pat learned through his molecular analysis had traces of honey, grapes, and barley in it.

There was also a petrified lamb stew in the tomb, which contributed to the odors that they encountered. We worked with Dr. Pat to bring this ancient ale back to life. We knew that the recipe came from an era 2,700 years ago when the tomb was built and sealed and that it predated hop cultivation. The climate in Turkey was also not conducive to hop growing, so we did the research of what other spices were growing in that area and saffron was the one that we believe was most likely prevalent. That is the spice that we use. You can imagine how expensive this 5-barrel batch of beer was. We sourced honey from Italy, saffron from India, and grapes from vineyards in California to make this beer. The most expensive beer Dogfish ever brewed. We thought we would only brew this recipe once, but we served it at a reenactment of Midas' feast at the University of Pennsylvania 6 months after that fated day when I met Dr. Pat. The Penn Museum caterers re-created the lentil and lamb stew and we brewed the beer. Numerous media outlets and journalists were invited to the event and they all fell in love with the Midas Touch beer and asked to write about it. When the *Philadelphia Enquirer* asked, "Will you ever brew this beer again?" I responded, "No, no, it's way too expensive, I can't afford the saffron and honey. It was just a one-off brew." By the next week, *People* and *Food and Wine magazines* were calling to do stories about Midas Touch. I could see it was in Dogfish Head's best interest to figure out a way to mass produce Midas Touch.

From the very first Cherry Brew beer I brewed in 1994 through 1998 with Raison D'Etre we were always seeking out world-class culinary ingredients from across America. We were inspired by the American food movement driven by luminaries like Alice Waters and James Beard. What made Midas Touch especially unique was that it was the first time that we looked globally to source exotic culinary recipes and culinary ingredients.

● in the money

"Sam has a reputation for doing things beyond the norm," wine critic Deborah Scoblionkov says of Calagione (at his Delaware brewery).

Go for the Gold

Beermaker Sam Calagione used grapes, honey, saffron and ingenuity to re-create King Midas's favorite ale

Sam Calagione is not your lite-beer kinda guy. In fact the Dogfish Head Craft Brewery owner's newest tipple could be labeled heavy metal. It's a re-creation of the ale served at the funeral feast of King Midas, who supposedly turned everything he touched into gold. Calagione, 32, got the ingredients from Patrick McGovern, 56, a University of Pennsylvania Museum scientist who found traces of barley, honey and grapes in jugs in the storied king's 2,700-year-old tomb in Turkey. How to prepare the golden grog was up to Calagione. "We're known as the guys that brew with weird stuff—like oregano, raisins and vanilla," he says, "but still make it taste good."

The brewmaster spent three months in his Rehoboth Beach, Del., brewpub mixing ingredients. Initial tastings by his wife and business partner, Mariah, 30, and the regulars at his restaurant got the thumbs-up. But the final say belonged to McGovern, who served the ancient ale at a benefit dinner. "I was surprised at how good it was," he says. "I ended up drinking at least four glasses."

Now Calagione, who lives in Lewes, Del., with Mariah and their son Sammy, 1, hopes to turn the stuff into liquid gold. Midas Touch Golden Elixir just hit stores nationwide. "A whole different group of people is looking at Dogfish Head," says his wife. "They're wondering what we'll come up with next." •

People.com For more on Dogfish Head Craft Brewery, go to **www.people.com** or **AOL (Keyword: People)**

PHOTOGRAPH BY SAM KITTNER

PEOPLE 6/11/01 103

The most expensive beer Dogfish ever brewed.

Dogfish Head
Midas Touch
ANCIENT ALE
between wine & mead, our original
is made with ingredients
2700-year-old drinking vessels in the
of King Midas - barley, honey,
muscat grapes & saffron
12 FL. OZ. | 9% ALC.

Namaste (4.8% ABV)

We made our own interpretation of an off-centered ale that also had the flavors of a Belgian beer. We called it Namaste. The idea and name for this beer came from my wife, who thought it would be cool if we did a Belgian-style white beer with lemongrass. I contributed the idea of using whole chunks of dried organic oranges instead of just the peel in the traditional manner. Mariah came up with the name and suggested the lemongrass, and the entire Dogfish Head community came together to make and sell Namaste. It was originally sold in a beautiful champagne bottle, and its origin is certainly a Wit, or Belgian wheat ale. It is its own unique thing within an existing variety of beer. Namaste is very flavorful but also extremely drinkable at a relatively low alcohol level of 4.8 percent. The Belgian-White beer style has grown to become one of the largest volume-style segments in the United States. For Dogfish Head, our Namaste is especially popular in the warmer months and we focus the sales geography for this along the coastal area of our backyard here in the Mid-Atlantic.

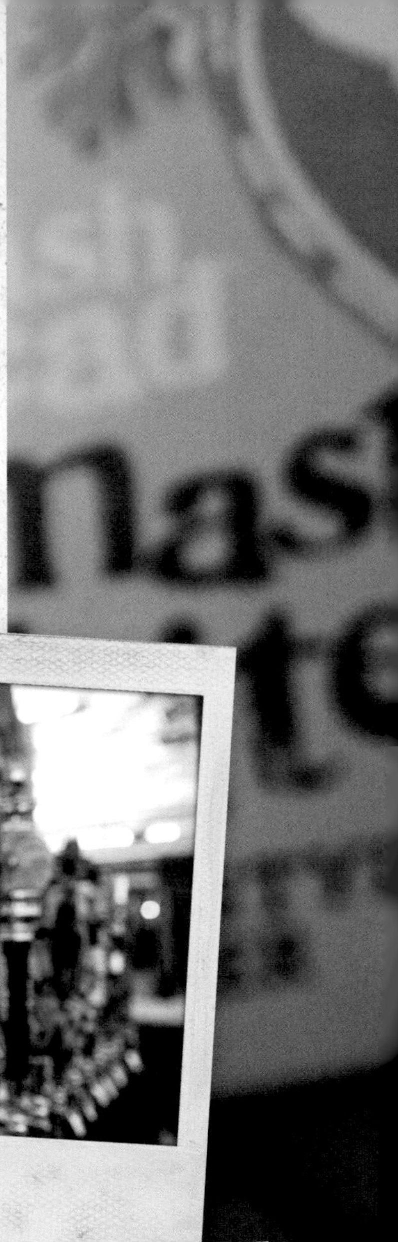

Namaste!

Brewer Liz Stairs preps oranges for a Namaste brew.

Dogfish Head
Namaste White
BELGIAN-STYLE WITBIER
Belgian-style White ale
with dried organic orange
peel, fresh-cut lemongrass,
coriander, peppercorns &
dose of good karma.
ALC. BY VOL.

90 Minute IPA (9.0% ABV)

In 1999 we brewed our very first test batch of 90 Minute IPA. That beer was inspired by a cooking show I saw. In the show, the chef was making a soup. As the soup was simmering, he was adding little pinches of crushed pepper throughout the entire 90 minutes that he simmered this soup. He explained that by adding pepper to the soup in tiny little pinches, in equal increments, throughout the entire time that the soup simmered, the flavors, the nuances, and the complexity of that pepper would be woven into the taste and aroma of that soup with more subtly and approachability than if you added that same volume of pepper all at once. I had an epiphany that maybe I could apply that technique to beer brewing. Traditionally in brewing, hops are added twice in large volumes during the brewing process—once early in the boil to add bitterness and then again at the end of the boil for aroma. I thought maybe if I add hops in tiny increments during the entire time the beer is boiling, I can add a lot more hops into this beer but keep the flavors nuanced and subtle with complexity and not bang the person over the head with them. I drove my pickup truck out to the local Salvation Army store where I go to buy my flannel farmer shirts, because I remembered that on the bottom shelf in the toy department of that Salvation Army was an old vibrating football game that a lot of people born in the '60s and '70s will probably remember, and bought it. I took that vibrating football game back to the brewery and put 2 two-by-fours on the long playing field of the football game. I then drilled holes into the bottom of a five gallon bucket, I duct taped that bucket to the two-by-fours and to the football game itself, then I filled the bucket with pelletized hops. I propped the bucket up on a stepladder that was positioned to be the perfect height that would allow it to be placed over the lip of the opening at the top of our boil kettle, so that just by changing the angle of the vibrating football game with a bucket propped on it, I could control the speed that the pelletized hops vibrated out of the bucket and down the football field into the boiling beer with a goal of having the pellets drop into the boiling beer, one at a time, continuously for the 90-minute boil. That was the day that Dogfish Head's innovation of continual hopping was born. And it worked. By adding hops to a beer in little increments continually you can make a beer that's intensely hoppy without being crushingly bitter. If we added that same weight and volume of hops in two stages, as was the standard in brewing, 90 Minute IPA would be unpleasantly and lingeringly bitter.

90 Minute

While my invention worked initially, within a couple weeks the game broke, so we had to manually add a pinch of hops every minute that we brewed that beer while we worked on designing the next generation of a continual hopping machine. Because of this arduous process, we quickly improvised a new continual hopping machine, which we dubbed "Sir Hops Alot." We're on our fourth iteration of continual hopping inventions, and it truly is an invention because it's rare to invent something in an industry today that's recognized as part of the spirit of our brand.

A version of that first continual hopping vibrating football game, along with our original 15-gallon boil kettle, can now be found in the permanent collection of the Smithsonian, the very same collection that houses the Wright Brothers' plane and the Apollo moon landing capsules. This obviously makes me and my coworkers very proud that our invention of continual hopping will live forever along with these other incredible American inventions.

Dogfish Head
90 MINUTE
IMPERIAL
IPA
Our continually hopped Imperial IPA whose powerful malt backbone stands up to the extreme hopping rate for a pungent, not crushing, hop flavor.
ALE | 9% ALC. BY VOL. | 12 FL. OZ.
TRU-ACTION ELECTRIC FOOTBALL GAME
TUDOR METAL PRODUCTS CORPORATION
NEW YORK, N. Y.

Indian Brown Ale

(7.2% ABV)

The next hybrid beer we brewed was our Indian Brown Ale. It is a hybrid of Americal Brown Ale, an IPA, and a Scotch Ale—three traditional styles of beer. It has the roasty, malty character of a brown ale; the high hopping rate of an IPA; and the caramelized and heightened alcohol of a Scotch Ale.

We named it Indian Brown Ale because in addition to the barley and organic brown sugar we add to the beer, we also added flaked maize to the recipe. Like 90 Minute IPA, the beer is also dry-hopped, adding a more citrusy flavor during the brewing process. We designed Indian Brown to be the ultimate beer pairing for a burger. It comes in at a little over seven percent alcohol by volume, so not quite as an intense as Raison D'Etre, the partner for steak. Indian Brown Ale is sort of Raison D'Etre's little brother.

INDE PEN DENT
Dogfish Head
Indian Brown
DARK IPA
IBA
about this ale:

OLDE SCHOOL
DOG FISH HEAD
A barleywine style ale
brewed with figs & dates.
15% alc. by vol. 12 fl. oz.

Olde School Barleywine (15% ABV)

Another iconic Dogfish beer that has stood the test of time, like 90 Minute where we've brewed it or have brewed different batches for over a decade, is our Olde School Barleywine, which we began brewing in 2002. This is sort of in the same family where superstrong beers like World Wide Stout play in, so we use that same sort of sadomasochist yeast regiment.

The inspiration for Olde School Barleywine came from reading a really cool book I bought from the website, Alibris.com, which sells rare and out-of-print books. I would browse the website every two or three months to see what brewing books they had acquired and oftentimes I would find obscure ones that would give me inspiration to resurrect an ancient style of beer that we would then put our new-world culinary thumbprint on.

Back in 2000, while browsing the site, I came across the image of a book that was written by a cellarman from eighteenth-century England. I paid the 20 bucks, bought this book written by this British cellarman, and waited eagerly for its arrival. A cellarman was a brewery worker who visited bars that were serving their cask-conditioned beers. Cask-conditioned beers were beers drawn from what's called a beer engine from a tank in the cellar of the bar through a hand pump. The tank the beer was stored in would still have active yeast in it, and the yeast would continue to eat what sugar was left in the beer while the beer was being served and the CO_2 by-product would get trapped in the tank and naturally carbonate that cask-conditioned beer. The practice was so inaccurate that the beers in the casks would often go flat, so part of a cellarman's job was to go around and figure out ways to re-carbonate these beers.

The book that arrived was not a book at all, but rather a handwritten journal—a slight, 16-page journal documenting the author's work as a cellarman. But in that handwritten cellarman's journal, he documented his secret for reactivating beer that had gone dormant and flat: He would tie strings to clumps of figs and dates and lower them into these tanks in the cellar. He was essentially fishing for the yeast in the bottom of the tank, moving the clumps around like a lure in a pond looking for fish.The activity of moving that string would stir up the yeast that had settled in the bottom of the tank. The yeast would find these clumps of dates and figs that were very rich in sugar, and the yeast would be reactivated by eating those sugars and would then re-carbonate the beer and salvage that batch of beer in the cellar of that pub.

The inspiration for Olde School Barleywine came from that journal. For centuries, English brewers have been making the barleywine style of beer, called barleywine because it's a beverage made with barley—the fermenting source of beer, but with the alcohol content of wine. Ours was even more of a hybrid because we introduced these dates and figs into the recipe using the same yeast regiment as we used for World Wide Stout. We were able to get Olde School Barleywine up to 15 percent ABV. As for the journal written by the wise yeast fishermen, it was unfortunately washed in a pair of dirty brewing pants. That ruined it and turned it into a puck of paper, which was stupid because it was probably worth a lot more than the 20 bucks I paid for it. I would love to have it now. I guess the beer is now a testament to the legacy of this journal.

We started brewing test batches in 2002. We started bottling that in 2003 using 750 ml bottles. For the Olde School Barleywine label's original artwork, I commissioned an artist living in Chicago named Jon Langford. I had bought one of his paintings of Johnny Cash that was hanging in a bar named Delilah's in Chicago. I loved it so much that when it came time to design the label for Olde School, I looked Jon up and commissioned him to do the artwork. Besides being a talented artist, Jon Langford played in the Mekons, a proto-punk band from England, and now plays with another great band called the Waco Brothers out of Chicago. Around that time I was also listening to a Library of Congress recording of an interview between famous folk singer and songwriter Woody Guthrie and the famous music historian Alan Lomax. In it Guthrie was telling Alan Lomax about the first time he and his train-riding hobo buddies brewed beer. He explained how he got a hold of a couple buckets of malt extract and some yeast packets intending to brew his own beer. The directions on the yeast packet read, "Add one packet to the malt extract, reconstitute it with water, and wait ten days." Woody Guthrie told the story, "So me and my friends got to thinking, why not add ten packets and wait one day and we drank that beer and golly we've never been sicker in our lives." I love that yeast story, and if you see the Olde School label, it shows a character that looks sort of like Woody Guthrie holding the yeast packets. The story of how that cellarman brought the yeast back to life reminded me of how ingenious Woody Guthrie thought he was with the way he used the yeast in that story.

Dogfish Head
Craft Brewery

A barleywine style ale brewed with figs & dates.
Dogfish Head Craft Brewery
OLDE SCHOOL
4 x 12 fl. oz. | 15% a.b.v.

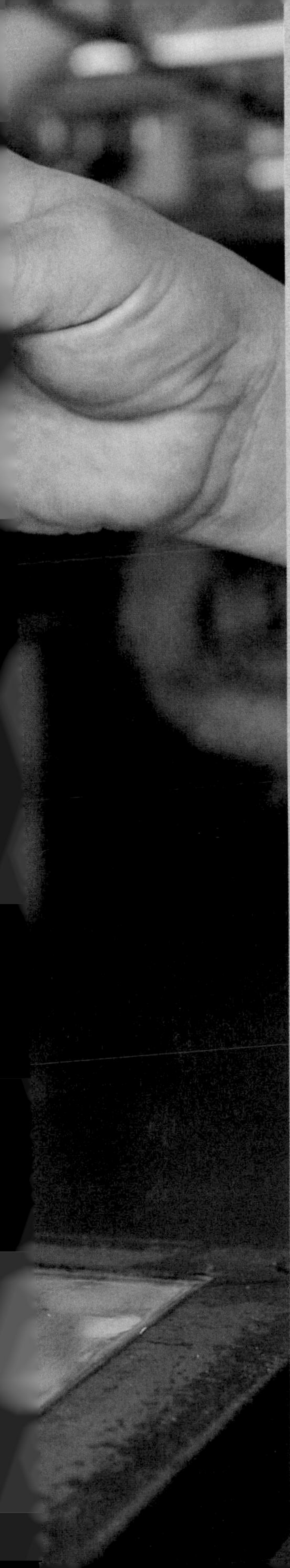

Jon Langford went on to do a number of iconic bottle label artwork for Dogfish, including the artwork for batches of 75 Minute IPA, Raison D'Extra, and Immort Ale. He also contributed art to our Analog-A-Go-Go record and artisan festivals we put on at the brewery every year for nearly a decade.

Jon Langford was really the first of a long line of supertalented and renowned artists that Dogfish Head was fortunate enough to work with before 2002. Up to this point I was designing all the labels myself—either I'd paint them or I'd cut and paste them together using our original doggy font.

Once we worked with Jon, we enjoyed that process so much that we began sourcing artwork from various artists. During that time, we started gaining some financial strength where I didn't have to design the labels myself out of necessity because we couldn't afford artists. Once we could afford artists, we started seeking out ones that inspired us—usually artists of my own age—to do fun, creative projects with me.

There's a great scene in Ernest Hemingway's book *A Moveable Feast* where the famous writer Gertrude Stein is showing Hemingway and his wife around her apartment, 27 rue de Fleurus in Paris, and she's showing them her collection of original Picassos and other painters who were maybe just a little bit older than Gertrude Stein. Stein was probably more than twice Hemingway's age and she gave Hemingway and his wife some advice: "Pay no attention to your clothes and no attention to all the mode, and buy your clothes for comfort and durability, and you will have the clothes money to buy pictures (paintings) ... Buy the people of your own age—of your own military service group. You'll know them. You'll meet them around the quarter. There are always good new serious painters." I think I took this story to heart because as soon as we could, the first thing we did was to invite coworkers who had complementary talents to Mariah and me to join our company, and the second thing we did with that financial strength was to seek out local non-profit groups and artists of our generation who inspired us to help amplify our creative journey and add their voices to it.

Nobody told me there'd be days like this

It was the end of the summer, early September 2002. I was scheduled to face another physically impossible workday. As our bottling crew loaded our undersized delivery truck with pallets of beer, I stood at a worktable constructing tap handles.

Most of the big breweries opt to order generic tap handles out of a catalog, but to be consistent with our off-centered motto, our brewery produces an off-centered tap handle. First, a local blacksmith bangs out a metal rod and welds bolts to the base of it; then a friend of the brewery who is a guitar maker designs and whittles a few dozen foot-tall wooden fish. The rods and fish make it to the brewery in paper bags and land on my workbench. Then I put them together by drilling a hole in the fish, filling the hole with epoxy, jamming the rod into the hole, and affixing a metal badge onto the fish that describes what style of beer is on tap. I then take these tap handles to potential draft accounts in the surrounding cities along with cold beer samples and try to convince them to put Dogfish on tap. When I'm making these tap handles, I always feel like a Zulu warrior, sharpening his spear before a big hunt. I'm thinking more about nailing a few new accounts and the thrill of the chase than about the incredible inefficiencies associated with making tap handles this way.

On this particular day, after completing the tap handles, I had to deliver a truckload of beer to Friedland Distributing in downtown Philadelphia, check in with a few existing accounts, drop off samples at a couple of potential accounts, and end my day hosting a beer tasting at a hip-to-be-square art gallery in downtown Philly. Since we had first begun distributing our beers in 1996, I had been playing the role of delivery guy-salesman-president-brewer with blurry and varied results.

Believing this to be a great way to kill a whole mess of birds with one heavy stone, I would schedule other appointments while in the city to drop off a delivery. I would drive the truckload of beer into the city, unload the truck by hand, head out into the city to solicit new business, patronize an existing account for an early dinner/happy hour tasting during rush hour, and then drive back to Delaware to be home in time to tuck my children in bed.

The first time I delivered to Friedland's (our Philly distributor, located in the absolute worst, sketchy and scary neighborhood in all of Philly), I got lost. Like a man with a death wish, I rolled down my window to ask some guy standing guard over a burning car for directions. He said he knew exactly where I needed to go but wouldn't tell me until I bought "something" off of him. I did as I was told out of fear and arrived at Friedland's 10 minutes later. When I described the freakish scene I'd just lived through, Eddie Friedland calmly informed me that he knew exactly the person I had run into, and quite frankly, the shit he was selling wasn't nearly as good as that being sold three blocks in the opposite direction. Welcome to the beer business.

I loaded a few cases of Midas Touch beer into the cab of my truck along with a bunch of posters and coasters for the art gallery event we were sponsoring later that evening. I had been contacted by a partner in a thirtysomething-run, self-described "edgy" and "young" PR firm. His company was putting together this extreme sport/skateboarding/art throwdown that was being covered by major magazines and cable networks. All we had to do was provide some product. How could we lose? It was the perfect demographic for us to showcase our over-the-top, edgy (that word again) beers, which, he added, he happened to love himself.

Dogfish Head
Craft Brewed Ales
namaste
look up!!!

And love himself he did. But it sounded like a good opportunity, so I said, what the heck, and committed eight cases of beer and my presence to the event. I called my college buddy Tom, invited him, and asked if I could crash at his downtown apartment if we had too much fun. He was on board. The plan was set. The truck was loaded. I hit the road.

As usual I was multitasking—driving, taking down a phone number on a scrap of paper, and talking to the brewery production manager, John, on the cell phone—as I came to the intersection for coastal Route 1, the primary road bisecting east and west Delaware. As I prepared to stop, my brakes failed and the box truck coasted out into oncoming traffic. I was composed enough to inform John what was about to happen. "Holy shit, I'm about to hit this car!" were the words he later informed me I used before he heard the sound of breaking glass. I threw the phone down and braced myself as a Ford Escort station wagon bore down on me from the southbound lane. I could see the driver's face clearly and his posture mirrored my own. White knuckles on the steering wheels, our wide eyes met. He was already braking and his 60 miles per hour speed was dropping. I thought if I sped up he would pass right behind me. Boy, was I wrong. As I accelerated he fishtailed into me. He nailed me right below my driver's side door. My window shattered, and I took a little glass shrapnel in the cheek. He had just missed my gas tank but took out my hydraulics and my electronics at the point of impact. So now, thanks to my brilliant decision to speed up, I was doing 30 miles per hour over the median and into the northbound lane, unable to turn or brake.

The first thing I noticed as I looked south at the oncoming traffic was that there were no cars within striking distance. My sigh of relief was choked by a fearful gasp in the next instant as I realized I was headed directly for a telephone pole on the shoulder of the road. I turned the wheel instinctively, which of course did nothing, but the impact of the accident had altered my course so that I was turning almost as much as I needed to. The telephone pole sheared off my driver's side mirror and scraped down the side of the box truck. More interesting I suppose was the way the telephone pole support cables sliced through the top of the box truck and opened it like a giant can of tuna. As I jammed to a stop to the sound of metal cutting metal, I looked out my nonexistent window and noticed the Escort had landed safely in the median and the driver was blinking in shock at the fully inflated air bag before him.

The engine was killed when I lost electric power, and as the symphony of destructive sounds faded from my ears I heard my name being called. It wasn't God. It was John. He was still connected on my cell phone. I picked up the phone and put it to my one unbloodied ear. First he asked if everyone was okay. He then informed me that the scene he'd just heard unfold—shattering glass, shearing metal, and lots of meaty cusswords—was more exciting than any episode of *Cops* he had ever watched. I promptly thanked him, hung up, and dialed 911 to fill them in on what just happened and where we were. I climbed out my window and ran to the median to check on the guy I had just hit. Thankfully he was all right. His nose was bleeding from where his eyeglasses had met the air bag, but otherwise he was not hurt.

As I was apologizing and explaining what had happened the police arrived along with an ambulance. They gave me a ticket and called a tow truck. The dealer from which I'd bought the truck was only 10 miles up the road. I called to inform the guys at the brewery that they should rent a moving truck and meet me at the dealership in half an hour. At the dealership they informed me that the frame was bent beyond repair, the electronics and hydraulics were shot, the axle was ripped, and the box on my box truck would never look like a box again. The guys from the brewery showed up, and we backed the U-Haul flush with the rear of our useless truck and unloaded and reloaded 350 cases of beer by hand.

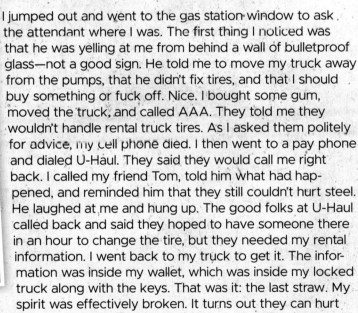

Two and a half hours after the moment of impact I was ramping onto the highway, back on course. I was sweaty, dirty, and a little bloody, but back on course. I called my friend Tom to inform him of what had just happened. He asked if I was sure I still wanted to come. I stiffened my upper lip and blurted, "You can't hurt steel," an old rallying cry of immortality from our college days. He responded, "Game on," as I had hoped he would. I hung up and called Friedland Distributing to inform them I would be a little late. The U-Haul I was driving was basically a glorified van with a box-truck back that was made to carry sofa sets and coffee tables, not multiple half-ton pallets of beer. It was doing this swervy dance all over the highway anytime I went over 52 miles per hour. Each time I hit a pothole, the back tires would bottom out and scrape the underside of the wheel wells in a cloud of smoke and burnt rubber stench. This happened until I was just north of Wilmington, at which point a back tire blew out and I careened off the highway. I managed to do a controlled dive onto an exit ramp and into a gas station at the base of the ramp.

I jumped out and went to the gas station window to ask the attendant where I was. The first thing I noticed was that he was yelling at me from behind a wall of bulletproof glass—not a good sign. He told me to move my truck away from the pumps, that he didn't fix tires, and that I should buy something or fuck off. Nice. I bought some gum, moved the truck, and called AAA. They told me they wouldn't handle rental truck tires. As I asked them politely for advice, my cell phone died. I then went to a pay phone and dialed U-Haul. They said they would call me right back. I called my friend Tom, told him what had happened, and reminded him that they still couldn't hurt steel. He laughed at me and hung up. The good folks at U-Haul called back and said they hoped to have someone there in an hour to change the tire, but they needed my rental information. I went back to my truck to get it. The information was inside my wallet, which was inside my locked truck along with the keys. That was it: the last straw. My spirit was effectively broken. It turns out they can hurt steel. I called my friend Tom and told him to please send lawyers, guns, and money ASAP. I gave him my coordinates. The sun was going down in the land of bulletproof glass, and I had a broken truck overflowing with mind-altering substances. It was like a robbery-scenario equivalent to The Perfect Storm. Tom left work and headed my way on a lifesaving mission.

To make a long story a little less long, I was back on the road a mere three hours later. I paid one company to unlock the truck, paid another to replace the tire, and purchased more gum than a bus full of sixth graders on a field trip for the right to stand my ground. Tom arrived to help me through all of this, ever mindful of the desperate eyes fixed on his late-model Audi.

I headed back onto the highway in a truck that was still way overloaded. I was covered in sweat, grime, motor oil, and exhaustion. It was enough to drive a man to drink.

I called Friedland Distributing and told them where I was. They said there was no way I was going to reach them before they closed and could I come back tomorrow. I laughed a little too maniacally into the receiver of Tom's cell phone (mine was long dead) and asked them if they were kidding. They weren't kidding. They felt my pain but would not acquiesce. I called my friends at Philadelphia's Yards Brewery. They were gracious enough to let me leave the beer at their place and have Friedland pick it up the next day. I dropped the load and raced to the art gallery. My contact there was antsy when he greeted me because the party was set to start in 10 minutes. He wondered why the beer wasn't cold yet and if I was really going to wear that to the party (he pointed to my dirty, bloody shirt). I started to describe my day to him as his eyes glazed over and he interrupted to say that while I iced the beer he would get me another shirt.

I was now wearing a too-small skater shirt, and I looked like an extra from an Avril Lavigne video. I was standing behind a Red Bull bar in a graffiti-stained art gallery preparing to serve beer made with grapes to a bunch of green-haired, multi-pierced trustafarians. I found myself wondering what August Busch III was doing at that very moment.

Tom and I went out to retrieve the last two cases of beer from the truck. When we returned, the pansy-assed public relations (PR) guru got in my face and started waving a bloody middle finger at me. He had broken one of the beer bottles while trying to remove its cork, and boy was he pissed. The corks weren't coming out of the bottles, and he didn't have time for this. I looked down at the empty beer cases and noticed they were marked "recork." These cases, I now realized, were from a batch we bottled with corks that were one size too big. Most of these cases were mistakenly distributed, yet their reception was a great indication of our customers' loyalty. The corks were supposed to pop out à la champagne, but since they were too tight you needed a corkscrew. Unfortunately, if you screwed down too far the bottle exploded in your hand, which, according to the number of irate phone calls and emails we received, happened quite frequently. We instituted an aggressive policy in which anyone who emailed us a picture of their hand bleeding received a Dogfish Head T-shirt. Anyone who emailed a picture of their hand with stitches received a hat. Our lawyer was more dumbfounded than impressed with this policy.

So I explained the situation to the PR guy, and he continued to give me the finger. I really wanted to pick this little wuss up by his over-coiffed hair and shake some backbone into him. In the past 12 hours I had lived through a car accident that totaled two vehicles, unloaded and reloaded 350 cases of beer by hand, swerved off the highway in my second runaway truck of the day, survived a lockout in one of the scariest urban combat zones outside of a third-world country, and continued on to Philadelphia in the very same death mobile just to make it to his little party on time.

But that's not what I did. Instead I walked around him to the bar. I opened up every bottle of beer that I'd brought with me except four. I told him his problems were solved and that I would send him a T-shirt (unless he required stitches, in which case I would send him a hat). At the end of the evening I lay awake on the sofa in Tom's apartment, alone with my thoughts and bruises. I couldn't really be upset with the bloody-fingered PR pansy. On a basic level he was right. I promised him the beer, and I had an obligation to make sure his patrons got what they expected.

Before leaving the art gallery I shared a beer with a guy who hadn't tried our Midas Touch beer before. He usually drank wine, and I explained the wine-like character of this beer to him. I described the day the recipe was discovered in King Midas's tomb in Turkey. The 2,700-year-old tomb was so perfectly preserved that, as the last rock obstructing the entrance was removed, the archeologists on hand literally watched the colors fade from the tapestries on the walls. He really liked the beer and asked where he could buy it in Philadelphia. I wrote out the address of the closest store as I walked out the door.

That night, as I lay there on the sofa thinking about this new Dogfish convert, I polished off the last glass of Midas. I thought about what a career-affirming moment it must have been for the archeologists as they walked into that tomb and stared at the fading walls. I thought about my day and all of the work that I had in front of me. I shut my eyes and fell sound asleep, looking forward to the next day.

Bryan Selders

Brewing Ambassador

Start Date: 2002

On this particular day in the Rehoboth brewhouse, Bryan is gearing up for a brew. He is surrounded by fermenters, each one with a different beer in various stages of fermentation. There is a Hazy Brown IPA, Faithful Companion, and a nitro beer inspired by the flavors in Cracklin' Oat Bran cereal. This will be a mild ale with toasted coconut, cinnamon, nutmeg, a bunch of oats, and molasses. No, he did not use Crackling' Oat Bran to make it. That would have been lazy and only good for useless Instagram fodder. We want this beer to be good! And finally, there is a Double IPA almost complete and heading to the taps in the other room for our guests. When you are around someone who is passionate about what they do, it is hard not to pick up on it. Bryan is no exception to this rule, especially on a brew day.

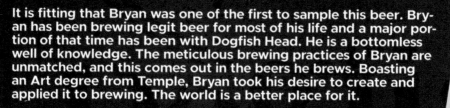

Bryan was working up at Nodding Head in Philly one day when a young Sam Calagione came walking through the door. He had a new beer he wanted everyone to taste that had a new hopping process he had come up with. That beer was 90 Minute IPA and would go on to change beer forever. Bryan knew Sam and got a taste. It was unlike anything else anyone was doing at the time, so when he got the opportunity to work for Dogfish Head, he jumped at the chance.

It is fitting that Bryan was one of the first to sample this beer. Bryan has been brewing legit beer for most of his life and a major portion of that time has been with Dogfish Head. He is a bottomless well of knowledge. The meticulous brewing practices of Bryan are unmatched, and this comes out in the beers he brews. Boasting an Art degree from Temple, Bryan took his desire to create and applied it to brewing. The world is a better place for it.

He started with Dogfish Head in 2002 when we were still located in our Lewes Brewery and getting ready to make the jump to the Milton facility. Because of this, Bryan has brewed beer on pretty much every brewing system we have ever had. The first-generation continuous hopper was the vibrating football game that is now making its way to the Smithsonian. The second-generation continuous hopper was our friend Sir Hops Alot. What people don't know is that there was a hopping device between these two engineering feats. That hopping device? Bryan Selders standing on a superdangerous platform with a pint glass dumping hops into a boil kettle for 90 minutes. He himself was a continuous hopper. You better believe he questioned his move down to Dogfish Head on some of those exciting days! This arduous and dangerous process had to go, so Sam and Brian created Sir Hops Alot. In that same year, Dogfish Head left Lewes and opened in the Milton facility.

Selders is also the one half of the dynamic duo The Pain Relivaz, a hip-hop group with Sam Calagione that drops some serious lyrical science interwoven with beer-geek knowledge, incomprehensible allusions, and some sophomoric humor unmatched by any other craft beer hip-hop group (because they are the only one that exists in this dynamic category). Recently, The Pain Relivaz have been killing some acoustic sets for Analog-A-Go-Go at the Dogfish Inn.

In 2011, Bryan knew the burnout factor was real and had to step away. In 2013, he got a wild hair and went on a "Rumshchpriga." He, his wife, Ally, and his two boys Charlie and Max packed up the Volvo and made their way west to Colorado to partake in

Coworker Profile

craft beer expansion. When he decided to make the move, Big Mama said, "You'll be back, honey." Big Mama was right (again), and we couldn't have been happier when this superhuman returned. Selders came back from his walkabout in 2017 to help build and run the new Brewhouse at Pub 2.0. Bryan has always been a brewer by title, but at one point when the CFO position was created and Nick Benz took on the title at Dogfish Head, Bryan decided to change his title to C3PO. Today, he is the Brewing Ambassador, and pretty much any Brewpub Exclusive you have at the Pub will be Bryan's doing. Standing in the new Brewhouse at Pub 2.0, you can see that Bryan is at home. When it comes to talking Dogfish Head history or beer geek knowledge, this man is hard to top.

Since Bryan has been around so many different beers, it is fun to know which beers he likes the least. That's a toss-up for him. One that stands out is Verdi Verdi Good. This was the beer we made for St. Patrick's Day. We wanted green beer, so we used Spirulina, a blue-green algae. Was it good? No sir. It had a bit of a pond flavor to it. Bryan is also not a big fan of a fan favorite: 120 Minute IPA. Sorry, 120 fans. It ain't for everybody.

One fateful day in Milton, Bryan was helping with a batch of Aprihop. At that time, we didn't have air-conditioning in the cellars. The fermenters are all jacketed so the fermenting beer holds the right temperature. Bryan needed to get a ton of Aprihop puree into the fermenters but the only way in was through the top. The best way up to the top of this 25-foot vessel? A forklift with a pallet on it, of course. Bryan was putting the puree in, lost his footing, and was off on Mr. Toad's Wild Ride sliding down the edge of the fermenter. Luckily, the forklift and pallet were up next to the fermenters. Bryan was able to throw himself off the edge of the fermenter and toss himself across the gap between the fermenter and the makeshift pallet deck. He pulled himself back up and wiped himself off. "Maybe we need a different way to do this?" he called out to the forklift driver. Nothing like a near-death experience to really help drive new and improved brewing processes.

"It is good to be obsessed, go down the rabbit holes, and explore," says Selders. He has always been obsessed with the saison and pilsner beer styles. When he was out west brewing with The Post, he won two medals at GABF in these categories. Bryan puts his heart and soul into what he loves, and it comes out in the liquid.

A direct interaction with the brewing process is what gets Bryan up and going. The new brewhouse at the pub is right where he needs to be. In the summer, he works hard to keep up with Covered in Nuggs, an IPA created to celebrate IPA Day in 2018. We can't keep it on tap at the pub in the summer because it goes so quickly. Just keeping up with this beer is a pain in the ass. It takes 18 days to make and is gone in 8 days.

If you are lucky enough to brew with Selders, you are sure to learn something new. You are going to laugh. He never stops learning, and when he gets riffing about beer ingredients or even just water, it seems there is no end to what he knows. What really stands out is how excited he is about what he does at Dogfish Head, and this excitement is contagious. Today you can book time with him in our "Beers with Bryan" program. This is a monthly experience where you'll have the chance to pick Bryan's brain and talk all-things beer—everything from brewing, Dogfish history, the future of Dogfish, food pairings, and a Q&A session that includes a tour of the brewhouse in Rehoboth.

If you were on a deserted island and could have one album to listen to and an unlimited supply of one beer, what would it be?

Beer: 60 Minute IPA
Album: Stevie Wonder, *Songs in the Key of Life*

Chapter 3

Think Global, Drink Local

The identity of our brewpub is centered around three things: original beers, original food, and original music. We make our own fresh beer locally and believe in doing things the same way in our kitchen. As we were formulating our menus before we opened, we took extra time to locate and meet with local growers and food companies with which we could do business. We knew that we would pay a premium to use locally grown products and that service might not be as regular as it would be from a national food distribution company, but we felt that this local, fresh connection was germane to our company identity. Not only did we gladly pay the premium for their wares but we set aside a large fraction of our menu space that we call Local Yocals. We use this section to list the different local mushroom growers, herb growers, dairy companies, and fish purveyors and tell a little something about their companies as well. There is obviously a great deal of harmony between Dogfish Head and these independent businesspeople, and I'm proud to say that many are customers as well as suppliers.

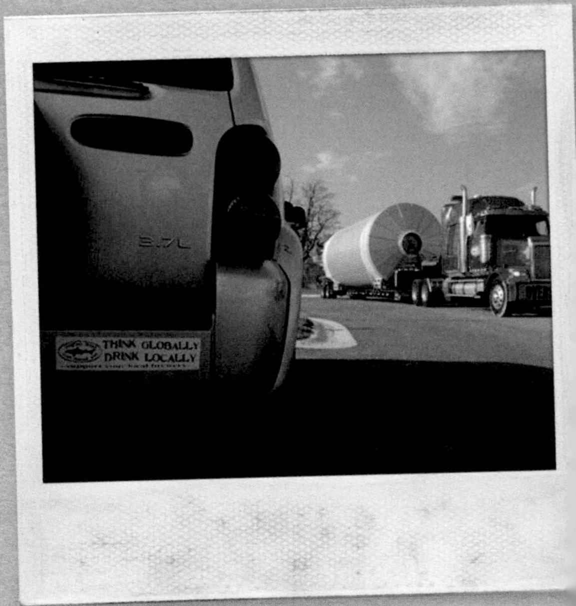

At Dogfish Head we look at other small indie businesses as allies putting something special or unique into the world. We spend more time, resources, and energy on the positive world of collaboration and much less on the negative, reactionary world of competition. The equity and harmony of these alliances can be measured using different metrics. Early on, we began working with a local farmer on an alliance project that is as unorthodox as it is exciting. In the brewing process, the largest fraction of solid waste is the barley grain and husk left over from the mashing. While a lot of the natural sugars and flavor are extracted from the barley during brewing, the remaining material is actually very nutritious and high in protein. It makes an ideal cow feed. So we give our grain away to a local farmer to feed to his cows. We went out to visit the cows with the farmer one summer evening to watch them literally run after the grain cart. You see, the juice left over with the grain undergoes a spontaneous fermentation as it sits in the summer sun, and the cows seem to really enjoy the extra kick they get from their food during the warmer months. The farmer brought us some meat one day and it was excellent. By utilizing our spent grain, the farmer could use a smaller fraction of cheap fillers and cereals to make up the balance of the cows' diet, and the result was higher-quality meat. So we shifted our purchasing of hamburger and steak beef away from a giant slaughterhouse and toward this local farmer. In this process we have closed a unique agricultural circle. Today, we are still sending out the spent grains to farms but we are no longer sourcing our burgers from this original local farm. With that said, we do source the beef we use at our pub from family-owned and operated Roseda Farms in Maryland, where they dry age all their beef. You are still going to like the burgers ... we promise.

Dogfish Head
What You have here is a bottle conditioned brown ale.
DIRECTIONS:
Open bottle. Pour contents into two snifters. Enjoy.
OR: Walk hand-in-neck with bottle into the middle of the woods.
Use a shovel to dig a 2 X 2 hole three feet deep.
Seal the bottle in a plastic bag.
Place in hole and pack with dirt.
Memorize location and leave.
Return exactly one year later.
Dig up bottle, open, and enjoy.
GOVERNMENT WARNING: (1) ACCORDING TO THE SURGEON GENERAL, WOMEN SHOULD NOT DRINK ALCOHOLIC BEVERAGES DURING PREGNANCY BECAUSE OF THE RISK OF BIRTH DEFECTS. (2) CONSUMPTION OF ALCOHOLIC BEVERAGES IMPAIRS YOUR ABILITY TO DRIVE A CAR OR OPERATE MACHINERY, AND MAY CAUSE HEALTH PROBLEMS.
Raison D'Extra
A bulbous brown ale.
1 Pint 9.6 ounces
Raison D'Extra
DEC 1 9 2002
This beer ages with the best of 'em
CT-ME-VT-DE-NY-MA-IA-OR 5 CENT DEPOSIT.
MI 10 CENT DEPOSIT. CA CASH REFUND
PH1.888.8dogfish www.dogfish.com
01 02 03 04 05

Original Raison D'Extra label

Sam with the Italian Grandmothers dinner

Lewes brewery

Article in the *Ale Street News*

October-November 2002 | Ale Street News | Page 13

Dogfish Head Steps up the Pace

New Brewery, Distillery On Line

By Lew Bryson

If you remember Dogfish Head as a little beach brewpub, you're out to sea. If your latest Dogfish Head memory is Immort Ale, wake up and smell the Chicory Stout. If you think Sam Calagione's still chasing Jim Koch's big beers, you've been left behind. Dogfish Head has broken out of the pack with a big new brewery, big new beers, and a big new endeavor: distilling.

I drove down to Milton, Delaware in September to see what was going on. I heard about the big new brewery, but I wasn't expecting what I found. With the 50 bbl. brewhouse out of Poor Henry's (which has undoubtedly already seen more use at Dogfish Head than it ever did in Philly) and a huge old canning facility building, Dogfish Head has five times the floor space, five times the bottling capacity, and three times the daily production capacity of their old Lewes brewery. The brewery is on track for 10,000 bbls. production in 2002, a huge jump up from the 6,500 bbls. they did last year. "It's been a big step up for us," Sam told me.

They haven't slowed down on the big beers, either. There's a special fermentation room for their big open tanks: Immort Ale, 90 Minute IPA, and a new barleywine, Old School, that's made with an addition of pureed figs and dates. This year's batch of World Wide Stout was bubbling away; I helped Sam "feed the bitch" with 100 lbs. of what Sam would only say was "special sugar."

Dogfish Head may still be making off-center ales for off-center people, but they've gotten serious about it. Head brewer John Gillooly is one reason. He has big-micro experience from Mendocino and Redhook, and a managerial touch that keeps this motivated and creative crew working together towards a goal of better, more consistent beers. That kind of thing is a must for a brewery that's growing this fast.

Where did the money come from for such a big place? "It's not that much money," Sam protests. "We got the equipment out of Ortlieb's for 18 cents on the dollar. The restaurant in Rehoboth is doing great, which convinced the bank to give us a big loan." It's not investment money; Sam and his wife, Mariah, still own 78 percent of the company. The building itself came as what Sam called "a sweetheart deal" with the developer. Dogfish Head is going to be the industrial cornerstone of a new planned high-tech community, Cannery Village, that will double the population of Milton.

The view out the front door looks like a war-zone right now, shattered earth and broken walls, but it's going to be the town square. Once that's up in 2004, Dogfish Head will open a restaurant and taproom in the front of the brewery, where the staff now have their kickball diamond. "We take kickball seriously," Sam said with an ironically huge grin.

A national beergeek buzz is building on Dogfish's big 90 Minute IPA and World Wide Stout, a buzz I haven't witnessed since Victory's HopDevil and Old Horizontal came to national attention four years ago. "90 Minute is growing fast," Sam admitted somewhat ruefully. "But the corking is a problem." The corking and caging machine is the next piece of equipment scheduled for replacement, but for now it gives the brewers fits.

The latest beer projects are the Old School Barleywine and bottle-conditioned 60 Minute IPA. Old School is from an old English strong ale recipe Sam turned up that included suspended bags of figs and dates in the brew. The brewers have modified that to a puree, and plan to age the 14 percent brew on a huge bed of Fuggles hops. The 60 Minute IPA bottled real ale is nothing short of brilliant, one of the closest approximations of cask ale in a bottle that I've ever had the pleasure to lay lip to. Both are coming soon, perhaps in November.

Of course, the big buzz — so to speak — at Dogfish Head is distilling. "We're working under our brewpub license," Sam explained. "I spent a lot of time up in Dover, but this is a small, business-friendly state. And we haven't blown anything up yet, so that helps."

Head brewer John Gilooley, packaging king Kevin Sundy, and the head of Dogfish, Sam Calagione in the new Milton brewery's fermentation hall

Former head brewer Jason Kennedy is back as distiller, working an internally-designed and built pot still that looks like a Mars lander. "We were driving around a scrapyard," Sam said with "doesn't everyone?" air. "We saw this stainless steel cone. I don't know what it was, they didn't know either, but we took it and welded a steam jacket on it, welded some the fittings on, and it works pretty well."

I'll say it does. Jason's making three spirits up on the second floor of the Dogfish Head brewpub in Rehoboth Beach: Dark Honey Rum, Wit Rum, and he's just stilled off the first batch of gin. He and Sam and I had an informal tasting of various batches of rum and the gin over dinner. The rums are triple-distilled out of table-grade unsulfured molasses, the gin is distilled four times. First the molasses is mixed with water and fermented with a clean distiller's yeast to about 11% abv. Then it is stilled down from 400 gallons of "wash" to 22 gallons of spirit that is cut to 80 proof.

The Dark Honey Rum is mixed with honey, and aged on toasted American oak chips for at least six months to yield a dark, rich rum. The Wit Rum is taken clear and charged with coriander and bitter orange peel, a spicing that yields a brisk rum delightfully tinged with an almost Cointreau-like orange character. The gin, which is planned for brewpub sales only, was quite nice...and I despise gin. There are only four botanicals: juniper, tri-color peppercorns, rosemary, and pineapple mint. "There are 1,093 botanicals allowed in gin," Jason noted. "I picked four for the four distillations — and to keep it simple." It's beautifully simple, crisp, brisk, and powerful.

Why distill? "Our momentum as a brewery was headed that way," Sam said. "We were pushing the alcohol envelope on beer, and that led right to it. We just have our toe in it now, and there's not the same level of expectation as with the beer, but it's still all about excitement. That's what sells it. I've always felt that our products themselves are our marketing campaign." A beautiful sentiment from a man who bases his business on poetic philosophy rather than business school axioms.

Milton

By 2002, excitement around our off-centered ales was expanding. Our early distribution started out by hand-bottling 22-ounce bottles of Shelter Pale Ale and doing draft of early beers like Immort Ale and Chicory Stout out of that 5-barrel brewery in 1996. By 1997, demand was such that we knew we needed to expand and open a second production brewery, so that's what we did. We used a bunch of old dairy and cannery equipment and we opened a 30-barrel brewery near Five Points Lewes. We operated that as our production brewery from 1997 until 2002, when we knew if we were to grow, we had to expand production further.

The town of Milton was an industrial town that had button factories where they made buttons out of bones of animals, and it was also a ship-building town. If you look at some of the houses in downtown Milton, they're asymmetrical because they were built out of the scraps from the shipyards by all the carpenters who lived in the town and worked as shipbuilders for a living.

Because it was also a big farming town, there were a couple of canneries. One of the largest canneries was the Draper King Cole Cannery, which operated as a vegetable and fruit cannery for over 100 years. The cannery had fallen on hard times in the late 90s and early 2000s, and couldn't compete with all the big, national canning conglomerates. It was on the brink of bankruptcy when Mariah's dad, Tom Draper, who was on the board of directors of Dogfish Head, decided to buy it. Tom was a really accomplished entrepreneur in his own right as the founder of Draper Communications, which owned radio stations and TV stations locally.

Tom razed some of the dilapidated buildings that were part of the cannery. He cleared the fields and started plans to develop a mixed-use community that would include residential properties and commercial businesses. Tom knew that Dogfish was kind of stretched to the limits of what we had in our little building in Lewes and he came to me and asked, "Hey Sam, I know you can't grow anymore in your location in Lewes, how would you like to move out to the old cannery that I just bought and be our anchor tenant of the commercial part of that?" He said, "I don't have any plans to sell it to, I'll continue to develop it, but I'll give you a cheap rent if you come and move out here."

So away we went and in 2002 we moved out to the former Draper King Cole Cannery in Milton. We purchased the brewing equipment of Ortlieb's Brewery, a brewery in downtown Philadelphia that went out of business in 2001, in preparation for our move and production expansion.

In the new brewery, we installed six 100-barrel unitanks that could be used for the fermentation or carbonation processes; two 100-barrel bright tanks, or pressure-rated, temperature-controlled tanks that could store beer waiting to be packaged; and a hodgepodge of the old shitty cannery and dairy tanks that we brought over from the old production brewery in Five Points Lewes. We also purchased and installed a bottling line when we bought that brewing system from Ortlieb's, which we installed here as well as a small kegging line.

Although we were open and brewing beer from 1995 until 2002, for those first seven years we never actually brewed beer on commercial brewing equipment. We were either making beer on our glorified home-brewing equipment or on used dairy and canning equipment that we MacGyvered into functional brewing equipment. The decision to grow that way played an important role in the history of Dogfish, because by repurposing used equipment from other industries that we bought for pennies on the dollar, it meant that Dogfish Head did not have to go into a lot of debt to start our brewery. We had some really difficult years in the early years, and if we had gone into debt buying a new, large brewing system, we probably wouldn't have been able to pay our bills and might not have made it through the rough years. So the fact that we had no money at the start actually made us financially strong, ironically enough, because we never went out over our skis with debt in those early years. Finally, with a real, commercial 50-barrel brewing system installed, we were ready to open our doors, and in 2002, we opened Dogfish Head Brewery in Milton, Delaware.

Sam: Andrew, you want to add anything before we go inside?

Andrew: When we did some of the upgrades here, we actually unearthed some of the abalone shells from when it was a button factory and a bunch of punch outs from the buttons made here.

Sam: Oh, that's right, they didn't use bones, they used shells. That's a little less macabre.

Dogfish Head Craft Brewery, Milton, Delaware

Rhythm

I have always loved music. I remember being a kid and pointing my magic Wiffle ball bat at my parents' radio and chanting hexes in an effort to get it to spit forth Laura Branigan's "Gloria." I remember being embarrassed crying tears of joy in front of my sisters one Christmas upon opening my LP copy of *Doctor Demento's Funky Favorites*. (I didn't say that I always loved good music, just that I always loved music.)

As I got older my tastes developed, diversified, and intensified, but my love for music goes back to my earliest childhood memories. Like many lovers of music, I longed to create music of my own. I wasn't willing to let my lack of tone or talent get in my way. Luckly, I was not the only one with this dream at Dogfish Head. So, in 2002, one of our brewers, Bryan Selders, and I formed a group called the Pain Relievaz. We bill ourselves as "Probably the finest beer-geek, hip-hop band of our generation." Of course, we are also the only beer-geek, hip-hop band of any generation. Bryan is actually a talented musician and we have set up a pretty sophisticated little recording studio in his house. He lays down the tracks, and we both write the lyrics.

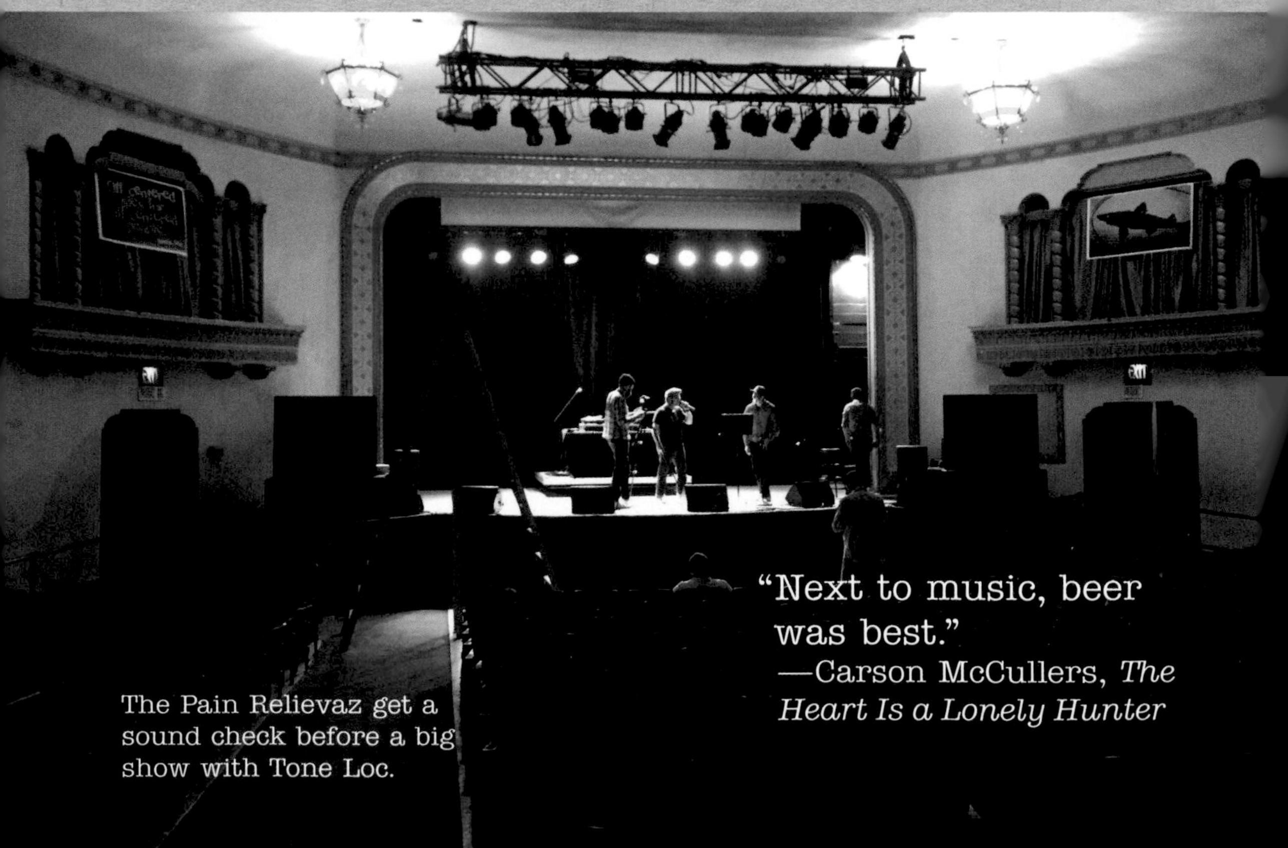

"Next to music, beer was best."
—Carson McCullers, *The Heart Is a Lonely Hunter*

The Pain Relievaz get a sound check before a big show with Tone Loc.

I could not separate my love of music from my love of Dogfish Head, so we sing songs with names like "Brewer's Bling-Bling," "Worst Brew Day Ever," and "I Got Busy with an A-B Salesgirl." We wrote the songs for the same reasons we make the beers and cook the foods that we do. It is basically off-centered music for off-centered people.

We have used the band as a promotional asset for the company. We did a multicity tour of great beer bars, set up our microphones and amplifiers, and sang our songs and served our beers. We drove from city to city and lived out our rock-and-roll dream. One of the highlights was playing the book release party for Ken Wells's *Travels with Barley: A Journey Through Beer Culture in America* (Free Press, 2004), a great social history of brewing in the United States that includes a whole chapter about Dogfish Head. In 2003, we cut a six-song disc on our own Dogfish Records label called *Check Your Gravity*, that has sold over 500 copies. As I've said, a sense of humor is central to the brand identity of Dogfish Head. Here's a sample of the Pain Relievaz new jack philosophy:

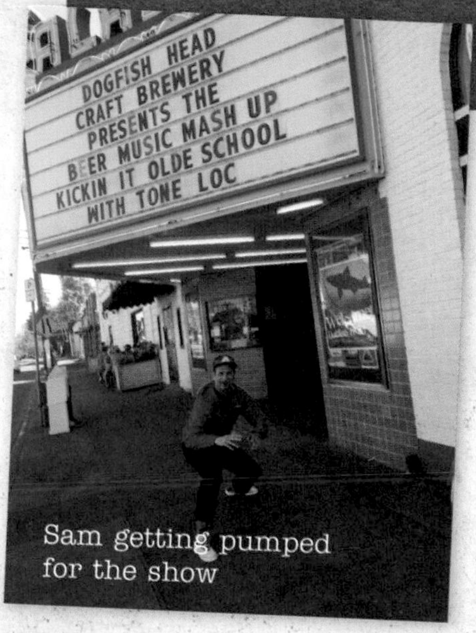

Sam getting pumped for the show

I've been rockin' phat beats since the boys in Mendocino
were sellin' all their ales from a Chevy El Camino.
And when I rock the mic you'll know that I'm serious
'cause my rhymes are more fruity than the beers of New Glar-e-us!

These lyrics might not make sense to most, but for those who follow the craft beer movement, Mendocino is home to some of the first microbreweries in the United States, and that New Glarus, a fine Wisconsin brewery, makes a world-class cherry beer. But we didn't record this album for the people who don't know about beer. We made it for ourselves, for true beer lovers, and for people just getting into good beer who want to learn everything they can.

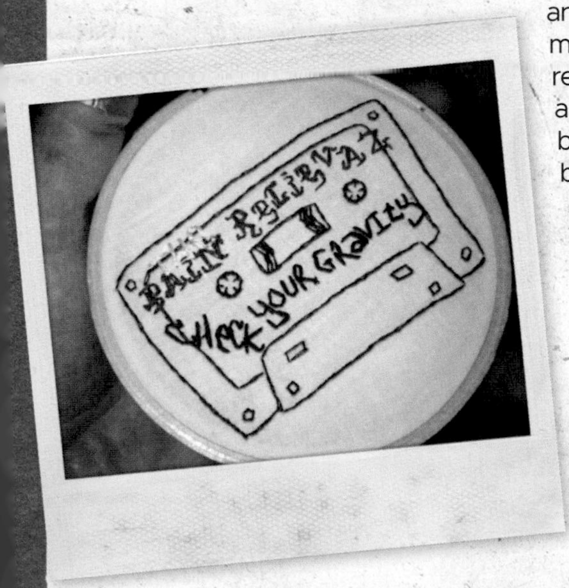

The Pain Relievaz aren't exactly in the middle of a record label bidding war, but we're not that bad, either. And I don't think the level of professionalism matters as much as the message that comes from such a project: Our off-centered brewery has found another off-centered method to promote what we do. There's nothing wrong with taking a risk and experimenting, especially if you don't take your experiment too seriously.

The Pain Relievaz released a second album, *Untether the Blimp*, in 2006 to rave reviews from our families and friends. We also have music videos that can be seen on YouTube that help us spread the word about Dogfish Head. It ain't Jay-Z, but I hope it represents the authentic, audacious, ambitious, exploratory image of Dogfish Head.

Breaking the rules of brewing

It was 2002 and I had just been stopped by airport security as I tried to board a plane to Chicago for a beer event. TSA officials had pulled me out of the security check and led me to a special room somewhere in the bowels of the Philadelphia International Airport. I was sitting at a table piled high with whole-leaf palisade hops and a two-foot-long plastic contraption. Things were looking pretty grim. Of the five people in the room I definitely held the minority opinion on whether a full-scale cavity search was really necessary. But I was also the only one in the room without a gun, so I did a lot of listening.

The officers made some valid points about how much the contraption I was traveling with resembled the bong to end all bongs. Their dog also did not like me or my bag of sticky hop buds, but he was German and probably partial to Hallertauer (a German hop variety). After hearing my impassioned speech on the role that dry-hopping plays in beer brewing, and the need for brewers in America to create beers that have a more bitter profile, they sent the dog away.

> "The free soul is rare, but you know it when you see it—basically because you feel good, very good, when you are near or with them."
> —*Tales of Ordinary Madness*, Charles Bukowski

One of the officers was from Wilmington, Delaware, and had heard of Dogfish Head; another drank Sierra Nevada regularly. In fact, all of them were beer drinkers. So I began to explain the story behind the invention of my contraption, which I explained was named Randall the Enamel Animal, pretty interesting. As craft brewers, we learn that educating people on the importance of fresh, quality ingredients isn't always easy but it is really important to do. Calmer, beer-friendly heads prevailed, and we all decided to forgo the cavity search. The hops were put in a special new bag. Randall was given a special new box. Each was plastered with very cool and highly collectable "Inspected by the Department of Homeland Security" tape. We were released from custody and loaded onto the next plane bound for Chicago. I was in the comfortable cabin and Randall sat in the cargo hold among the suitcases and snowboards.

A few months earlier, I had been invited to captain an East Coast team of craft brewers in a brewing competition against a bunch of West Coast breweries during an event called the Lupulin Slam (after the flavoring oils in hops). Dogfish Head, Old Dominion, and Capitol City represented the East Coast, while Pizza Port, Oggi's, and Avery hailed from the West. The competition was set for back-to-back nights at RFD, or Regional Food & Drink, located in Washington, D.C., and the sister location of the Brickskeller Dining House and Down Home Saloon, which formerly held the Guinness Book of World Records' title for bar with most beers available in the world.

The West Coast is where most of the American hops are grown, so I knew the brewers from the West would bring some seriously hoppy ales from Boulder and San Diego. For the Lupulin Slam, I planned to feature a giant version (120 minutes, 20 percent alcohol by volume) of our India Pale Ale. While it was hoppy enough for most occasions, I thought that it could use a booster shot for the big event.

I got to thinking about an alternate use for a stainless steel filter I'd bought at a scrap yard, and I designed some fittings and a flowchart that outlined my intentions. I shared this diagram with our brewers, and they went to work modifying the filter. As usual, they were up for this unorthodox challenge; these are the kinds of projects that remind us what Dogfish Head is all about. The night before the contest we packed this reconstructed filter that we named Randall with whole-leaf Cascade and Willamette hops and flooded the chamber with 120 Minute IPA. Randall did exactly what we "hopped" it would.

The original Randall

By hopping the beer at the moment when it's being poured, the alcohol in the beer strips the oil off the hop leaves packed into the Randall on the way to the tap. The beer comes out the other side of Randall soaked in natural hop flavor and natural compounds not present in beers hopped only at the brewery. The reference to "Enamel" in the name "Randall the Enamel Animal" comes from the gritty feeling of hop resins on your teeth.

The West Coast beers were pretty amazing as usual, and the Old Dominion and Cap City beers were stellar. But a Randallized keg of Dogfish Head 120 Minute Imperial IPA took the belt and hipped the West Coast beer folk and hop-heads to the reality of hardcore East Coast IPAs: maybe not better, but certainly equal in quality to the West Coast counterparts.

Randall in the O.G. pub

Dozens of voters came up to me over the course of the two nights to tell me they had never tried a freshly hopped beer and were amazed at the flavor. Nearly every beer-centric publication in the country covered the event, and Randall got his 15 minutes of fame with a front-page story and picture in the Dining section of the *New York Times*. So Randall was a hit and Dogfish Head's beer won the title, but the story of this event doesn't stop there. We expected that we would only use Randall for this event and then put him out to pasture. But upon seeing Randall in action, we received lots of interest from brewers and bar owners who wanted to test out dry-hopping with their beers and in their establishments.

Since that event we've gone on to sell Randalls to bars and breweries throughout the country and as far away as England and Sweden. In a way, Randall represents the democratization of the hop leaf, but it also represents the perfect ingredient in a successful publicity event—a focus on the product and its uniqueness in the market. Randall is really nothing more than a tool to educate people on hoppy beers and to allow brewers to show off and describe their beers. We hope it will continue to be used as a tool to educate consumers on the importance of hops in beer—something the big three brewers couldn't care less about doing. It's pretty amazing to realize that many beer lovers have never even seen a real hop leaf before, much less watched the pint of beer they're about to try flow through a see-through filter full of hops. Dogfish Head has decided to sell Randall at cost. We believe that making innovation like this accessible to others will only benefit the whole beer industry (open-source hopping). Kind of like the Linux scene, Randall is an evolving experiment. If brewers or bar owners have ideas on how to improve the design or suggestions for events to use Randall, they can email them to us and we'll get the word out in online updates.

Pangaea (7.0% ABV)

In 2003 and we released a number of really exciting beers. This was the year of Operation Shock and Awe and the invasion of Iraq under the Bush administration. I remember being on vacation in Montana skiing with my family. old then and we came home from skiing, the only thing as we were clicking around the T.V. most of the channels were just showing the bombing going on and I didn't feel good about watching that with my son Sammy, who was about four years old then. I passed him the remote and said, "Put on what you want." He found a channel that had a cartoon with dinosaurs on a time-traveling train. This was much better than the bombing in the news.

The cartoon panned out to an image of the era before continental drift when there was really just one giant land mass called Pangaea. As I watched that with my son and thought about what a fractured, tumultuous world we were living in—as shown by the images of us bombing another continent—an idea came to me. I thought, "Wouldn't it be cool to bring the world back together at least in liquid form, bring this fractured world back together." I started googling information about the supercontinent and I spent a chunk of my vacation evenings the rest of that week searching interesting ingredients that I thought would be complementary to each other from every continent in the world, and brew a beer called Pangaea to reunite all the continents inside of one bottle that included ingredients from every continent.

I found ingredients like crystalized ginger from Australia, basmati rice from Asia, but the hardest continent to find an ingredient from was Antarctica. I don't know whose idea it was to make Antarctica a continent, but my research showed I pretty much had two choices, one being penguin shit and the other being reverse osmosis iceberg water. Thankfully I was able to get in touch with an American military base on Antarctica and they happened to have heard of Dogfish Head from some documentary film we were in, and they were home brewers since they were stuck in this remote area themselves. I sent them a mixed case of Dogfish Head beer and in return they sent me two 5-gallon buckets of reverse osmosis Antarctic water that got added to the Pangaea so that it could have one ingredient from every continent in it.

Dogfish Head
Pangaea
A flavored malt beverage
brewed with crystallized
7% Alc. by Vol.
1 pint 9.6 ounces

Festina Lente (7.0% ABV)

One recipe that was integral to Dogfish Head's experimental reputation and our first foray into sour was for Festina Lente. Because Delaware is famous for its peach orchards and for exporting delicious peaches to nearby states, we decided to brew a peach beer in 2003. There's a famous peach farm not far from our brewery called Fifer Orchard. We had brewed different Belgian-style beers and brewed beers with Belgian yeast, like our Raison D'Etre, but I wanted to create a new-world, off-centered take on the traditional Belgian style known as Lambic. Unlike other countries in Western Europe, such as France, Italy, and Germany, Belgium doesn't have a climate conducive to growing grapes, so they don't produce the volume of wines that the other countries in the region do. However, the air in certain regions in Belgium holds a magnificent cocktail of wild yeast and bacteria. So Belgians brew a very complex, beautifully balanced, very food complementary alcoholic beverage incorporating the natural elements from the region.

Lambic is brewed by making a traditional prefermented wort out of grains and water, adding hops to it as you traditionally would, but instead of adding a single strain of yeast to it, Belgian brewers pump beer into shallow tanks that are as wide as the brewing barn. They installed louvres in the roof that they could open to allow the micro flora and fauna in the air to fall into the beer. By opening up their windows and roofs and allowing air carrying this micro flora and fauna into the room housing a giant tray of cooling beer, the beer would be naturally inoculated with this blend of wild yeast and bacteria that would do the fermentation process. This would add a lot of very complex, spicy, phenolic, sometimes horse-blanket-like characteristics to the beer.

We wanted to do a beer at Dogfish that used local ingredients but also incorporated the Belgian process of using wild yeasts and bacteria in the beer. I chose the name Festina Lente, which means "make haste slowly" in Latin. I drew a rough draft of a hand on the label intentionally so you couldn't tell if it was illustratively signaling go or stay. We brewed the beer and got the wild yeast and bacteria for it from overly ripe peaches that were left over on the farm at Fifer Peach Orchard. I guess you could say Festina Lente is the great grandson of our Cherry Pale Ale, my first ever home brew, because it was the second time I found overly ripe fruit that had fruit flies all over it when I added it to a beer.

All of that wild yeast and bacteria did the trick with Festina Lente. It turned the beer sour, which is a desired characteristic of a Lambic-style beer, it makes it acidic, drops the pH and makes it pleasantly tart, but the addition of local peaches and the sweetness and fruitiness from that was a nice counterbalance to the souring that came through the bacteria and wild yeast.

We bottled the beer into 600 big champagne bottles and hand corked them to drive home the fact that it was going to be wine-like in its complexity, but the Festina Lente label that I hand drawn only said on the front of it, "It's a right lusty ale made with honest to goodness peaches." It didn't call out that this was an intentionally sour beer, because in 2003, sour beers were not very popular.

Something like 30 percent of the bottles that we sent to distributors and retailers ended up being sent back to us! I received a lot of angry emails and calls from retailers and distributors saying, "Hey asshole, your beer went sour, you suck at brewing! You need to take all this shit you sent us back." So we took back all the inventory of Festina Lente that didn't sell and we actually sent bottles of it to the World Beer Cup, the world's single-largest beer-judging competition.

Festina Lente won a silver medal up against famous sour beer brewers like Rodenbach and Cantillon, so through that award we got some redemption in the world of brewing. Soon after that, sour beer started to come into favor. Starting with that fated first brew of Festina Lente, Dogfish Head is now the largest producing brand of sour beers in America.

Today, that same brewery that we got a medal next to, over a decade and a half ago, is our partner brewery Rodenbach in a new kettle sour called Vibrant P'Ocean that Dogfish and Rodenbach released together in 2020. In their 200-year history, Rodenbach had never done a collaboration with another commercial brewery until they decided to do this collaboration with all of us here at Dogfish Head.

60 Minute IPA (6.0% ABV)

When we first came out with beers like 90 Minute IPA at the turn of the millennia, IPAs were not a popular style of beer in America. If you research what were the most recognizable, highest-volume microbrewery beer styles in that era—before breweries were even called craft breweries—the big microbrew beer styles back then were amber ales, seasonal beers, and craft lagers. It is probably unexpected for today's younger craft beer aficionados who are maybe in their 20s or 30s to think that IPAs were until recently a niche craft beer style. It wasn't until the early 2000s that beers like 90 Minute, 60 Minute, Victory Hop Devil, Stone IPA, and Harpoon IPA took off that the IPA style moved from the fringe into the mainstream.

Our 60 Minute IPA actually came about in 2003—three years later than 90 Minute. The 90 Minute is, of course, nine percent alcohol and continually hopped for 90 minutes to 90 international bittering units. It was the first Imperial IPA brewed, bottled, and packaged anywhere in the world, but some people felt like they wanted a beer that had the continual hopping character, so superhoppy but not crushingly bitter in a more sessionable lower ABV recipe. That's why we brewed 60 Minute. It uses the same continually hopping technique that was born from that converted, vibrating football game, but for 60 Minute we only continually hop for 60 minutes and make a beer that's six percent alcohol and 60 international bittering units. Of course, this went on to become our best-selling beer and still is today.

Dogfish Head
60 Minute IPA
6% ALC. BY VOL. | 12 FL. OZ.
Dogfish Head
60 Minute
IPA

Increasing Production

Shortly after releasing our 60 Minute IPA, we were unable to produce enough beer to keep up with consumer demand. Sounds like a great problem to have, right? I'm sure in the long run we'll look at this period with perspective and see that the unfulfilled desire for our beer created a heightened level of excitement for our brand. But in the short term, I must say it wasn't very pleasant. When our customers run out of beer, that means our retailers run out, our distributors run out, and our brewery runs out. Everyone is frustrated.

We have customers who would have driven across state borders to find our 60 Minute IPA. They'd ask at every store if the beer is available there, and when the retailer says they are out of stock these customers just go to the next store without buying anything. So then the retailer calls the distributor and yells at them for being out of stock. Of course the distributor calls us to let us know that we are costing them money by being out of stock. We could have just said it wasn't our fault that our beer was selling faster than we could make it, or that we were working on it and they'd have more beer when it was ready. But we recognized our responsibility to everyone affected by the situation and tried to keep people informed on how we were responding.

We sent letters to all of the retailers who complained, and we apologized. We asked them not to blame the distributors that they bought from, that it was our fault and we were in the process of buying new tanks to help us catch up with demand. After these bigger brewing fermentation tanks were in place, we emailed pictures of them being installed to our distributors and asked that they share them with their salespeople and retailers so that they could understand the investment we were making to rectify the situation.

Between the letters of apology, the pictures of bigger tanks, and the empty shelves, we had a makeshift marketing program that cast a positive light on our failure. Our customers, retailers, and distributors were willing to stick by us and hold out for our beer if we made good on our word and worked out our production woes soon. Mariah and I collateralized the only property we owned that had any value against a bank loan that would allow us to buy the equipment we needed in order to keep up with growing demand. We did everything we could to correct the problem, but it took a long time. Seven months passed from when we first recognized the situation, ordered the tanks, and installed them, before we had enough beer flowing to catch up. We were missing budget, our salespeople and our distributors' salespeople were missing commissions, and our retailers were missing sales. Matt, our sales service manager, and Devin and Allen, our regional sales managers, spent the better parts of their workdays calling and running from retailer to distributor, apologizing and putting out fires. It wasn't pretty, but it could have been worse. It could have been a disastrous situation, but we took the responsibility not just to admit that it was our fault but to explain how we were going to correct it.

Dogfish Head
60 Minute IPA

Raison D'Extra
Brewed with an obscene amount of malt, brown sugar & raisins.
12 FL. OZ. | AGES WELL

Raison D'Extra
(16% ABV)

In 2003 we also first brewed Raison D'Extra, which is another play on words. For this beer, we basically took the Raison D'Etre recipe and doubled it, adding extra malt, extra hops, extra beet sugar, and extra raisins using the same yeast regimen. By adding extra sugars, combined with those high-alcohol-tolerant, sadomasochist yeast strains that we used in World Wide but applying it to the strong Belgian ale called Raison D'Extra we were able to achieve that 16 percent alcohol.

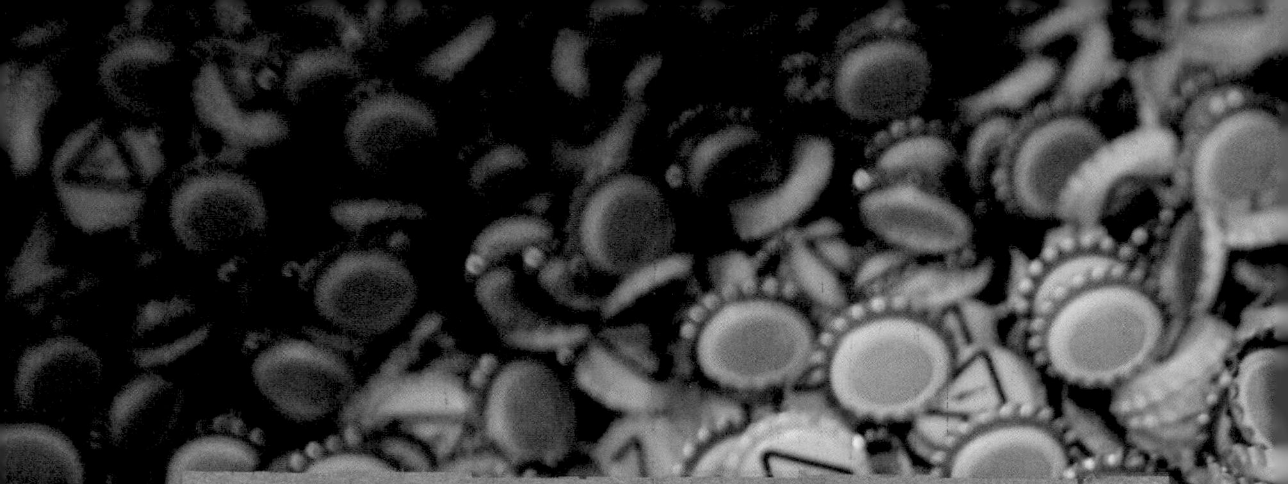

Bottlecaps

You might notice in this book or on the shelves of your favorite beer retailer that some of our beers have a really bright and noticeable yellow cap that has Dogfish's version of the danger symbol you see on dangerous roadways. These are our caution caps. We started using these yellow caps in the early 2000s because retailers were letting us know that ethically challenged consumers were going into stores, taking six packs of our Chicory Stout, which was five percent alcohol—and probably ten bucks for a six pack back then—and going to the shelf where single bottles of our more expensive beers—beers that cost $12 and $14 per bottle—and swapping the Chicory Stout bottles for World Wide Stout bottles in the Chicory Stout six pack. The checkout person would scan the code of the 6-pack of Chicory Stout and the customer would get away with $80 worth of beer for a $10 6-pack. On the advice of outraged retailers, our beers that are over 12 percent alcohol, and more expensive as a result, now carry a bright neon cap that has the danger sign. This is both to remind the consumer to be careful: this is a strong beer that they should really think about splitting with a friend in a snifter instead of drinking it themselves all at once, and also, that superbright color is meant to be easy to identify in retail stores so that customers don't swap the beer by putting it in a less expensive beer's six pack.

Burton Baton (10% ABV)

Burton Baton was first brewed in 2004. By then, Dogfish Head's 90 Minute and 60 Minute really started taking off, and those two beers along with Midas Touch and Raison D'Etre started getting distributed from coast to coast. Our little brewery in Delaware was now experiencing annual, double-digit growth. The hot shit breweries from the West Coast like Pizza Port, Russian River, Stone, and Sierra Nevada, while they were great friends of mine, jokingly teased us that Dogfish Head was getting famous for brewing hoppy beers when they believed hoppy beers were the hallmark of West Coast brewers and that the West Coast deserved to be celebrated as the rightful geography to pinpoint the epicenter of American hoppy beers.

To help remind the American craft brewing community that the East Coast was the home to many hop-forward beers long before West Coast breweries focusing on IPAs opened—we released a beer called Burton Baton. The name is a homage to the P. Ballantine & Sons Brewery, which opened in 1840 in Newark, New Jersey. Back in the '40s, '50s, and '60s, the Ballantine Brewery was a real pioneer of strong hoppy beers. They brewed a beer called Burton Ale that they didn't even distribute. With just one batch being produced every year, it was so coveted and rare that they hand numbered and labeled every bottle. Oftentimes they even hand wrote on every bottle who the recipient of the bottle would be: it might be a famous politician or actor or an important retailer or distributor in their network. The brewery was acquired many decades ago by one of the large international brewing conglomerates, so that coveted brew is no longer available.

We crafted and brewed Burton Baton basically as a friendly middle finger to the West Coast brewers who were saying that they were the inventors of American hop-forward beers on the West Coast. I wanted to brew this to show them that long before the West Coast breweries opened, Ballantine, an East Coast brewery, was brewing a really hop-centric beer and they would actually age that superhoppy beer in giant wood tanks, so that also informed the production method for Burton Baton, which is aged on oak. Burton Baton clocks in at ten percent alcohol as an oak-aged imperial India Pale Ale. It's a classic liquid iteration of the West Coast/East Coast battle that rages on in music, art, fashion, tattoos, real estate, and even theme parks.

BURTON
BATON
DOGFISH HEAD
An oak-aged Imperial India Pale Ale
10% alc. by vol. 12 fl. oz.

Fort (16% ABV)

In 2005, we decided to take everything we know about brewing superstrong beers and combine it with what we learned about Belgian beers. We had brewed a version of a Belgian red beer with grapes in Raison D'Etre, and we brewed a version of a Belgian sour beer with Festina Lente. Next we wanted to brew the world's strongest fruit-infused beer to go along with the our world's strongest stout, World Wide Stout.

We ordered truckloads of pureed raspberries be delivered to our brewery and we began brewing a big Belgian golden ale, something similar to the base of Duvel Belgian Ale. Throughout the brewing process we kept dosing in pureed raspberries and re-oxygenating the beer as it fermented so the yeast stayed active. We named it Fort, the world's strongest fruit beer fermented to about 16 percent alcohol.

Being as much music geeks as we are beer geeks at Dogfish Head, we decided to engage another rock-and-roll artist for the design of this label. We had so much fun working with artist Jon Langford, who came from the world of rock and roll and designed our Olde School Barleywine label, that we decided to find another artist with an overlap in the music scene for our Fort beer. I came across a gig poster for the Melvins, the legendary Northwest punk band that Kurt Cobain was a roadie for before he started Nirvana, and I thought the characters in that poster were the perfect style for the label. Tara McPherson, a New York-based artist, had created that poster. So she did a beautiful job bringing this woman to life as the centerpiece of the label art for Fort—a woman who's not blowing kisses toward the viewer, she's blowing fistfuls of fresh raspberries because when you open a bottle of Fort and decant it into a snifter and put your nose in that snifter, that image on the cover of Fort perfectly captures what experiencing the aromas of Fort is like for the first time. The word fort was a playful and legal way for us to infer that this beer was ageable and bulletproof, like a fort would be, but the word "Fort" in Latin and the romance languages also means strong. In the rules around beer labels, we can include ages of the beers, but we can't include certain words. One of those words we can't use to describe beers is "strong"; however, we can use the term, "Fort."

For many years, the beer aficionados influencing what people were drinking were mostly the Gen-X and Boomer demographic. They fell in love with the concept of beers being designed to deliver a more high-end experience while being available at a more affordable and approachable price than high-end wine. They loved that certain styles of our beers could age as well as the world's finest wines but only cost a fraction of the world's finest wines. Dogfish was among the first breweries in the country to start releasing these strong beers in 750 mil wine-or-champagne bottles to drive home the fact that they were designed to be enjoyed fresh or to be stored in a wine cellar or beer cellar to see how the flavor changed over time. We regularly get emails and calls from people today telling us they'd celebrated a tenth anniversary or that they were celebrating the wedding of a son or daughter and they'd broken out a five, a ten, or a fifteen-year-old World Wide Stout, 120 Minute, or Fort. This is a niche within the craft brewing world that Dogfish Head's played a really prominent role in, working to convince beer lovers to not be afraid to lay down and age stronger beers as they would a world-class wine.

"When they give
you lined paper,
write the other way."
—Ray Bradbury,
Fahrenheit 451

Chateau Jiahu (9.0% ABV)

Chateau Jiahu is in a historic context, perhaps the most existentially important beer recipe of all time in that it is the oldest known beer recipe in the history of civilization. Chateau Jiahu is one of our famous beers from 2006. For this beer, we reunited with Dr. Pat McGovern, the molecular archeologist who we worked with on Midas Touch back in 1999.

Chateau Jiahu refers to the Neolithic village of Jiahu where the oldest known fermented beverage molecular evidence has ever been found. The Chateau Jiahu recipe was based on Dr. Pat's analysis of residue found in a vessel during an archaeological dig in the Henan Province of China. The Chateau Jiahu dig site is believed to be about 10,000 years old—this would be the era when humans as a species shifted from hunting and gathering nomadic people to settling down into the earliest communities. It's believed that the impetus for this shift in how our species lived was a result of the discovery of growing crops. Humans learned that instead of having to be out risking our lives in the wild, hunting down live prey that might also have their brothers and sisters trying to hunt down and kill us, we could hang out together in a village, put a fence around that village, and grow crops to sustain us. It's also unknown if we made this leap because we wanted to grow crops to make bread with or we wanted to grow crops to make beer.

This tomb was so perfectly preserved in China that it also contained the oldest salvaged and playable human-devised musical instruments, next to the shards of crockery that held the liquid. There were hollow bird bones that had different-sized, perfectly round holes carved into them that when you blew into them, they played close to the equivalent of modern musical scales. These Chinese artisans were making beer, making musical instruments, and I envision they were having a hell of a party, a hootenanny the night they closed that tomb and chose to put the musical instruments and remnants of their funerary feast, including the remnants of this beer, into that tomb as sustenance for their fallen leader. These tombs were usually built to hold the skeletons of famous or important people, and they would fill the tombs with their best food and beverages because they believed once the tomb was sealed, that famous person could use that food and beverage on their journey to heaven or the afterworld.

Chateau Jiahu is brewed with sake yeast, sake rice, and hawthorn fruit along with white grape juice, a variety we believe was similar to the wild grapes that grew in that region 10,000 years ago. It's also cool to think about, you know, today in America, how the beer world has morphed to include beverages sold in beer stores and on beer taps that aren't by definition modern beers. Most experts agree, the modern beer era started in 1516 with the Reinheitsgebot, the Bavarian beer law that said beer had to only have water, hops, and barley in it, yeast had yet to even be discovered. It is funny that thousands of years ago, before the internet, before Reinheitsgebot, every culture just defined beer by what grew on the land they lived on unique to their geography, that they could combine and turn into a fermented beverage that made them see the gods when they drank it and made them feel close to their loved ones and their ancestors. Today it's cool to see that there's a lot of beverage companies that are helping to broaden the definition of beer into the realm of alcoholic seltzers or ciders or canned cocktails that have a broader array of natural ingredients in them. Dogfish Head's proud to have been one of the real pioneers in expanding the definition of beer with all the different hybrids and fermentable sugars that we've been adding to what we make in our breweries and in our distilleries for well over two decades.

The News Journal – 5/19/05

Del. brewmeister has treat on tap for Big Apple

A8 THE NEWS JOURNAL ••• THURSDAY, MAY 19, 2005

The News Journal/SCOTT NATHAN

Sam Calagione, owner of Dogfish Head Craft Brewery in Milton, entertains patrons Sunday at his Rehoboth Beach restaurant. Calagione was celebrating publication of his new book, "Brewing Up a Business."

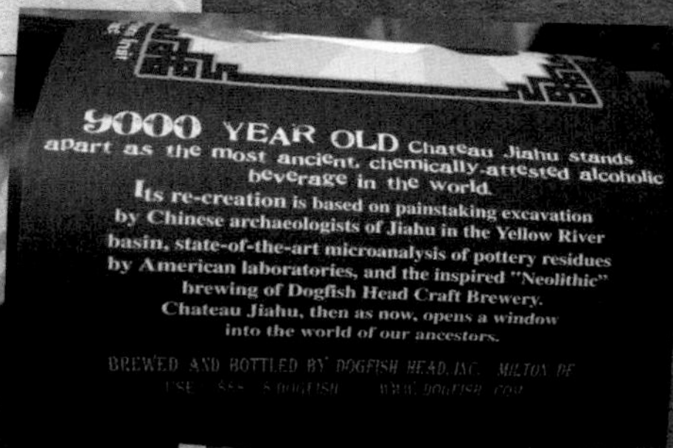

9000 YEAR OLD Chateau Jiahu stands apart as the most ancient, chemically-attested alcoholic beverage in the world.
Its re-creation is based on painstaking excavation by Chinese archaeologists of Jiahu in the Yellow River basin, state-of-the-art microanalysis of pottery residues by American laboratories, and the inspired "Neolithic" brewing of Dogfish Head Craft Brewery.
Chateau Jiahu, then as now, opens a window into the world of our ancestors.
BREWED AND BOTTLED BY DOGFISH HEAD, INC. MILTON DE

Dogfish Head creator to unveil new, er, old concoction

By PATRICIA TALORICO
The News Journal

Tonight at Manhattan's swanky Waldorf-Astoria hotel, Sam Calagione is hosting a keg party for 120 people. The beer: His interpretation of a prehistoric Chinese concoction believed to be the world's oldest fermented beverage.

It's the first public tasting of Chateau Jiahu, Calagione's re-creation of a rice, honey and fruit drink unearthed from a 9,000-year-old tomb.

Journalists from "Good Morning America," The New York Times, The Wall Street Journal and Food & Wine magazine are expected to raise glasses at the event.

It's "so Sam," say friends and colleagues of the national attention focused on Calagione, owner of Dogfish Head Craft Brewery in Milton, one of the fastest-growing breweries in the United States. They know that nothing this 35-year-old Lewes resident does is *ever* on a small scale.

"I'm not a shameless promoter of myself," Calagione stresses, "but I am a shameless Dogfish Head promoter."

Media curiosity and kudos long have surrounded Calagione and his Sussex County

See BEER — A8

book "Brewing Up A Business" (Wiley, $35) – yep, he even scored a major book deal – that young entrepreneurs should drum up business them-

your company, farm out the n't catch the voice as well as you agione, whose s been to make les for off-cen-

rowin'

marketing has, f-centered. omote plans to is Dogfish Head beyond mitted to resort- alled "a shame- nt." He built any skiff and ow it across er from Lewes to deliver the eople showed ter the 5½-

gh, were beer- and soap for me popular ers who say beer make a e kind of ," Cala-

good looks ning him opportuni- pose for such famed photographers as Bruce Weber and the late Richard Avedon.

He's sheepish about his cover-boy appeal.

"I never really did it much," he said of the modeling.

Did he have to say that?

And he's learned to take some ribbing. When he appeared on the "Today" show five years ago to promote his Midas Touch Golden Elixir, a honey-flavored medieval-style drink made from a recipe culled from organics found in a 2,700-year-old tomb in Turkey, Katie Couric said the beer appealed to women because of its sweet taste. Matt Lauer then called it "a chick beer" and Calagione cringed.

Calagione said his phone began to ring immediately.

"All my friends were saying, 'You're making a chick beer?'" he said, rolling his eyes.

But he said beer experts have recognized there's something special about his product beyond "just some dog and pony show."

"If the beer sucked, we'd only sell a little bit of it," he said. And for a brewery his size Calagione sells a lot of beer. He currently is brewing 33,000 barrels a year, an increase of almost 21,000 gallons from 2003.

In his book, Calagione writes that beer "has always played an important role in my life."

When he got kicked out of his Massachusetts prep school in the late '80s, two months before graduation for an "accumulation of offenses," which included beer drinking, friends gave him a send-off by blaring Frank Sinatra's "That's Life" out of the window. Later, he enrolled at Muhlenberg College in Allentown, Pa., and became an English major who "minored in beer drinking."

While there, he designed a reclining chair with a hidden compartment for a keg and invented a beer-drinking game in which contestants dressed only in tube socks and ski goggles.

After college, he moved to New York, enrolled in writing courses at Columbia University and scored some minor acting gigs. But he continued to nurture a love of obscure, imported beers while working as a waiter at Nacho Mama's Burritos in the city's Upper West side.

Sorry, Ricki

At age 23, Calagione decided on his future career and broke the heart of former talk-show host Ricki Lake all in the same night.

He held a party in his New York apartment to unveil his Cherry Brew, a homemade pale ale made with cherries. One of the guests was Lake, whom Calagione knew after appearing on her program. But Lake left the party soon after Calagione introduced her to his girlfriend, and now wife, Mariah. "Ricki had a little crush on me, but I had no idea. I guess I bummed her out."

But Calagione's bee hit of the party. The M tive decided that night his obsession into his hood. In 1995, he move Mariah's hometown of hoboth Beach and star Delaware's first brewp fish Head Brewing & E name comes from a M peninsula, where his f a summer house.

Dogfish Head beer. And Calagione's willingness to do almost anything it takes to make his business successful is part of the attraction.

"To be honest, to some degree he steps in it and he gets lucky," Trostle said of Calagione's media attention, which has included splashy articles in Forbes, Details, People and Men's Journal; stints as a model for a Levi's clothing company and Abercrombie & Fitch; and an appearance on the former "To Tell the Truth" TV show.

"He tries to row across the Delaware River and the next thing you know he's selling Levis and is on 'The Today Show.' Everybody wants something new and unique. Sam understands that. But he also makes great beer," Trostle said.

Calagione has never used a public relations firm in his 10 years in business. He stresses in his new, funny and unflinch-

Ryan Mazur

Quality Assurance Supervisor
Start Date: 2005

Janelle Mazur

Social Media Specialist
Start Date: 2011

With a degree in Marine Biology from Kutztown, Ryan moved to Delaware and really wanted to work for DNREC (Department of Natural Resources and Environmental Control). They were on a hiring freeze, so he fell back on what helped him get through college: working as an irrigation technician at a golf course. In 2005, his buddy told him about a job at Dogfish Head that had come up. We were looking for a forklift operator. Lucky for us, DNREC was on the hiring freeze, and he was sick of digging holes, so he applied. At the time, the brewery was essentially a garage. He really wanted the job, so he put on his khakis and a tie to formally apply for the position. HR gave him the full shakedown. There was a new policy of drug testing, and Ryan was the first Dogfish Head coworker to piss in a cup. With his fancy tie and clean urine sample, Dogfish Head had a new forklift operator. We had no A/C in the cellars, there were birds flying around, and the gig paid $9 an hour. Ryan was in paradise. That forklift gig lasted two months.

The brewmaster at the time caught wind of the marine biologist on the forklift. Back then, the quality lab was no more than a closet with a microscope. We had broken 20,000 barrels that year, and growth was smacking us around. The quality lab had to grow, too. Between Ryan Mazur and Chad Collier, the quality lab stepped up its game fast. Ryan has been in the lab ever since, and while he didn't know much about beer when he showed up to Dogfish Head in a tie, his beer knowledge has taken him to Jedi status. That lab has a hell of a lot more going on in it now than just one microscope.

As the years progressed, we were having 100 percent growth year after year. The trajectory was nuts. With Ryan's grit and know-how, the quality lab kept pace through all of it. The timing was perfect and he was having a blast. But there was more in store for the marine biologist at Dogfish Head.

In 2011, Janelle was going to live in Ocean City, MD, for the summer. Janelle looks back fondly on that summer as one that altered the trajectory of her life. She thought an internship at Dogfish Head would be a good way to spend her time between semesters, so she tweeted at Dogfish. Sure enough, she got a response. She didn't know it at the time, but she was tweeting with Mariah. There was no internship available, but Dogfish was thinking about creating one. A month went by, and she tweeted again. Dogfish responded with a job posting, and she got it. After the internship and graduation, Janelle came on full time. Ryan remembers thinking, "Hey! We got that blond intern back!"

Up to this point, Mariah had done pretty much all of the social media, and Janelle fit right in. Mariah gave Janelle the freedom to really take on all aspects of social. Having the autonomy to make decisions and experiment with our social media channels from the get-go was paramount for Janelle. Mariah gave her the freedom and the foundational support that allowed Janelle to really own it. Also landing on Janelle's plate? Customer complaints. We scheduled a weekly meeting with Ryan in the quality lab to help Janelle understand the beer side of things to deal with these complaints.

Enter Kvasir: our ancient ale we did with Dr. Pat McGovern. This Scandinavian liquid time capsule is Ryan and Janelle's favorite—and for good reason. While a Festina Peche or a 75-minute on cask at the pub are high on their list, Kvasir wins out. It was a Friday at Beer:30 (when the taps are opened at 4:30 PM for all of our coworkers) and Janelle and Ryan were partaking in a few Kvasirs. A glance here, a leg touch there, and the cat was out of the bag. In 2017, the two were married.

With all the time Ryan has spent tasting and dissecting beers, and Janelle being on the front lines of social media, they have a great shared perspective about some of our beers that have failed. Au Courant is on the list. Black and Red reared its head, too. Black and Red was hard on tap lines everywhere, leaving a minty residue for the beer that followed it.

Between the two of them, Ryan and Janelle have some great memories from their time at Dogfish Head. For Ryan, one of his most memorable days was when we got air conditioning in the cellars. It was a game-changer. Tanks were cold and sweaty, and the cellars were superhot come August. Not only was it a challenge to just be working the cellars, it was a pain from a cleanliness standpoint. "Looking back, I don't know how the hell we made good beer. But the beer never sat around long. It was all sold the moment we had it," he recalls.

Janelle will never forget the day Pitch Perfect came to life at the brewery. The a cappella group from the University of North Carolina came through on a tour. It was a beautiful spring afternoon on a Friday. Beer:30 was kicking up, and coworkers were all outside drinking pints and playing bocce under the treehouse. The group performed "Africa" and Janelle remembers the feeling of the day. These moments are what make the hard days easier and remind us that what we have going at Dogfish Head is damn awesome. The key is to take the time to stop and take it in.

Coworker Profile

If you were on a deserted island and could have one album to listen to and an unlimited supply of one beer, what would it be?

Beer: Ryan: 60 Minute IPA (a beer he can crush all day)
Beer: Janelle: Seaquench Ale
Album: Ryan: Guns and Roses, *Appetite for Destruction*
Album: Janelle: Fleetwood Mac, *Rumours*

But not every day can be like this. Like the day consumers started getting their Randall Jrs. The launch was picked up by publications, so we sold a ton of them. It was a great launch, but it ended there. This new batch was made of glass, so when people filled it with beer and whatever ingredient they wanted to infuse into that beer ... BOOM! They would explode. People were calling and emailing, and bleeding, and it was a hot, hot, mess. Janelle was the frontline on this one. No Toto a cappella "Africa" that day.

Two of the hardest-working people you will ever meet, it just makes sense these two ended up together. Looking back on all these two have contributed to Dogfish, Janelle is often the person behind the camera or the tweets or posts you see on social media. Ryan is the reason that 60 Minute is right where it needs to be so you can taste that same outstanding beer every time. Pay no attention to these two behind the curtain. They are just helping us be the best we can be every single day and reminding us that while beer is an amazing industry to work in, the relationships that come from working in it are what it is all about.

Chapter 4

The OG Craft Beer Evangelist

It was 2006 and I was attending one of the dinners hosted by the Rare Beer Club out West. Michael Jackson, the British beer writer and OG craft beer evangelist, not the one-gloved music icon, created the Rare Beer Club and members of the club would be invited to events around the country. This particular event was a rare beer and rare wine dinner, so there were some amazing winemakers there, too. Known as the Beer Hunter, this Michael Jackson actually had the first modern craft beer television show, which aired on the Discovery Channel, called *The Beer Hunter*. Michael Jackson was a pioneer in beer journalism and is responsible for jump-starting the international renaissance of craft beer by writing books about the different styles of beer brewed around the world in the late seventies and eighties.

Michael Jackson was an early champion of Dogfish Head beer and our approach to adding culinary ingredients to our recipes, even defending us against a number of journalists who, back then, thought we were being heretics for including culinary ingredients in our beer.

"I have always depended on the kindness of strangers."
—Tennessee Williams,
A Streetcar Named Desire

Michael Jackson and I became great friends because of these events. He would host events in Washington, D.C. and Philadelphia every year, so I would meet him in D.C., participate in the event, then after I would drive him to Philly for the next event. He frequently featured Dogfish Head beers at his dinners. But between events, he'd be so tired of talking about beer, because that was his job and I guess mine, too, that once we got in my pickup truck we said, "We can't talk about beer the rest of the trip." And we would talk about jazz, Beat poetry and writers, which we both loved, and he liked some weird esoteric form of rugby. When he talked about rugby I would try to humor him but I would always angle to get him back to jazz and the Beat poets. He knew as much about those worlds as he did beer. That was where our friendship grew deeper.

When we opened the first incarnation of a Dogfish-themed hotel—which was really just one Dogfish branded room within a hotel that we did not own—I thought it'd be awesome if Michael Jackson would be the first guest, thereby christening that room. This was the Dogfish Head 360 program. I put out some nice stationery for him, filled the fridge with beer, and filled the CD player with some of his favorite albums from Coltrane to Miles Davis and told him, "Please, as you stay here just write something commemorating your stay."

Charlie's Pubs

Dogfish Head
Small Batch Spirits

DOGFISH ALLEY

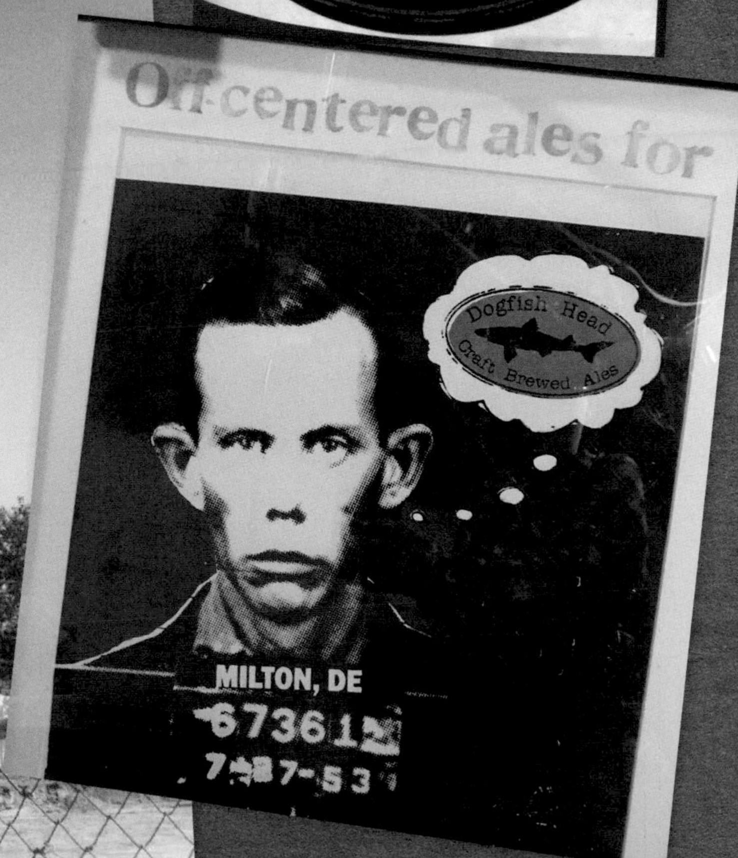
Off-centered ales for
Dogfish Head
Craft Brewed Ales
MILTON, DE

Below is the article he wrote in *All About Beer* magazine. That was the first real national article where someone highlighted Dogfish Head's approach of bringing culinary ingredients in the beer. Michael once said, "What Dogfish is doing isn't disrespectful to modern brewing traditions, it's actually the most respectful approach to the ancient tradition of brewing which is the definitions of beers should have no bounds."

Say it again, Sam

On stage with the poet-brewer March 28 and 31 in Philadelphia, I recall our first meeting

The young woman with whom I had dinner was envious. "You are spending the whole day with Sam Calagione. Tomorrow!? He's the Robert de Niro of brewers!!" She told me that he not only had the good looks of a movie-star but also the sensitivity of a poet. He even took Walt Whitman to bed with him. I think she meant a book by the laureate, though I am certain she had no first hand knowledge of this.

Outside the fancy hotel where a client had accommodated me, the pompously-uniformed, top-hatted, doormen looked less impressed with Calagione when his muddy Ford Lariat rattled to a halt amid a snakepit of shining stretch limos. The top hats distracted themselves with other duties, such as whistling cabs for invisible, but apparently impatient guests.

The doormen's view was obviously that, if the lariat were to be uncoiled, either I or Calagione could do the dirty deed. Calagione did. He opened the door to help me in, and offered me a cup of tea. A very thoughtful touch, that, but I have been a caffeine junkie since I dated a French Canadian 30 years ago. Englishmen are supposed to be polite, so I apologised like a stereotypical Anglo for not being one.

He apologised for the mobile junkyard. I reassured him. Most brewers' cars are full of kegs, tapping systems and the like. Tidiness, cleanliness and godliness are focused on the brewery itself.

The Calagiones seem to be practical people. The grandparents, on both sides, were from Calabria, Italy. They came to Milford, Massachusetts, to quarry pink granite. Among the next generation was a quarryman with a more personal pursuit: an oral surgeon. He is also a gentleman farmer, who makes his own wine and cultivates maple syrup. It may rot the teeth, but son Sam has found good use for the syrup.

This was not his original plan. Sam was an English major, and took courses in fiction and poetry. Perhaps he was just too romantic. He was thrown out of one school for playing ice hockey in the nude in the middle of the night. Somehow he finished up busing tables in a nightclub in Australia, developed a more than passing interest in beer, and home-brewed pumpkin ale.

"I do creative work, too—I formulate beers."

"I did start writing, but it was a business plan," observed Sam. "I do creative work, too—I formulate beers." In 1995, Sam opened a brewpub. "It is an opportunity to express myself, to create something that had not existed before. I get up every morning and do what I love. It is a romantic notion. Hopelessly so, but I a happy to pursue the struggle."

He named his brewpub after a promontory in New England: Dogfish Head, site of a lighthouse in Booth Bay, Maine. His family has a weekend place there.

The jump in the purpose of writing, and creativity, seemed a lengthy leap, I noted. I was thrown this reply: "Believe what is true for you in your private heart is true for all men. Speak your latent conviction and it shall be the universal sense."

These did not seem to be the nature of sentences commonly utters in a Ford Lariat hurling down the interstate. Scarcely has that thought registered than Sam added a silent dash and an attribution. "—Emerson," he said.

All very fine, I countered. I understood the poetry of brewing, but was the notion not limiting? "What of beauty I see now," he intoned, "has grown from within, out of some unconscious truthfulness, without ever a thought for the appearance. Beauty of this kind is destined to be preceded by a like unconscious beauty of life." This time, the attribution was Thoreau.

Was beauty enough? "Art-art does not support the space it takes up. Business-art does. Or it goes out of business." —Andy Warhol. The quotations rolled out effortlessly as Sam swung the lariat round each bend in the road. We were heading south, past Philadelphia now, crossing waterways as we entered the flat, open, landscape of Delaware's

bean-growing country. While the Calagiones come from one town called Milford, Sam's wife is from another of the same name, in Delaware. He established his brewpub in that state, but farther south in Rehoboth Beach, "summer capital" for Washingtonians.

Local fish is grilled over hickory and oak, and the beer is pulled by tap-handles made by a blacksmith in the area.

On a road lined with outlet stores and restaurants, a home-made model of the Dogfish Head lighthouse marks out the pub, three blocks from the boardwalk. The otherwise utilitarian building had previously accommodated a succession of failed restaurants, and for a time a successful crab house. Sam gave the interior a touch of style by creating a bar and wainscoting in wood salvaged from a Victorian bar in Massachusetts. The agricultural touch is heightened by blow-ups of photographs from the Farm Security Administration. Local fish is grilled over hickory and oak, and the beer is pulled by tap-handles made by a blacksmith in the area. What Sam describes as the "self-reliant, artisan approach," is evident everywhere.

The brewhouse was assembled from vessels acquired at an auction when a local cannery closed. Supportive local farmers refrained from bidding. Sam's wife, a former television news producer, runs the pub, and there are two sweat-equity partners. One is his college roommate and best friend John Rishko, who previously farmed clams. The other is Jason Kennedy, who was cellarman at Wild Goose when that operated as an independent brewery on the Western Shore of Maryland.

In this Mid-Atlantic region, Dogfish has begun to win a reputation for its extraordinarily adventurous beers.

The nearest thing to a conventional brew is the oddly-named Shelter Pale Ale, at 5.0 per cent alcohol by volume. "Your home-base, your shelter, the place to which you return," explains the poetic Sam. The grist of this ale contains a small proportion of Delaware-grown barley, kilned in the pub's pizza oven. With its deep golden color, Shelter Pale has a firm malt background, becoming almost slippery in its smoothness. It starts dry, then develops a clean sweetness, with lively flavors. The hops—Willamette, Cascade and Columbus—provide an earthy, cedary aroma and powerful bitterness.

On a number of occasions I had already greatly enjoyed Dogfish Chicory Stout (5.3). In addition to granulated chicory root, this contains locally-roasted organic Mexican coffee and St John's wort, sometimes known as "nature's Prozac," as well as smoked barley malt, wheat, and oatmeal. The brew has a sweet, fresh, flowery, aroma; a relatively light but smooth, rounded, body; a gentle dryness; and a suggestion of aniseed in the long, faintly medicinal finish.

I could not resist the pun in a beer called Raison d'Etre (7.5), based on a brown ale. This contains green raisins and dark candy sugar, and has a primary fermentation with an English ale yeast and a secondary with a Belgian culture. It starts winey, with suggestions of sweet oloroso sherry, developing spicy grain notes in the middle, then finishes with a soft, almondy dryness.

Near the brewery is the site of a colonial settlement called Zwaanendael (old Dutch for "Swan Dale"). This has been punned into Zwaanend Ale (9.5). The crimson brew contains equal amounts of barley, corn and dates. The corn lightens what might otherwise be an overwhelmingly rich and rummy brew, but this is still a deliciously syrupy dessert beer.

The Dogfish word-plays are endless. Immort Ale (11.0) is another of my favorites. It contains peated barley, demerara sugar, maple syrup, vanilla beans and juniper berries; has a secondary fermentation with Champagne yeast; and is matured over oak chips from Chardonnay barrels. This heady, fruity, brew starts with a rich sweetness, becoming firmer, then lightly smoky and woody.

Bizarre though these beers may be, their sales have been sufficient to encourage the opening of a 30-barrel Dogfish micro five mile away in the town of Lewes. To held justify this, Sam has moved into "export" markets. The energy he puts into sales has impressed me greatly. His first shipment to New Jersey—a sixpack—was transported by small boat across Delaware Bay, requiring seven hours for the 20-mile journey. He rowed the boat himself. He also built it. No wonder the women are impressed.

Published Online: MAR 7, 2001
Published in Print: JULY 1, 1999
In: All About Beer

With thanks to Paddy Gunningham and Sam Hopkins, Executors to the Michael Jackson Estate

The article was influential because after it was published, the other journalists stopped taking potshots at our creative process because Michael Jackson, the then lord of beer journalism, endorsed our direction. This was pivotal in shifting our momentum in the early 2000s.

When I published my first book, *Brewing up a Business*, Michael Jackson was generous enough to write the Foreword:

THE PASSION OF THE INDIVIDUAL

The cheerful chap on the cover of this book has every reason to smile. The military-looking vehicle behind him delivers only the matériel of sociability. People love him for it.

Sam Calagione does not aspire to sit among the suits at a boardroom table and be a slave to the military metaphors of marketing. He fights his own battles, on behalf of people with individual tastes and against the tyranny of timidity, conformity, and the lowest common denominator.

When I first took my pen to the same cause 30 years ago, my colleagues asked if I had given up serious journalism. Did I no longer want to change the world? Almost all of them took beer seriously, but they nonetheless thought that writing about it was a frivolous pursuit.

Like Sam Calagione, I can simultaneously have fun in my job but pursue it with serious intent. Those of us who are truly demanding about our beer are a minority, but we are by no means insignificant in number, and we are willing to pay more for a brew we like.

For us, good beer is essential to the quality of life. People who love wine or bread or cheese, for example, would take the same view. These are all perfect products for the entrepreneur, but so are scores of others. In my view, a passion for the product is the first essential. If you have a passion, look at that first. Whatever excites your passion, there are surely others who feel the same way.

Passionate beer-lovers are seeking character, with its own individualistic interplay of flavors. Big breweries have the technical know-how to make such products but their kettles are too large for our market. Their cost accountants want to produce beers low in raw materials and high in acceptability. Their marketing people believe they can think small, but they cannot; well, not small enough. To have individualistic beers, we need small breweries. If you are not passionate about beer, you may be unaware of the renaissance of craft brewing in the United States since the late 1970s.

When I began writing about beer, there were fewer than 50 brewing companies in the United States, almost all of them making very similar beers. Today, there are more than 1,500, brewing beers in more than 100 styles. Many of those beers are highly individualistic, but none more so than Dogfish Head's.

Their individuality is suggested by their names. I especially like Raison D'Etre (both the name and the beer); then Dogfish Head exceeded it with Raison d'Extra.

As his verbal dexterity suggests, Sam was an English major. He studied fiction and poetry. I'm told he takes Walt Whitman to bed with him, though I learned this from a young woman who has no firsthand knowledge of that. I think she wished she had. "You are spending the whole day with Sam Calagione?! Tomorrow?! He's the Robert De Niro of brewers!" He hasn't made a feature film yet, but he has been a Levi's model and made a rap record.

Sadly for female admirers, he seems to have found the perfect wife while still at college. He has the ingenuity to invent new equipment for the brewhouse, and the muscle to row his beer across the Delaware River.

Now it turns out he can write a book, too: brisk, readable, and instructive. A man of such diverse attributes, abilities, and achievements sets an example that makes us all look deficient.
What can we do about this? I can write a Foreword, which aggrandizes myself: I become someone whose blessing he needed. And you? Read the book and brew up your own business. You don't have to make beer. Just make a million....

—Michael Jackson

Michael Jackson is the world's best-selling author on beer and whiskey. His most recent books are *The Great Beer Guide* (New York: DK Inc.) and *The Complete Guide to Single Malt Scotch* (Philadelphia: Running Press).

Self Guided Tour

Our goal here at Dogfish Head Craft Brewery is to make great, original beer. Our ales are brewed with the finest whole leaf hops, and two-row English barley, just like other esteemed micro-brewed beers. But, we take extra steps… we use roasted chicory and organic Mexican coffee in our Chicory Stout, Delaware-grown barley in our Shelter Pale Ale, and pure Massachusetts maple syrup, whole vanilla bean, and champagne yeast in our Immort Ale.

We built our brewery by hand. We converted used dairy and cannery stainless vessels into a brewery. We reconditioned a 1969 Sumac bottle filler that, at 50 bottles per minute, easily fills our needs. We built this system on the cheap. We don't have enormous debt or a board of directors telling us to sell more beer. It is only us reminding each other to brew great beer!

1.888.8DOGFISH
www.dogfish.com

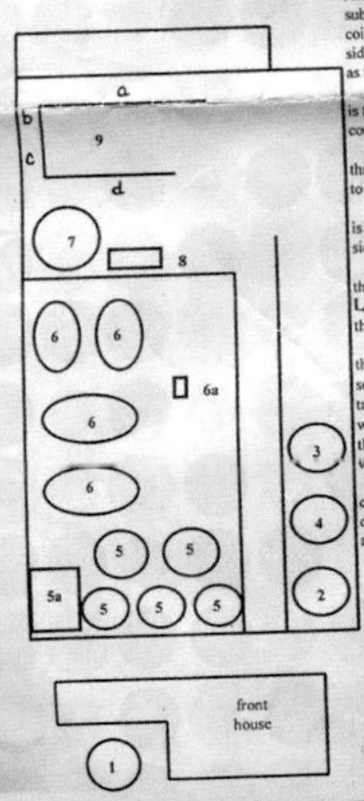

Getting ready to brew a batch of beer begins when our grains arrive and we suck them from the tractor trailer into our **Grain Silo** (1) out in front of the house.

We start the actual brewing process by heating the water in the **Hot Liquor Back** (2) and add phosphates to attain the proper pH level.

Once the water is at the optimal brewing pH, we transfer it to the **Mash Tun** (3) using one of the electric pumps you see on the wall.

After adding the water, we suck the proper amount of grain from the silo into the grain hopper above your head, and into the mash tun. Inside the mash tun, the water and grains heat until the sugars are removed from the grain.

At that point, the wort (or pre-fermented beer) is transferred from the mash tun into the **Boil Kettle** (4). The spent grains are taken from the mash tun and given to a local farmer to be used as cattle feed (it's got lots of protein and the cows love it!). Once the mixture is pumped into the boil kettle, the hops are added and the whole thing is brought to a boil.

From the boil kettle, the beer-to-be is hosed into the enclosed room and into a **Fermenting Tank** (5). All of the fermenting tanks are lined with a coil. A cooling substance runs from the **Ice Builder** (5a) through those coils and allows us to maintain an exact temperature. Inside the fermenting tank, our mixture finally becomes beer as the sugars become alcohol.

After a few days in the fermenting tank, the beer is transferred into a **Conditioning Tank** (6) where it continues to settle.

Once the beer is ready for bottling, it is run through the **Filter** (6a) to remove any yeast particles and to clarify the beer.

Once the beer makes it's way through the filter, it is pumped into the 3000-gallon **Bottling Tank** (7) outside of the cold room, where it is carbonated.

From the bottling tank, the beer can go either to the **Kegging Station** (8) or right to the **Bottling Line** (9). If the beer is put into a keg, the keg is filled and then stored along the wall to your right.

If the beer is to be bottled, it is pumped right into the bottling machine. The bottling machine begins by sending empty bottles through the **Rinser** (9a), then takes the bottles through the **Filler** (9b) where it is filled with the beer, through the **Crowner** (9c) where the bottle is capped, and finally through the **Labeler** (9d), where the neck and body labels are applied.

Once the bottles are packed into the six packs and cartons, they are sent out the back door onto the loading dock, then put into a truck, and (hopefully) transported to a store near you!

Dogfish Head
Craft Brewery

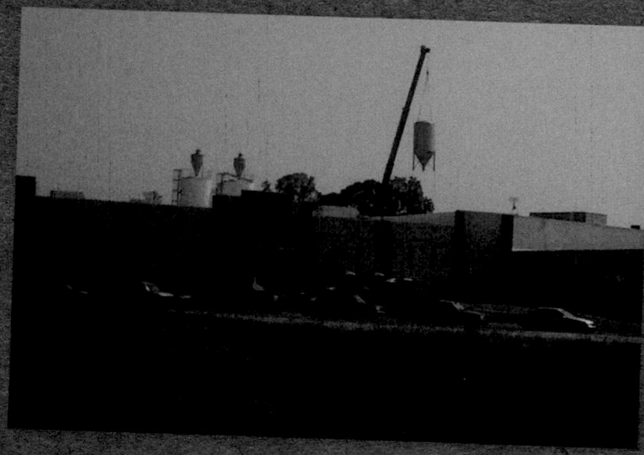

REBECCA 503

stood there, looking at me, that slow smile on her face, her eyes wide open . . ."

Maxim's voice had sunk low, so low, that it was like a whisper. The hand that I held between my own was cold. I did not look at him. I watched Jasper's sleeping body on the carpet beside me, the little thump of his tail, now and then, upon the floor.

"I'd forgotten," said Maxim, and his voice was slow now, tired, without expression, "that when you shot a person there was so much blood."

There was a hole there on the carpet beneath Jasper's tail. The burnt hole from a cigarette. I wondered how long it had been there. Some people said ash was good for the carpets.

"I had to get water from the cove," said Maxim. "I had to keep going backwards and forwards to the cove for water. Even by the fireplace, where she had not been, there was a stain. It was all round her where she lay on the floor. It began to blow too. There was no catch on the window. The window kept banging backwards and forwards, while I knelt there on the floor, with that dishcloth, and the bucket beside me. [illegible] does not remember [illegible] rain on the [illegible]

And the rain on the roof [illegible] fast. [illegible] half-past [illegible] roof. It [illegible] the boat," he said, "it must [illegible] no moon. The [illegible] "I carried [illegible] was quite dark. There was [illegible] eleven by the [illegible] nearly twelve. It was quite dark. [illegible] carried her down to the cabin and left [illegible] wind was squally, from the [illegible] with [illegible] dinghy [illegible], and beat [illegible] there. Then I [illegible] me but it came [illegible] out of the [illegible] over of the headland. I remember [illegible] puffs, and I was [illegible] half-way up the mast. I had not done [illegible] you see [illegible] got the main-sail jammed [illegible] out with Rebecca. [illegible] for a long time. I never [illegible] the tide, how swift it ran and [illegible] into the little [illegible] "And I thought [illegible] the headland like a funnel. I got the boat [illegible] cove. The wind blew down from the headland [illegible] beyond the beacon [illegible] I tried to go out into the [illegible] I got her [illegible] of rocks. The little jib fluttered [illegible] I could not sheet it about, to clear the ridge [illegible] out of my hands, went twisting in. A puff of wind came and the sheet tore out of my hands, went twisting round the mast. The sail thundered and shook. It cracked like a whip above my head. I could not remember what one had to do. I could not remember. I tried to reach that sheet and it blew above me in the air. Another blast of wind came straight ahead. We began to drift sideways, closer to the ridge. It was dark, so damned dark I couldn't see anything on the black, slippery deck. Somehow I blundered down into the cabin. I had a spike with me. If I didn't do it now it would be too late. We were getting so near to the ridge, and in six or seven minutes, drifting like this, we should be out of deep water. I opened the sea-cocks. The water began to come in. I drove the spike into the bottom boards. One of the planks split right across. I took the spike out and began to drive in another plank. The water came up over my feet. I left Rebecca lying there, on the floor. I fastened both the scuttles. I bolted the door. When I came up on deck I saw we were within twenty yards of the ridge. I threw some of the loose stuff on the deck into the water.

Dogfish Head
against the tide.
Craft Brewed Ales

Palo Santo Marron (12% ABV)

For nearly all alcoholic beverages aged on wood, the de facto wood variety is oak. It might be French oak, or it might be American oak, but whether you're aging whiskies or wines or rums, universally the wood of choice for barrels and tanks for aging alcoholic beverages is oak.

We were lucky enough that by the mid-2000s our reputation for being fearless with ingredients and fermentation and aging processes was well-known in the beer geek circles we traveled in. Still today lots of beer lovers who choose to visit us at Dogfish will bring ingredients from their region of the world that they think would make for great additions in our off-center recipes. Sometimes it works, and sometimes it doesn't, but in the case of Palo Santo Marron, it worked out really well. At one point we had some wonderfully crazy hippie visit us from Santa Fe that brought all these crystals with her and said who if we brewed and submerged the crystals in the beers it would essentially give the drinkers, you know, superpowers of some sorts. That was a collaboration we did not embrace. In this case of Palo Santo Marron there was a great Dogfish fan who lived in Baltimore named John Gasparine, who was a high-end flooring salesman and he would source exotic woods from around the world to make these superlush, expensive hardwood floors for people. He was on a work trip in Paraguay and he landed in this village. He got out of the taxi and he's like, "Whoa." The first thing he noticed was how it smelled. He inquired about the smell and was told it was coming from this very rough lumber mill in the village that was processing trees into lumber from the local wood called Palo Santo wood. He could tell by the aroma that it would be, could be, something really interesting to introduce into beer. So he smuggled home some chunks of that Palo Santo wood and brought them to me at Dogfish Head and said, "Hey, Sam. I know you're aging beers like Immort Ale and Red & White on oak. What would you think about trying something with this exotic wood?" I smelled the shavings of wood and agreed that they had a beautiful incense-like, spicy smell to them.

We brewed a big strong brown ale and added a special sugar called sucanat, which is the abbreviation for sugar cane natural. The sucanat bumped up the alcohol content because the yeast ate the sugar in addition to the barley. I put in that strong 11 or 12 percent base in a fermenter and then added cheesecloth sacks filled with shavings of the Palo Santo wood

When we tasted the beer, it was just beautiful. And so in 2007 we released our beer called Palo Santo Marron.

that John had brought me. The alcohol in the beer acted as a solvent and stripped the natural oils and resins out of the Palo wood.

When you drink a beer aged on oak barrels it has these sort of toasty vanilla notes to it, but when you drink a beer that's aged on Palo Santo it has these spicy, sweet, resiny, deep notes that are unlike any other beer. We fell in love with the Palo Santo so much that we commissioned John to return to Paraguay and harvest more of this sustainably harvested Palo Santo wood and ship it back to us on a container boat. The wood in this particular tree was so dense that when John Gasparine went to Paraguay, the local wood salesman would prove that it was truly Palo Santo wood by standing in front of the tree and shooting it with a .22 caliber pistol, to prove that the bullet would bounce off the tree or barely pierce the tree's outer surface and would not penetrate the tree. That just showed how dense the wood really was. We built giant wooden tanks out of this Palo Santo wood, each tank costing over $100,000 dollars. We have two of these Palo Santo tanks that we use for beers like Palo Santo and Bitches Brew.

Wood tanks, whether oak or Palo Santo, were not common to have—especially the scale of the barrels that we had commissioned. For the Palo Santo project we got to collaborate with a father and son team from Upstate New York called Arrow Tanks. They are one of the last companies in America handcrafting giant wooden tanks. Their primary business is building the giant wooden tanks you see on the rooftops of buildings when you're in New York City or other cities that hold the water, but they accepted the challenge of making beer tanks from this Palo Santo wood, which I should also say feels more like iron than it feels like wood. The wood is superdense, heavy, and difficult to work with, so it was a real challenge for them to build those tanks.

Red & White (10% ABV)

At that Rare Beer Club event where I first met Michael Jackson, he and I were sitting at a table with some of the winemakers and we had a sort of, "Your chocolate is in my peanut butter" moment with them. We started mixing some beautiful Oregon pinot noir with the white beer that we had at our table—I think it was a Hoegaarden—and the blend of flavors tasted beautiful. That inspired me to create a beer that would weave that juicy pinot noir grape character into an imperial white beer so that it would have the strength and food compatibility of a pinot noir wine but also have the refreshing lower-body character of a traditional Belgian-style white beer.

Artist Sarah Lamb

We were not creating a revolution, we were embracing and bringing attention to the renaissance of creative brewing that's existed throughout the history of civilization.

The beer resulting from that event, our Red & White Ale, is an extension of our beer-wine hybrid legacy that began ten years earlier in 1996 with our Raison D'Etre. It is an oak-aged Belgian-style white ale fermented with pinot noir grape juice. This beer is brewed with coriander and orange peel but then fermented with pinot noir juice. After fermentation, a fraction of that batch is aged in our giant 10,000-gallon oak barrels. This beer was inspired by that very first evening of drinking and eating with Michael and the winemakers and it has as much wine terroir as it has beer terroir.

I
Voted
Today!
Dogfish Head
red
&
white

Black & Blue (10% ABV)

In 2007 we released Black & Blue. Black & Blue is a sort of sister beer to Red & White, which we began brewing the year before. While Red & White is a Belgian-style white fermented beer with very red pinot noir grapes, Black & Blue is a Belgian-style golden ale that we ferment with blackberries and blueberries. While some breweries use artificial fruit flavoring, we use real pureed berries. When artificial flavoring is used, you are able to smell the aroma of fruit, but you don't taste it in the beer. You also get that super synthetic flavor that come forward like you find in a Jolly Rancher or bubble gum. When you use real fruit, the yeast eats the natural fruit sugars and weaves the complexity of that fruit into the taste of the beer. That's the big difference. When you brew with real berries that have real fermentable sugars it gives more depths and complexity to the whole beer.

The label art for Black & Blue and Red & White also came from a mom and pop duo. The portrait painter David Larned did the painting of the gentleman on the Black & Blue label and his wife, Sarah Lamb, did the still life of the beer glass and grapes that became the label for Red & White.

Portrait artist David Larned

Dogfish Head Craft Brewed Ales

Black & Blue

ABV: 10% IBU: 25

Black and Blue is a lightly hopped bold golden ale with a slight reddish/purple hue. It's not your typical fruit beer – Black and Blue is a beer first and foremost, but a beer that pays homage to the powerful and delicious world of the berry. It has the body of a big malty ale exceptionally balanced by a subtle fruit bouquet with tart berry notes and spiciness in flavor. This comes from literally tons of American malted barley and a heavy hand of blackberry and blueberry added to the beer in both the Brewhouse and Cellar all complimented by domestic northwestern hops and the use of a robust Belgian yeast in fermentation.

To learn more about Black & Blue, visit us at www.dogfish.com.

Food Pairing Recommendations:
Spicy pork, toasted nuts, chocolate

Cheese Pairing:
Good with most cheeses, especially roquefort

Wine Comparable:
Medium-bodied red: Zinfandel

The Big Ol' Beer Bottle

When Dogfish Head began bottling beer in 1996, we were hand-bottling 22-ounce tall bottles of Shelter Pale Ale. The first semi-automated bottling line we bought was for the more standard 12-ounce beer bottles, and from 1997 when we installed that bottling line, up until about 2000, we were only running 12-ounce glass bottles. But when we started brewing these more exotic beers that were more wine-like in their complexity, their alcohol by volume, and their ageability, we thought it'd be cool to actually present them in a wine bottle to show that they deserved their place next to fine food the way great wine did. Since we couldn't afford new equipment, we

scoured used wine equipment websites and found a used sparkling wine bottling line in California that we bought pretty cheap. We transported it back to Delaware and began filling 750 milliliter bottles. The first beers bottled on the automated bottling line was Midas Touch and 90 Minute IPA. Soon after, we had a whole line of beers being bottled on the 750 milliliter bottling line.

This larger-format bottling was a great way to market and sell these beers. Dogfish was among the first. I've got to give props to Stoudt's, a lager-centric brewery from Central Pennsylvania founded by Ed and Carol Stoudt. They were one of the first to market in Philly and PA with these champagne bottles even earlier than we did. But we were really the first brewery that I know of shipping champagne bottles of beer coast to coast starting around the year 2000.

Dogfish Head 75 Minute
A bottle-conditioned India Pale
with maple syrup.
7.5% Alc. by Vol. • 1 Pint 9.4 fl. oz.

The Mullet

Several years ago, the *Today Show* did a piece on Dogfish Head that brought the brand a lot of national attention. That piece begot another in *People* magazine, which begot an appearance for me on the NBC show *To Tell the Truth*. Now I'm not sure how many high-end beer buyers are tuning into this B-rated daytime game show. Its host was the actor John O'Hurley, who had played J. Peterman on *Seinfeld*, and I had to grin and bear it as some flunky from the series *Designing Women* tasted our beer and informed the studio audience that it "ain't no Heineken." On the flip side, the show's staff left me alone in the makeup room for a moment too long and I scored a really cool mullet wig that I still enjoy wearing to parties. But all of this attention certainly helped to increase national interest in Dogfish Head and didn't cost us a cent. I received a few calls from other brewery owners who congratulated me on the coverage and asked if I wouldn't mind sharing the name of the public relations company I use. They were a little surprised when I told them that we didn't use one and never had. I do admit, though, at Dogfish many of our coworkers look forward to events where we get to meet up, dress up, and rock a mullet wig, a fake 'stache, and what not. We take the art of brewing seriously but we don't take ourselves too seriously.

"Science has not yet taught us if madness is or is not the sublimity of the intelligence."
—Edgar Allan Poe

Another Sam hairstyle nobody asked for

Kenny Thorpe

Brewer, PhD (That's Player haters Degree)
Start Date: 2007

Walking through the cellars, you might come across Kenny cleaning lines, brewing in Brewhouse 1, or dropping rhymes as he occupies his mind with some of the more mundane tasks that come with being a brewer. This is what makes Kenny so "Kenny." Everything is an opportunity to grow and learn. Everything.

Kenny Thorpe

It was 2007, and Kenny Thorpe had no brewing experience. He was looking for a job after taking some classes at the local community college. Dogfish was hiring and needed some help on the keg line. Not even 21 at the time, the job sounded different and fun. He was right. Working the keg line was not an easy job and the odds of needing a snorkel and a mask were a reality. While this work was not for everyone, Kenny had no problems with it at all. He wanted to learn and grow so we tried him on the packaging line. He picked that up no problem. After three years he had learned everything he could and had covered almost every base there was to cover in packaging. Then, third shift brewing needed some help so we looked at who could step up. Kenny was it. Cleaning tanks, doing dry hops, and spraying floors. Not a brewer yet but growing every day and supporting where he could. When you keep throwing work at someone and they eat it up, it is hard not to keep feeding them. Kenny has grit. He lives for the hard work. "Just give me a chance," he says. Time progressed, and he was trained on the D.E. filter. A little move here, a little learning curve there. Today? Full-blown Brewer. Degree? School of Dogfish Head, straight outta Milton.

"There is always room to advance. Always room to grow," says Kenny. He puts himself in spots where he can make mistakes, and that's one reason Kenny has come so far. If we as a company are not growing people, ALL of our people, then we are failing. That growth relationship has two sides to it. On one side, the indi-

Coworker Profile

vidual must be willing to fail, learn, and grow. On the other side, the company must be willing to be patient, teach, allow for mistakes, and grow with the individual. For Kenny and Dogfish, the ties run deep. It is a 200 percent game that takes drive from both sides. Dogfish had to be willing to invest 100 percent in Kenny. Kenny had to be willing to put 100 percent into Dogfish. With 200 percent, anything is possible.

When he turned 21, Kenny had his first beer at Dogfish Head: Shelter Pale Ale. He loves Raison D'Etra and for years it was his go-to on the payday case circuit. Every two weeks all the coworkers at Dogfish Head get a case of beer. Kenny said Raison was king for him for a long time. When it comes to brewing beers, he loved making Olde School Barley-wine and grinding up the figs for it. Kenny has had his hands in a great deal of our history.

Looking back, Kenny loves to look around the brewery and think about how much it has changed over the years. When he gets talking about it, he realizes that it has never stopped. The change and transformation in the company is what feeds Kenny, like many of our other coworkers. Change, while difficult, spurs growth. Standing with Kenny by the wood room, he can see the place as it once was and smiles. What he doesn't realize is that his transformation from 2007 to today has been just as fast-paced and drastic. As the building transformed, we transformed with it, and Kenny embodies that growth. Guys like Kenny make us who we are and define our Off-Centeredness. We hire brewers with all sorts of sweet degrees ... but, we also home grow them. In-house. Delaware native style with a PhD. That would be his Player Haters Degree.

If you were on a deserted island and could have one album to listen to and an unlimited supply of one beer, what would it be?

Beer: Slightly Mighty (because he can drink it all day)
Album: Jay-Z, *Reasonable Doubt*

Chapter 5

The Great Communicator

When I first met Mariah, she was a 16-year-old sophomore standing in the dining room of Northfield Mount Hermon. She was filling hundreds of pastries with cream. I put down my paring knife and stepped over to her. I believe I told her she looked good enough to eat, and then I learned that she was the girl with the heirloom brownie recipe.

Since that very first day when I decided I wanted to build a brewery named Dogfish Head, Mariah has been the first person I went to for advice and support on the challenges we faced in the early years at Dogfish Head. She became my true partner in the company in 1997, our third year in business, and has been as committed to guiding Dogfish Head toward where we are today as I have been. Since then, we've worked side by side to grow Dogfish Head, although she is much more focused and practical than I am

There are a million reasons why I love Mariah, one of which is that she is undoubtedly the only person in the world who has higher expectations of me than I have of myself. She is never surprised when we achieve great things; she would expect nothing less.

In a lot of ways my wife Mariah and I share the job of articulating the voice of our company hand in hand. I'm usually the person at Dogfish Head who is driving the strategic decisions on what we are going to do next. We need all the talented people we work with to bring the idea to reality. Then Mariah gets the word out about what we are doing. She does this by cheerleading and evangelizing in the virtual world while I do much of it in the physical world. Whether that means hosting an Ancient Ales dinner, serving beers from behind our booth at a festival, speaking at a convention, or hosting a television program, it's all part of the same world for us.

Mariah joined Dogfish full time in 1997. One of the biggest impacts Mariah has had on the business since then is our push on social media. Mariah has been the voice of Dogfish Head in our online community and is a big voice in where we are today.

Mariah is effective at having a dialogue with the most people in the most authentic and consistent way. Even if I'm standing behind the Dogfish booth at the Great American Beer Festival and there are over one hundred people lined up to talk with me about our beer, my work is not nearly as effective as the work Mariah does in her online outreach. For example, she has personally built our social media community to the point where, when we announce in that world that a new beer is hitting the shelves around the country, hundreds of thousands of people will get that message.

She has built such a large presence online that when she types a sentence, a giant community gets it, and who knows how many people they talk to or text about it and how much it grows from there? It's not like our online community just spontaneously erupted. Mariah has built it up from just a handful of friends and followers. And she has done this by speaking in our off-centered voice, by actually listening and responding to our followers, and by focusing more on what we represent rather than what we are trying to sell.

We have jokingly called her the queen of all media. She might not have the reach of Oprah Winfrey or Rupert Murdoch, but in the world of Dogfish Head she wears this title well. Over the years she has taken our static website and turned it into the hub for all of our marketing efforts. It is now a portal to the robust and diverse Dogfish community and a jumping-off point from which she has given Dogfish a significant impact and relatively loud voice in the online beer community in the context of our size.

While she no longer posts everything herself, she works closely with our small team of storytellers. Mariah and her team updates our community on what we are doing today, what we are doing next, and about the other communities and companies around us that inspire us—as well as chiming in on general current discussions in the worlds of beer, food, and spirits. She has earned the respect of this community. Whether or not the person to whom she is responding realizes it, the online Dogfish voice is informed by Mariah's, on behalf of all 400 Dogfish Head coworkers. Her dedication and commitment to our followers is at the heart of our success in this world.

Here's Mariah to tell you more:

The Voice of Dogfish Head

Q: Let's talk a little bit about the one thing that has been, I think, difficult for the book so far. We talk about brewing a lot, because that's obviously what we enjoy.

Mariah: Turns out we like beer.

Q: Turns out we like beer—and we brew a lot of beer, but as we were collecting all these great artifacts from the history of Dogfish Head, and we came across a lot of amazing pictures, we found ourselves asking, "Where's Mariah? Where are the pictures of Mariah?"

Mariah: <laughs> Right. There's nothing to see here. <laughs>

Q: Yeah, there are no photos of Mariah.

Mariah: These are not the droids you're looking for. <laughs>

Mariah explains

When Sam and I first opened the brewpub I was working another job, which was in TV news. I wasn't pulling shifts as a server or bartender in the restaurant, I was more coming in on the weekends to be a host or bus tables or fill in as a server. On weekends when we weren't in the restaurant, Sam and I would travel to beer festivals to showcase our beer. Sam is obviously the extrovert, and I'm definitely more the introvert, so I was never the one walking up to groups of people saying, "Hey, let me tell you all about our beer ..." Well ... maybe after a couple beers, but in the beginning Sam was the one out in the crowds engaging people and pulling them in with his dynamic personality to come to our stand and taste our beers. I would be the one behind the tap, filling pints with whatever beers we brought to the festival, passing them across the tap box, talking to people, and asking them for feedback.

Dogfish Head Craft Brewery
Mariah Calagione
Vice President
Marketing & Distribution
1-888-8DOGFISH
www.dogfish.com
22 NASSAU COMMONS
LEWES, DE 19958

As online social media channels emerged, I went from evangelizing about our beers to festival attendees to connecting with people both near and far to educate them about our beers. Back in 2008, just a couple years after Twitter had launched, a fan of Dogfish reached out to us and said, "Hey, you guys should be on Twitter." Right around that same time, another fan reached out and said, "I grabbed the @dogfishbeer handle and set up an account. Here's the password. I also put your logo up there." I thought to myself, "Okay. Well, who the heck wants to hear from us on Twitter? That's weird."

At first, I just started following other accounts. I'd follow the accounts of different tourism destinations, obviously other breweries, wineries, places where people would go, food companies, and I just sort of started watching what kind of conversations were happening on Twitter. I stuck my toe in and started posting little things here and there. As more of an introvert I enjoyed engaging with folks on digital platforms. Around the same time, I found a Dogfish Head Facebook group that a woman in Texas had started that had thousands of followers. I didn't know who she was, but I thought, "This is kind of cool." So I reached out to her and said, "Hey, it is awesome that you started this group. I work at the brewery and I'd love to also post here and get some more information to your fans," and so she made me an administrator.

I sent her a box of awesome Dogfish swag, but didn't hear from her again.
So whoever you are, thank you!

From that homegrown Facebook account, we were given an opportunity to engage with a very dedicated Facebook group of Dogfish Head fans. And just as the over-the-tap-box conversations we had at beer festivals were so integral to establishing and engaging fans back in 1995 and 1996, the conversations we began having on social media became just as fundamental in engaging beer fans and spreading the word about what we were doing.

And so we began engaging craft beer fans on social media in the same way we engaged customers that we were handing a beer to across the bar. We've never been the type to be like, "All right. Here's your beer," and walk away. If you've ever been to an event with Sam, you'd know he loses his voice every time, because he will not hand someone a beer without personally explaining what the beer is. Sam's never going to be like, "Oh, here's your beer. Next. Here's your beer. Next." Even though it's on the sign behind him, Sam will tell you, in his own words, the story behind each beer because he wants people to know about the beer they're drinking. But it's not just talking about beer for Sam, it's about creating an experience for the beer drinker attending an event. So when we can't engage fans at a beer event, social media provides another opportunity to engage our beer-drinking fans. We often find ourselves saying, "Glad you like that beer. Here's the story behind it."

Sam often traveled, being his extroverted self, doing events and beer festivals and selling beer, which was critically important, so because of social media, I was able to engage fans

and have the same kinds of conversations that we'd had when we were talking to beer lovers at beer festivals, except online. I began posting real-time photos of Dogfish Head coworkers in action, sharing details around what we were working on, and connecting with Dogfish Head fans all over the country.

The cool thing about social media was that I could be home taking care of our young children—we had little kids at the time—or working at the brewery, yet still be very engaged. I wanted to make sure if someone was reaching out with a question or trying to engage with us, that we were responding. I could be at home, or working at my desk, or just checking my phone on nights and weekends and engage with fans looking to connect.

As it turns out people who drink beer are drinking beer on nights and weekends and talking about it on social media while drinking our beer, so it became an all-encompassing endeavor making sure that when people were engaging us, we were responding. While we were unique, geeky beer people, the early adopters of social media were more the unique, geeky, technology people, and it turns out there's quite a lot of overlap.

Part of why our community is so strong, and our fans are so engaged, is because we began engaging our communities on social media early and gave beer fans an opportunity to help define how we engaged with them. We often talk about the fact that the belly of the brand is not only our people, our products, and the storytelling we do here—it's just as much about the people who are a part of our off-centered community.

From the beginning we focused on cultivating a sense of belonging within our online presence. When people came to our pages, it was me just talking to them and posting pictures and videos. I'm not a trained photographer or videographer. I did not have the skill set to take professional photos. I would literally open my little flip phone and I'd say, "Okay, Sam, I'm going to say, 'Three, two, one.' You talk for 25 seconds or so, and don't mess up, because I don't know how to edit," and so we'd shoot a little video and post it online. So it was real content that was captured on the fly at the brewery.

We want to show people what it's really like here, what it really feels like here, what it tastes like here, what it sounds like here, and it isn't a slick marketing campaign that they're going to get from a big ol' brand that is really good at making slick marketing campaigns. That's just not our DNA, that's not where we came from. When we have veered in that direction a little bit, we see that, you know, people aren't as excited about our content and don't engage as much, don't ask questions. They're like, "Oh, yeah, nice." Scroll right on by. But if we're showing our people, like, fans love to see our coworkers, they know our coworkers. The fans will call out our coworkers by name in the post and create deeper engagement not only for them, but for us as well.

We are also very spontaneous. If we want to post something, we usually say, "We need a picture of someone pouring a beer in the tasting room. Hey, let's go downstairs and, oh, hey, Lars, can you pour a beer while we take a photo?" We take a picture and post it. To us, Lars is a coworker. But to the people who see the picture, he's their tour guy. So, people will comment, "Hey, I know Lars because he was my tour guide and he was awesome." So just like that, we make a connection through people, which is the best connection, and that happens with brewpub too. People say, "Olivia is my favorite server." It's one of the many ways we connect to our community near and far. We maintain that real, and I hate the word authentic, because it's overused, but authentic look behind the curtain of who Dogfish is. We give that community glimpses of what we're doing each day. I also think people like the idea of off-centered. That everyone is aspirationally off-centered, even if they're sitting in, like, their corner office in a three-piece suit in a big city. Somewhere in the back of that person's mind, she wants to be off-centered. So, to be a part of what we do and connect with us through our posts, our people, our liquids, and our stories gives them a channel to be off-centered, too.

"Mariah came up with the name and suggested the lemongrass, and the entire Dogfish Head community came together to make and sell Namaste."

Theobroma (9% ABV)

Theobroma, first brewed in 2008, is another collaboration between Dogfish Head and Dr. Pat McGovern, the Scientific Director of the Biomolecular Archeology Laboratory for Cuisine, Fermented Beverages, and Health at the University of Pennsylvania Museum. Theobroma, another Ancient Ale, is a celebration of cocoa, which was considered to be the food of the gods. The recipe for Theobroma is based on chemical analysis of pottery fragments that were found in Honduras that revealed the earliest known alcoholic chocolate drink used by early civilizations to toast special occasions. The discovery of this beer predates the earliest recorded use of cocoa for human consumption by more than 500 years earlier than what was thought at the time to be 1200 BC.

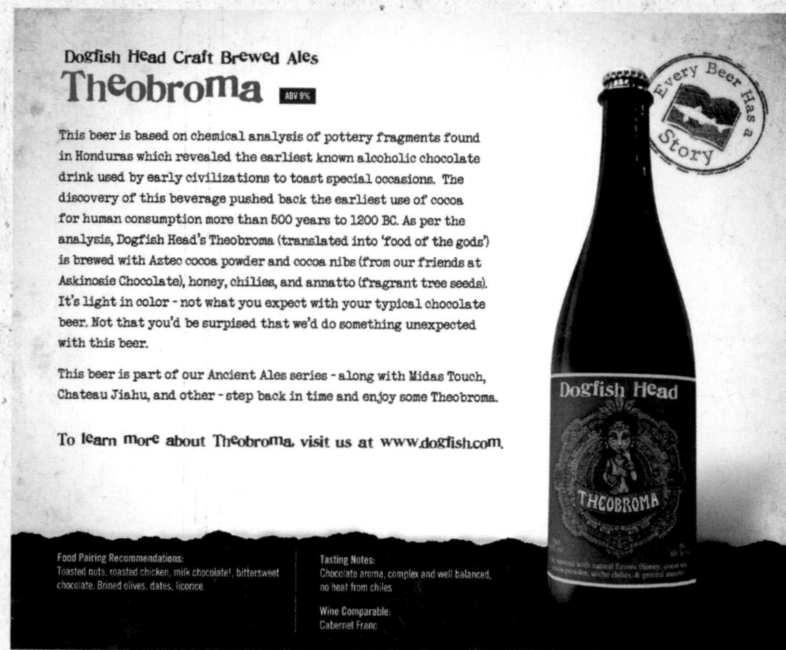

Dogfish Head Craft Brewed Ales
Theobroma
ABV 9%
This beer is based on chemical analysis of pottery fragments found in Honduras which revealed the earliest known alcoholic chocolate drink used by early civilizations to toast special occasions. The discovery of this beverage pushed back the earliest use of cocoa for human consumption more than 500 years to 1200 BC. As per the analysis, Dogfish Head's Theobroma (translated into 'food of the gods') is brewed with Aztec cocoa powder and cocoa nibs (from our friends at Askinosie Chocolate), honey, chilies, and annatto (fragrant tree seeds). It's light in color - not what you expect with your typical chocolate beer. Not that you'd be surpised that we'd do something unexpected with this beer.
This beer is part of our Ancient Ales series - along with Midas Touch, Chateau Jiahu, and other - step back in time and enjoy some Theobroma.
To learn more about Theobroma, visit us at www.dogfish.com.
Food Pairing Recommendations:
Toasted nuts, roasted chicken, milk chocolate!, bittersweet chocolate. Brined olives, dates, licorice.
Tasting Notes:
Chocolate aroma, complex and well balanced, no heat from chiles
Wine Comparable:
Cabernet Franc
Every Beer Has a Story
Dogfish Head
THEOBROMA

Theobroma is brewed with Aztec cocoa powder and cocoa nibs provided by our friends at a local artisanal chocolate producer called Askinosie Chocolate. The beer is brewed with honey, chilies, and annatto, which is a fragrant tree seed that is native to Honduras as well. It's relatively light in color, which you might not expect from a typical chocolate beer, but we wanted a base that would allow reddish hues derived from the annatto, the fragrant tree seeds, to come through because the reddish hue is an homage to another tradition Dr. Pat and I learned about, which is that before people were actually eating chocolate they were drinking it. The drinks would be fermented, and they were used in religious ceremonies where the Aztecs would encourage members of their community to jump into active volcanoes to appease their gods. To give them the courage to make the jump the leaders would ply them with giant chalices of this fermented cocoa beverage. They would slice their hands open and add drops of blood to what they were drinking. We envisioned that it would give the beverages a reddish hue, which we wanted to acknowledge in the recipe. This is why we added the annatto tree seeds to it, which gives it the reddish tint we imagined Aztec tribes would have observed in the chalice before drinking it.

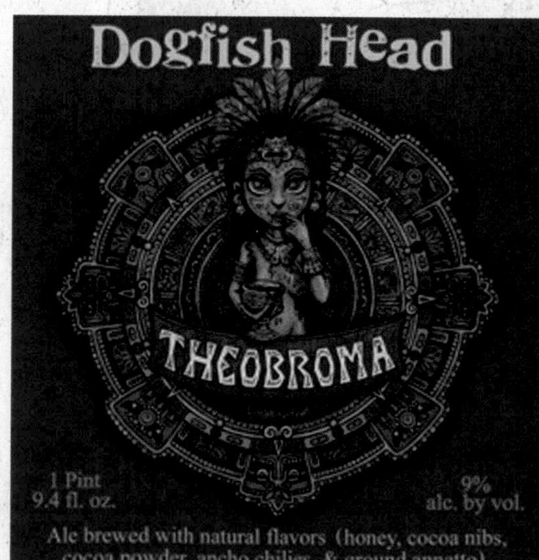

Dogfish Head
THEOBROMA
1 Pint
9.4 fl. oz.
9%
alc. by vol.
Ale brewed with natural flavors (honey, cocoa nibs, cocoa powder, ancho chilies, & ground annatto).

Dogfish

My Antonia

(7.5% ABV)

Another killer collaboration we did in 2008 is called My Antonia. The beer is named after the 1918 novel of the same name by fiction writer Willa Cather. This beer began as a collaboration between Dogfish Head and Birra del Borgo, a craft brewery outside of Rome, Italy. Originally brewed in collaboration with Birra del Borgo in Italy for the Italian market, this was the first time we ever incorporated our proprietary continual hopping process to the brewing of a lager-style beer.

There are two classes of beer: ales and lagers. Ales are brewed at warmer temperatures with a top-fermenting yeast. The warmer temperatures mean they usually are more estery and fruity—and they ferment quickly, warmly, and vigorously. Then there are lagers, which are brewed cold with a bottom-fermenting yeast that ferments more slowly. Lagers tend to be more mellow and refined. My Antonia applies the explosive hop-forward process of continual hopping that we typically incorporate into our ales resulting in what's considered a lighter, nuanced beer style of pilsner, which is a type of lager.

We also decided to bump up the alcohol by adding more barley which means more fermentable sugars. Traditional pilsners are usually between 4 and 5 percent alcohol. After the collaboration with Birra del Borgo in Italy, we began brewing it in Delaware for U.S. distribution in 2010.

Sam and his father

Dogfish Head Craft Brewed Ales

My Antonia

ABV 7.5%

Dogfish Head has been an ale-focused brewery since we opened in 1995, but we do have room for an off-centered lager every now and then. My Antonia, the only lager we package for distribution every year, is a continually-hopped imperial pilsner first brewed with Birra del Borgo near Rome in 2008. Named after the Willa Cather novella, it has roots in our Golden Era and Golden Shower lagers.

My Antonia starts with Pilsner and Carapils malts. It then gets boatloads of Noble and Pacific Northwest hops before primary fermentation with a Czech pils yeast strain. Dry-hopped, unfiltered and bottle-conditioned, My Antonia has earthy, bready and spicy notes in the nose and is a perfect match to cedar-plank salmon or a Reuben on pumpernickel.

The label for My Antonia features a cityscape melding the Old World architecture of Rome with the modern skyline of Manhattan, symbolizing the collaborations we continue to do with Birra del Borgo at Eataly New York's rooftop brewery.

To learn more about My Antonia, visit us at www.dogfish.com.

Every Beer Has a Story

Food Pairing Recommendations:
Raw Oysters, Grilled Sausages, Lasagna

Cheese Pairing:
Havarti with Dill

Wine Comparable:
Bordeaux-White

Sah'tea (9% ABV)

In 2009 we released Sah'tea. This beer was based on the recipe of an ancient ale from Finland named Sahti. A Finnish beer, Sahti was known to be popular in the eighteenth century but its origins can be tracked back to casks found aboard sunken Viking ships dating as far back as the ninth century.

We researched and brewed our first iteration of this beer back in 1997, before we began analyzing and reviving recipes for ancient ales with Dr. Pat McGovern. This was a beer we designed and brewed all by ourselves by researching historical documents rather than analyzing molecular evidence, which is the process we use when we work with Dr. Pat.

For Sah'tea, the wort, or prefermented beer, is processed in a way that was indigenous to how beers in Finland were brewed in the ninth century. Beer was brewed with local rye in a cauldron likely made of wood or pottery. They did not use steam in the brewing process back then, so instead would heat rocks in an open fire and drop those white-hot rocks into the cauldron of beer. The rocks would sizzle and steam and that is what would generate the heat to boil the beer. For Sah'tea, we did the same.

From there, we fermented beer with a German weizen yeast, which throws in a lot of phenolic peppery notes, in addition to juniper berries that were foraged from the Finnish countryside. We also included black tea during the boil, which is not a traditional ingredient in traditional Sahti, thus it's kind of a hybrid between a tea and a beer, so we spell ours Sah'tea.

Once we tasted the original batch of Sah'tea we brewed, we immediately recognized the great earthy, smoky complexity the beer developed from heating rocks in a wood fire and submerging them into wort to get the beer to a boil. We decided that would be a significant step in any future batches of the beer. As a result, we have one tank in particular in the Dogfish Head Milton location that is especially banged up because it bears the scars of being the tank we brew Sah'tea in.

When we brew new batches of Sah'tea, we wheel out this old wood grill, which was our original wood grill from our brewpub that's all beat up now. While we heat the rocks for Sah'tea batches we also have a barbeque for our coworkers and serve wood-grilled hotdogs while we heat the wood-grilled rocks for Sah'tea.

Dogfish Head
Craft Brewed Ales
SAH'TEA
Dogfish Head
1 Pint 9.4 fl. oz.
SAH'TEA

The spicing pots

Incorporating culinary ingredients into our brewing process began presenting technical challenges as our brewery grew. When we first began, I would just dump handfuls of herbs, spices, and fruits into our 15-gallon brewing system. When we jumped to a 5-barrel brewery, I would put the specialty ingredients in cheesecloth and tie it off with rope and add that to the boil pot. Eventually, when we jumped to a 50-barrel brewery I would buy women's pantyhose, which are porous and sterile in the package, and I would cram them full of hops, herbs, and spices, along with blocks of food-grade stainless steel so they would sink to bottom of the tank rather than float on top and toss them into the tanks.

After a boil, when we would empty a giant tank that was filled with beer, hops, and stuffed pantyhose, it would look like the site of a cult murder because there would be all these lower torsos at the bottom of the tank, which were the pantyhose filled with hops and different fruits and spices.

Not many breweries go through the pains of using whole culinary ingredients in their brewing process, but we believe it can make all the difference in the taste of our beers. It is yet another example of our innovation in beer ingredients driving innovation in the beer-making process.

The cold storage

During most traditional brewery tours there's probably a cold box that has kegs in it and a box of hops, and that's the entire inventory of the cold box. When you come to Dogfish Head, first you notice that our cold box is almost as big as our brewery itself. It's a massive warehouse, and when you walk into it, it smells like you've been transported to a fresh-air market in Cairo moved to Antarctica. It's freezing in there, but it smells beautiful because in addition to the rows and rows of pallets of hops, there's saffron and coffee and licorice and pumpkin meat and junipers and giant tanks full of honeys and grape must, molasses, and all kinds of other ingredients. It's a pretty diverse inventory of culinary ingredients. Mariah often jokes, if the zombie apocalypse goes down, we're going to lock ourselves in this brewery and we'll be able to live for a long, long time just off our beer and brewing ingredients.

Instead of throwing it away, we hand-loaded the cases into our truck one layer at a time. We sold some at our brewpub at a reduced price, and most of it went out to the beer festivals that we attend most weekends in the summer, where we gave the bottles away as free samples for beer lovers to try.

We went to work brewing another batch and found a source for better caps. I served some at a festival in Massachusetts and was amazed by the response. People loved the beer. They loved the fact that a 40-ounce malt liquor could actually have a lot of flavor and be served bottle-conditioned and fresh. They also liked the hand-stamped bag that came with every bottle and the irreverent name that we gave the beer—Liquor de Malt—French for malt liquor.

Again we proved that we could take our beer very seriously without taking ourselves too seriously. The beer was flying out the door at our brewpub, and people were lining up at our booth to try it at all the festivals.

The next batch came out great and the new caps worked perfectly. By now all of the free samples of the first batch that we had given away had worked their magic. Beer lovers were calling their retail stores and our distributors looking to buy bottles of Liquor de Malt. Every case that we made was presold before it even came off our makeshift bottling line.

Normally, a 40-ounce bottle of malt liquor costs about $2 at the corner liquor store. We were selling Liquor de Malt for $7.99, four times the price of traditional malt liquors, and it sold out immediately.

People recognized that the bottles exemplified our philosophy of beneficial inefficiency. They understood that we paid more for the exotic corn, we spent more time in the brewing process and in bottle conditioning and then hand-bottling this beer than the big breweries ever would. They knew that we hand-stamped the brown bags that came with every bottle and that the person who designed the comic in every case worked at a liquor store in Madison, Wisconsin, that had named Dogfish Head its favorite American brewery of the year.

We spent a lot of time sharing the glory of our inefficiency with our customers, and they believed in the choices we made. A number of newspapers and magazines ran stories on our Liquor de Malt project. My favorite was from Kerry Burns of the *Boston Herald*. He wrote that Dogfish Head had "shown an ability to take something esoteric and abnormal and turn it into something special and coveted."

We still make a small batch of Liquor de Malt every so often, but draft only ... hand bottling 40 ounces is brutal.

Chicha (3.1% ABV)

Another beer that we released in 2009 is called Chicha. Chicha's another form of an ancient beer style. For this beer, we did research on the ancient Central and South American chichas—the word chicha is kind of the universal generic term for beers fermented with corn from Central or South America, and each of the countries that make chicha in those regions have put their own spin on it. The primary fermentation sugar source is always maize or corn, but depending on the region, a brewer might also include fruit, spices, vegetables, or seeds in the brewing process.

I took a trip to Peru and researched the way they made chicha and was blown away by the tradition. Probably the most compelling and memorable step in the traditional method of making chicha is that people chew the maize before they brew with it. The tradition of brewing chicha existed before the work Louis Pasteur conducted revealing the process of bacterial fermentation and pasteurization. It was through trial and error that early humans in Peru and other cultures discovered that if they chewed on cereal grains the enzymes in human saliva would do the work of converting the starch in the maize into fermentable sugar. They would chew on maize, make a cake out of it, and leave it out in the sun. The enzymes would do the rest!

While in Peru, I got to observe the process of making chicha, as all these native Peruvian women formed these cakes and brewed this beautiful chicha from those cakes. When I returned home, I thought it'd be really fun to make a traditional chicha in the United States, but chewing enough corn to do this on a commercial scale meant that I had to be like Tom Sawyer painting his fence: I'd figure out a way to entice a bunch of my coworkers to chew all that corn with me. So we got a bunch of buckets and put them next to people's desks at Dogfish. I had one full of corn and one empty one for each coworker and asked them during the course of their day at work if they could chew an entire bucketful of corn, make the cakes out of it, leave it out overnight, and then the next day we would collect all the cakes from all of our coworkers, crumple them up into our mash tun, add hot water, and begin our boil. In addition to the corn, we also added strawberries to our version of chicha. It also had a tree seed in it, called a pink Peruvian peppercorn.

Dogfish Head has brewed Chicha a number of times throughout the years. It usually takes us as coworkers a few years to forget how painful it is to chew all that corn, and then after a few years of not doing it, a newer coworker says, "We should make Chicha again," and we fall for it, and the Sisyphean cycle begins all over again. The last batch we made we required all coworkers showing up to our End-of-Year Hootenanny to chew up a cup of corn before they could come in and get crazy. This means that last batch was made up of the spit of all the Dogfish Head coworkers. We do love to collaborate anyway we can. What's better than a big batch of coworker-made Chicha?

Dogfish Head
CHICHA
A sweet and tart ale brewed with masticated Purple Peruvian Corn.
R&DFH
2018 SERIES
YOU ARE HOLDING
BOTTLE ___ OF ___
BOTTLED IN MILTON, DE

Saison du BUFF (6% ABV)

In 2010 we brewed Saison du BUFF. This beer was a collaboration between Dogfish Head, Stone from Escondido, California, and Victory Brewery from Downingtown, PA. The idea behind this collaboration actually came together seven years earlier, at an ill-fated tasting event. In 2003, back when Dogfish, Victory, and Stone were all very small breweries, we all used the same distributor in Massachusetts. The distributor invited us to participate in an event at one of the liquor stores in Boston. Bill, one of the founders of Victory, Greg, one of the founders of Stone, and I rolled into this beer store, and set up coolers with each of our beers, preparing to serve samples of each of our beers to anyone who would come into the store.

Brewed with parsley, sage, rosemary, and thyme

Sam with Bill Covaleski, cofounder of Victory Brewing Company, and Greg Koch, founder of Stone Brewing

There were posters in the windows saying the founders of three craft breweries would be there from 5 to 7 p.m. For and the entire two-hour event the three of us outnumbered the number of customers that came to try our beer. We stood there in the corner drinking each other's beer and laughing about the fact that we were essentially in a race to go bankrupt with each other because no one gave a shit about the beer we brewed.

During the time of that event, we were all worried about the futures of our breweries; however, over the next months and years, all three of our companies really took off in growth, and we were each named to the prestigious club of the Brewers' Association's Top 50 Craft Brewers in America. We often reminisce about those years and how lucky we were to go on the journeys we have since those years, and so, in 2010, the three of us came together to brew Saison du BUFF.

All three of us love that sort of spicy, phenolic Saison style that comes from Belgium and France, but we also wanted to put a unique spin on it. All three of us also love music, so we decided we should do a play on the Simon and Garfunkel song that references parsley, sage, rosemary, and thyme, so those were the ingredients that we decided to add to our Saison du BUFF beer.

We also used a very egalitarian method of brewing and distributing the beer. Typically if breweries collaborate on a beer, they all brew it together in one place and figure out how to share the profits from the beer that they brew and package and distribute all from one of the breweries. For Saison du BUFF, we thought it'd be fun since it was a three-way collaboration of just trusting each other and leaving it to each brewer to make that recipe every year and take turns, so Dogfish brewed the batch in 2010, 2014, and 2017, and on different years Victory and Stone brewed theirs. By the end of it all, we even had a coworker in our Brewery in Milton who had previously worked for Victory and Stone before he came to work with us at Dogfish Head, and he knew all about Saison du BUFF. His name is Justin Brunda or Saison du BRUNDA, as we liked to call him. This beer has become a cool tradition for a unique brew that captivated a lot of attention of the brewers, coworkers, and beer lovers in 2010.

Ta Henket (4.5% ABV)

This ambitious beer, which was another ancient ale informed not by molecular evidence, as were Chateau Jiahu and Midas Touch, but by a trip I took to the Tomb of Ptah—a famous tomb on the outskirts of Cairo. This tomb is significant because it houses the earliest known human-drawn depiction of the brewing art form. Here, it was discovered that the original glyph for beer was also the original glyph for bread. The two were synonymous. The image simply meant liquid bread or solid bread. It showed how central beer and bread were to that ancient civilization. There are lots of references in ancient brewing to the intertwining of the two arts—brewers would first make loads of bread and then add hot water to the broken-up chunks of bread and then ferment that combination of bread and hot water resulting in a mash, or oatmeal-like consistency.

We first decided to brew this beer after learning of the original hieroglyph of brewing and baking. To incorporate some of the traditional elements originally used in the ancient brewing process, we bought beautiful fruits, herbs, and spices from an outdoor market in Cairo that we believe would have been available in that area back when the pyramids were being built. When we returned, we also roasted loads of wheat on an outdoor hearth at the Milton location. In addition to soaking wheat bread in water to make mash, Ta Henket is also brewed with chamomile, doum fruit or palm fruit, and a medley of Middle Eastern herbs called za'atar. Most uniquely, to collect the ingredient that would help ferment this earthy ancient ale, I visited a date palm farm in the shadows of the pyramids outside of Cairo. Using Petri dishes lined with this chemical compound that was essentially fruit fly cologne or perfume to fruit flies, I set out to capture local yeast. The smell of this chemical compound attracted these fruit flies to the Petri dishes. Once the flies landed in the dishes, I quickly sealed them and shipped them off to a yeast lab in Belgium.

At the lab the scientists took the fruit flies and they swabbed their tiny little feet and captured the wild yeast from the date farm. They isolated the healthy yeast cells, grew them, and sent the yeast to our brewery. It is very similar to the native beers of Egypt that were used as payment for the people who built the iconic pyramids that still stand there today.

Dogfish Head
Craft Brewed Ales
ta henket
dog
fish
head
beer
Beer brewed with Za'atar, Doum Fruit, and Chamomile.
4.5% Alc. by Vol. • 1 Pint 9.4 fl. oz.

JAN FEB MAR APR MAY JUN JUL AUG SEP OCT NOV DEC
Dogfish Head
Craft Brewery
BREWED BY DOGFISH HEAD
CRAFT BREWERY
#6 CANNERY VILLAGE
MILTON, DE 19968
Net Contents:
15.5 U.S. Gallons
5.16 U.S. Gallons
5.17 U.S. Gallons
(1) ACCORDING TO THE SURGEON GENERAL, WOMEN SHOULD NOT DRINK ALCOHOLIC BEVERAGES DURING PREGNANCY BECAUSE OF THE RISK OF BIRTH DEFECTS. (2) CONSUMPTION OF ALCOHOLIC BEVERAGES IMPAIRS YOUR ABILITY TO DRIVE A CAR OR OPERATE MACHINERY, AND MAY CAUSE HEALTH PROBLEMS.
ATTENTION - READ BEFORE TAPPING
THIS KEG MAY RUPTURE AND CAUSE INJURY IF OVER-PRESSURIZED WITH COMPRESSED AIR OR CO2. TAPPING SYSTEM AND PRESSURE REGULATOR SHOULD EACH BE EQUIPPED WITH A PRESSURE RELIEF (BLOW OFF) DEVICE. IF YOU ARE NOT FAMILIAR WITH TAPPING EQUIPMENT, CONSULT YOUR RETAILER OR LOCAL BEER DISTRIBUTOR.
ta henket
BEER BREWED WITH ZA'ATAR, DOUM FRUIT, CHAMOMILE, AND EMMER FARRO'

Bitches Brew (9.0% ABV)

Bitches Brew was one of our first beers inspired by music. We decided to brew this beer in honor of the 40th anniversary of the release of the iconic 1970 Miles Davis album, *Bitches Brew*. When I was drafting the business plan for Dogfish, I would listen to music, and *Bitches Brew* was an album I listen to a lot. That record was a paradigm-shifting landmark album in that it was really the first album that combined jazz and rock, hence the term fusion. It is recognized as the first jazz album that the term fusion was applied to, so to commemorate such an iconic album, we knew we needed to create a recipe for a beer based on the concept of a fusion.

For inspiration, I read Miles Davis's amazing autobiography titled *Miles*. If you are a music or art fan, I highly recommend it. In it, he describes this smoky chili that his second wife used to make for him, which was his favorite dish in the world. After reading that, I knew I wanted to brew a beer that would be the perfect partner for Miles Davis's favorite chili. It would need to have a roasty, sweet, and strong flavor to stand up to a spicy chili dish. I got the idea to brew an imperial stout—a strong, inky, dark, beer.

Because the album itself takes inspiration from African culture, including the iconic cover artwork, we decided to incorporate African ingredients in the beer. We blended it with a version of the traditional Ethiopian-fermented honey wine called tej. Back when Dogfish was really small in Rehoboth, I brewed a simple version of tej honey beer, so I thought it'd be cool to bring back and brew the tej—which is essentially fermented mead that gets its bitterness not from hops but from a tree seed—for Bitches Brew.

We brewed a big vat of tej, but then in a separate vat we brewed a more traditional imperial stout. Much like jazz fusion, which blends different musical styles, our Wood-Aged Bitches Brew is a fusion of three beers: the Imperial stout aged on oak; the African honey-wine, Tej; and both combined were aged on Palo Santo barrels. The result is a brew chock-full of aromas of vanilla, licorice, and chocolate with flavors of roasted coffee.

Bitches Brew was among the first music-inspired beers that we brought to a national stage. Music has always been such an important part of my life but is also woven into the DNA of Dogfish, from writing the business plan for Dogfish while listening to *Bitches Brew* and beyond. This is one of the things that started off the thought of collaboration and just intrinsic work with music. And those similarities lead to a partnership with Sony Music and eventually the creation of Bitches Brew. My good friend, Adam Block, was senior vice president and general manager of Legacy Records, one of the imprints at Sony, and I worked with him on creating Bitches Brew. We also worked with him on other projects like Hellhound On My Ale, which we'll get to next.

MILES DAVIS' BITCHES BREW
Ale brewed with honey and gesho.
1 Pint 9.4 fl. oz. · 9% alc. by vol.

Hellhound (10% ABV)

In 2011 we also brewed a beer called Hellhound On My Ale. This is another music collaboration we did with our friends at Sony Legacy. The year 2011 would have marked the hundredth birthday of Mississippi Delta Blues legend, Robert Johnson, who according to legend sold his soul down at the crossroads in a midnight bargain and changed music forever. To brew this beer, I researched a lot about Robert Johnson and who his influences were, and his biggest influence was a Texas-based bluesman named Blind Lemon Jefferson, so I wanted to pay tribute to Robert Johnson's hero. I built the recipe around hop varieties that had lemon and citrusy character because I also wanted to use dried organic lemon peel and lemon flesh to add aromatics and additional fermentable sugars to this beer. The name, Hellhound On My Ale, is a reference to Robert Johnson's most famous song, which is *Hellhound On My Tale*, and goes back to the legend that he sold his soul to the devil to gain his epic guitar-playing skills. Hellhound is a super hoppy ale that hits 100 International Bitter Units in the brewhouse and comes in at 10 percent alcohol even, all those tens and zeros are meant to commemorate that it was brewed for the hundredth anniversary of his birth. It's dry hopped with 100 percent centennial hops at a rate of 100 kilos per 100-barrel brew-length. Yes. There are a lot of hundreds in there.

Every Beer Has a Story

Dogfish Head Craft Brewed Ales

Hellhound on My Ale

ABV 10%

Robert Johnson's
Hellhound
On My Ale
Ale brewed with lemons

2011 would have marked the 100th birthday of Mississippi Delta bluesman Robert Johnson, who according to legend, sold his soul down at the crossroads in a midnight bargain and changed music forever.

Working again with our friends at Sony Legacy (yup, the same folks we did our Miles Davis-inspired Bitches Brew with), Dogfish Head pays tribute to this blues legend by gettin' the hellhounds off his trail and into this finely-crafted ale.

Hellhound is a super-hoppy ale that hits 100 IBUs in the brewhouse and 10% ABV. It's dry-hopped with 100% Centennial hops at a rate of 100 kilos per 100 barrel brew-length. Can you tell we're stoked for this mighty musical centennial?

To accentuate and magnify the citrusy notes of the Centennial hops (and as a shoutout to Robert Johnson's mentor Blind Lemon Jefferson), we add dried lemon peel and flesh to the whirlpool.

To learn more about Hellhound on My Ale, visit us at www.dogfish.com.

Food Pairing Recommendations:
Beef, jambalaya, Thai

Cheese Pairing:
Bierkase

Wine Comparable:
Citrusy chardonnay

Dogfish Head Craft Brewery

Robert Johnson's
Hellhound
On My Ale

Dogfish Head Craft Brewery

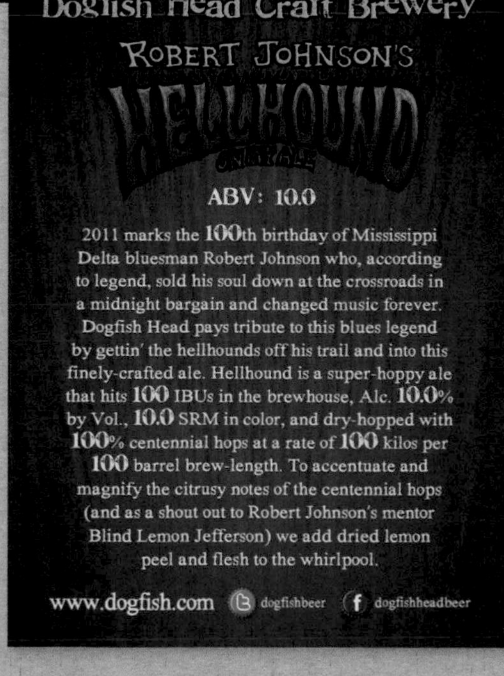

Robert Johnson's
Hellhound
On My Ale
ABV: 10.0
2011 marks the 100th birthday of Mississippi Delta bluesman Robert Johnson who, according to legend, sold his soul down at the crossroads in a midnight bargain and changed music forever. Dogfish Head pays tribute to this blues legend by gettin' the hellhounds off his trail and into this finely-crafted ale. Hellhound is a super-hoppy ale that hits 100 IBUs in the brewhouse, Alc. 10.0% by Vol., 10.0 SRM in color, and dry-hopped with 100% centennial hops at a rate of 100 kilos per 100 barrel brew-length. To accentuate and magnify the citrusy notes of the centennial hops (and as a shout out to Robert Johnson's mentor Blind Lemon Jefferson) we add dried lemon peel and flesh to the whirlpool.
www.dogfish.com
dogfishbeer
dogfishheadbeer

Faithfull Ale (7% ABV)

Faithfull Ale is a celebration of Pearl Jam's 20th anniversary, one of my favorite bands, and it's celebrating the 20th anniversary of Pearl Jam's debut album, *Ten*. We got to work with Pearl Jam on this beer because Eddie Vedder, the lead singer, is a huge Miles Davis fan, and he found our Bitches Brew. Through his manager, Eddie reached out and asked if we would do something special to commemorate the 20th anniversary of their epic album, *Ten*.

Eddie shared with me his desire for what the beer should be in an email that said:

> "Hey Sam, Love what you guys did with Miles. For our band's beer, on stage the two things we drink almost exclusively and in huge volumes is either fruit-forward Oregon Pinot Noirs or a shit-ton of Corona. Can you make something that tastes like a combination of those two things?" –Eddie

I thought, "Oh, geez. I don't know if that would be good or not, but here we go."

So what I decided to do was brew a beer that had the exact same color on the Lovibond scale of Corona, and it had the same IBUs or bitterness, hop bitterness, as Corona, but then we dosed in black currants into this Belgian-styled golden ale. To give our nod to the album *Ten*, we did 10 incremental additions over the course of the one-hour boil of the black currants, which gave it its red, wine-like color and fruitiness while being very mildly hopped, the way Corona is. Faithfull is a super-drinkable beer that you could have on the stage or in front of the stage listening to Pearl Jam.

todays tasting
PUNKIN' ALE
7% ABV
INDIAN BROWN ALE
7.2% ABV
OLDE SCHOOL BARLEYWINE
PEARL JAM
ithfull Ale
Brewed with

Positive Contact (9% ABV)

Positive Contact was our next really fun music collaboration. This was a hybrid between a cider and a beer. This beer was part of our music series, and it's an amalgamation of hip-hop, beer, cider, and a DIY culinary experience. It's named Positive Contact after my favorite song from the discography of the awesome hip-hop band Deltron 3030, which is a collaboration between famous San Francisco-based producer, Dan the Automator, and the rapper, Del, the Funky Homosapien. I met Dan the Automator, who named his son Miles (Miles is a common thread once again) to discuss an opportunity to work together. We linked up on the rooftop of the Eataly restaurant where Dogfish Head helped to create the brewing program. We sat there with tea strainers and cheese graters, and we brought up all of Dan's favorite culinary ingredients and found the combination that was most exciting for Dan's palate. It was a pretty epic afternoon and the recipe ended up having Fuji apples, roasted farro, cayenne peppers, and fresh cilantro. Positive Contact was a Belgian-style dubbel beer, or golden ale, as the base, and both the cayenne and the alcohol gave it a bit of a warming note with the fresh cilantro waved over the top of the boiling wort at the end of the boil.

When we first released this beer in 2012 we actually packaged every case of six 750 ml champagne bottles with 10-inch vinyl EPs that had 4 new Deltron 3030 remixes that Dan made exclusively for the project.

On the cover of the album, you'll find five Deltron 3030-inspired recipes from some of the best chefs around: acclaimed chef and TV personality Mario Batali, loud and fast Joe Beef chefs Frederic Morin and David McMillan, Momofuku's influential David Chang, supercreative Homebrew Chef Sean Paxton, and West Coast luminary James Syhabout.

Coworkers hand-packing the beer with the vinyl

Release in the tasting room with apple cider doughnuts and apples from Fifer Orchards

Positve Contact LP!

POSITIVE
CONTACT

Nora Sheehan aka Big Mama

Brewceptionist
Start Date: 2008

It is a fluke that Nora ended up at Dogfish Head. Before Dogfish, Nora was on the admin team for Gore in Cherry Hill and was looking to relocate down to Sussex County, Delaware. It was 2008. Nora had a coworker up at Gore, and the two loved to laugh and mess with each other a bit. She knew Nora was looking to relocate down south, so she sent Nora's resume to Dogfish Head as a joke. "What is Dogfish, and why would you do that?" Nora said.

Her friend Brooke answered, "Because they are looking for an off-centered receptionist, and you are the most ridiculous person I know."

They laughed at each other about it, and then got on with the day. Nora never gave it another thought. A few weeks later, Brooke was messing with Nora again. They were in the office, and she had Nora laughing so hard that she couldn't talk, and the phone rang. Nora answered and couldn't catch her breath. She finally did, and she had the job the moment HR heard that laugh coming through on the other line.

When Nora came down for the interview, there was an intergalactic bocce tournament going on, so the front lawn was loaded up with people in costumes. "Oh, yeah ... this is for me," she thought.

During her interview, she remembers being asked how she feels about burping, farting, and cursing. Again, "Oh, yeah ... this is for me." They gave her a scenario of the phone ringing, the UPS man is standing there, and a coworker is asking you a question. What are you going to do? Her answer? "Is the UPS man hot?" Big Mama had our number from the get-go, and she is still rocking it with us today.

When Nora started, her title was receptionist and she changed it to Brewceptionist. There was never a manual for what the job entailed. It, like Dogfish Head and all of its people, is in a state of constant evolution. Today, our many departments and amazing coworkers keep us focused on our exploration of goodness. Back when Nora started, she was part of almost every department.

Where did the name Big Mama come from? We first got radios at the Brewery, because we were at the point where we could no longer yell across the room to each other. It was a fun day, but damn it, we were going to take this seriously! Yeah, right. The orders were clear. "No messing around on these. We are using them for legit communication only. You can't go asking if anyone has seen Mike Hunt. It is not funny!" Yeah, right. That lasted, hmm ... 10 minutes tops, and it was go time. Everyone needed a radio name. Some names we can't print in this book, but it was that day Nora came to be known as Big Mama. But why has the name stuck? She cares deeply for every single coworker at Dogfish Head. Her hugs are profound, and you can feel them in your soul. If a coworker has a rough day and Nora knows, she is going to pick them up. If a coworker finds success and is promoted, she is going to be there cheering them on. She knows when to wrap people in love and when to tell them to get lost. Much of our coworker culture at Dogfish Head is treating each other like family. Nora is the Big Mama of the Dogfish Head family.

Looking back at her 11 years at Dogfish, Nora says, "It has been home, honey. Home. There has been good and there has been bad, but there is nothing but love and family at Dogfish for me." This love for all our coworkers really sets Nora apart. When our people are invested in each other at this level, there is no limit to what we can accomplish. The key is to bring on people willing to go that deep. Nora goes there every day and she takes others with her. Our strength in our beer is a direct reflection of the strength of our people and the bonds they build working together. Big Mama knows the ties that bind.

Coworker Profile

If you were on a deserted island and could have one album to listen to and an unlimited supply of one beer, what would it be?

Beer: Tweason'ale
Album: Bee Gees, *Greatest Hits*

Big Mama loves a cold beverage, and according to her, the best beer we ever made was Tweason'ale—and she could put 'em back, folks! There was always a cold 4-pack in the fridge of the tasting room stashed there for Nora. Raison D'Etra is on her no-no list. At a beer:30, she had three big-girl cups of Midas and was feeling it. She got home and wanted a night cap. There were some Raisons in the fridge, and that put her over the edge. Sadly for Raison that day, Big Mama was done with you.

Early on, Nora was in love with Sam, but she caught him picking his nose one day and that was it. The crush was over. She moved on to bigger and better ones. Trey Bowden, a dreamy, muscular, tattooed, IT genius was next on the list for the crush. For some reason, Big Mama kept needing tech support.

Just like with family, there are tough days, and the day Tom Draper (Mariah's father) passed away was without a doubt the hardest day Nora faced at Dogfish. "We lost a family member that day. Tom was so vital to who we are at Dogfish. He taught Sam and Mariah and all of us so much, and that to be successful, we need to put back into the company what we get from it." Tom was right and his lessons resonate with all of us to this day. Tom did not like the name "Big Mama" and always called her Nora. He also taught her not to believe everything that came out of Oprah's mouth.

Robert Plant and Big Mama

To this day, Nora is relentless in all she does. Her sense of humor is as strong as ever, and there is still a chance to see her in a skin-toned bodysuit, if she can get it from Lars in the tasting room. There are some guarantees. If you need something and you are not sure the answer to the question, start with Big Mama. She may not have the answer, but she is going to do everything she can to help you find it. If you are having a bad day, Big Mama is going to help pick you up, get your ass dusted off, and help you get back in the game. If you are getting promoted? Big Mama is going to be there cheering you on. If you decide to leave Dogfish Head, Big Mama is going to give you a hug you will never forget, and you will know in that moment that Dogfish Head is a family and that family includes all of the coworkers past, present, and future.

Chapter 6

Brew Masters

By 2010, craft beer had evolved from its origins as a beverage on the fringe of the brewing industry to becoming an increasingly popular selection for customers in bars and liquor stores coast-to-coast. As craft beer began to receive more mainstream acclaim, Dogfish Head was fortunate enough to be one of the craft breweries frequently profiled in books, magazine articles, documentary films, and television shows as one of the leaders in the craft brewing movement. Writers and producers were drawn to the unique culinary-centric approach to brewing and distilling that was core to the Dogfish brand.

One media opportunity—the one that gave America a front row seat to the craft brewing movement—also became a catalyst for a very unexpected development in the beer industry.

In early 2010, a NYC-based production company called Zero Point Zero (ZPZ), came to us with an idea for a reality-based television series that would profile various small, creative craft breweries around the world and give viewers a glimpse into the craft brewing industry. Called *Brew Masters*, the concept for the show centered around a global exploration of the burgeoning craft brewing movement and how collaborative we were, through the point of view of a relatively small but creative brewery that just happened to be located in rural Delaware.

ZPZ was the production company behind many award-winning television shows, including those hosted by Anthony Bourdain, so we were flattered by the invitation, but ultimately we said to them, "Well, we don't really have time to do anything other than what we're already doing...." We told them about our plans for the year ahead which included installing a giant, beautiful structure called the Steam Punk Treehouse, built by the Five Ton Crane artist collective in Oakland, California. We told them about the new beer we planned to make in collaboration with the Grain Surfboards company, a small surfboard manufacturer in Maine that makes its boards by hand with sustainably harvested cedar wood, and that we were going to use the scraps of its wood in the aging process for a beer called Grain to Glass. We showed them the Miles Davis Bitches Brew project that we'd been working on with Sony Records that would be a mash-up of styles—a fusion of an imperial stout made with Mauritius brown sugar and Tej, which is the native African honey beer fermented with geisha root—to represent the fusion that is symbolic of the Miles Davis Bitches Brew album—the seminal fusion of jazz and rock. We outlined all of these really exciting projects that we already had on our dance card, and they were like "This is awesome!"

So, instead of having us go on the road and peek into breweries around the world, ZPZ decided to follow us on what we were already doing at Dogfish Head—because our world already intersected with so many other interesting entrepreneurial and artisanal companies. It was a great reminder to us that as far as we've come in scale since our last book—and certainly since we opened Dogfish Head over 26 years ago—we really haven't had to change too much of what our company is about. In other words, our original mission of "off-centered ales for off-centered people" still resonates as much (if not more) at this moment as it did when we came up with it over 26 years ago. The only difference is that in that era we were the smallest craft brewery in the country, and today ours is one of the top 20 craft brands in the United States, out of over 8,000 breweries.

ZPZ loved the plans for the year and offered to capture the stories of the collaborations already underway. So we got to work fleshing out shooting scripts, TV show or no TV show.

It was our passion for what we do, our determination to create something special, and our dedication to the craft beer industry, that led to that opportunity. But the fact that a major cable network chose to create an entire series around beer culture was a powerful statement about the rapidly expanding popularity of craft beer in general.

It exemplified how exciting a moment it was in the timeline of craft beer.

Over the last decade, craft beer's market share continued to grow, and as a result, sales of light lagers from international beer conglomerates continued to decline. And so, *Brew Masters* was born. A documentary film crew accompanied me around the world to produce six episodes about some of our more exotic beers already established, made in collaboration with other small companies, artists, and scientists.

We had a blast making the series because we liked the production company, and we were already planning on doing the projects they filmed, so the footage was authentic and real and not forced or manufactured like much of what you see on reality television.

The first episode premiered in November of 2010 to positive reviews. Unfortunately, what seemed to be the start of a successful new television show turned into a cautionary tale for craft beers about just how competitive and aggressive big beer conglomerates could be....

What Happened?

This next section about the fate of our TV show is based on my perspective. The suits, and the network, and the international beer conglomerate involved may have different perspectives and they can share those when they write their books.

About one week before the first episode aired, the network told us that one of the largest international beer conglomerates had bought out each of the ad blocks at the front end of each segment of each episode of our craft beer show. I was outraged, but as the network reminded me, I had no say over the ads that air during the commercial breaks. So, in those blocks would run ads for one of the quasi-craft beer brands that consumers might believe was a fellow craft beer. In actuality, it's a beer dressed up like a craft beer, but created and owned by an international beer conglomerate. The international beer conglomerate purchased the prime ad space. Their advertising agency created ads that seemed like ads a fellow craft beer brand might run. The design of the ads looked very much like the design and branding aesthetics of our show. So, to a viewer less familiar with the craft beer landscape, this might appear to be simply another craft beer brand advertising and supporting a fellow craft beer. To a viewer well-versed in craft beers, well....

Just as we anticipated would happen, a social media firestorm broadsided us when the show premiered, and the leading advertising spots profiled a quasi-craft beer brand—a beer that appeared to be a craft beer, but that is owned by an international beer conglomerate. Craft beer lovers began reaching out via social channels asking why Dogfish Head would participate in a series presumably about the indie craft brewing community but whose production was funded by advertising dollars from an international beer conglomerate.

Anthony Bourdain
@Bourdain
Replying to @TheAtlHealth
@TheAtlanticLIFE Big story there. Brewmasters goes-
our ads do.
1:51 PM · Mar 29, 2011 · Twitter for iPad

While we had no say over which corporations bought the advertising space for our show, what we could control was how we responded to the confused and disappointed fans reaching out to us. And so we did. When

> "A number of folks have been reaching out to me today about this twitter stuff. I'd rather focus on positive stuff than negative at this point. So this is what I will say: No comment. Other than I'm a big *No Reservations* fan.
>
> And now more than ever—support your small, truly indie breweries! Last night I had two Prima Pils and an Aprihop. Today I had cask-conditioned Thyme Pale Ale, Baladin Nora, Birra Del Borgo ReAle, and am enjoying an Indian Brown Ale as I type this.
>
> Focused on the goodness inside the bottle instead of the weirdness outside the bottle. Cheers."

What Happened?

beer lovers expressed disappointment that our show had been co-opted by these ads, we responded and we let them know we, too, felt it was misleading. We very publicly explained to Dogfish Head fans and beer lovers we engaged with online and in person the truth about what had really happened.

Representatives from the invested party immediately reached out to the network saying that they were infuriated by our attempts to set the record straight and call bullshit on their misleading through our social media channels, and threatened to pull the millions of dollars of advertising from the entire network unless the network deemphasized the appeal of our show.

There were a total of six episodes in the first season. The first episode aired Sunday night. By episode 3 our slot was moved to Monday night. For episodes 4 and 5, the show was moved yet again, to Thursday night. Viewers struggled to find the time that the show was on from week to week. The final episode was delayed because it was supposed to be filmed at the grand opening of Dogfish Head's new brewpub on the rooftop of the New York City restaurant and marketplace, Eataly. Delays in the brewpub's opening resulted in delays in completion of the episode. Although the rooftop brewpub eventually opened, the accompanying final episode never aired.

The network was contractually obliged to air all six episodes, but they effectively killed the show by changing the time slot from one week to the next with no messaging about it, confusing the audience. They even intentionally scheduled the show at the same time as Monday Night Football, one of the highest rated programs of the season—and then blamed the cancellation on bad ratings.

As a result, the series only ran for one season.

Bourdain: Brew Masters Was Canceled Because of Big Beer

by Paula Forbes | Mar 31, 2011, 6:20am EDT

SHARE

Left: Travel Channel, Right: Discovery

Beware the power of ad dollars: word is that Dogfish Head founder **Sam Calagione's** Discovery Channel show *Brew Masters* has been canceled, and that "Big Beer" is responsible. And who do we have to thank for this information? Why, **Anthony Bourdain**, of course.

Before Bourdain started aggravating the entire internet with his thoughts on food journalism earlier this week, he let slip a couple tweets responding to an Atlantic story about beer legislation. The *No Reservations* host tweeted: "See what happened to Dogfish/Discovery deal. Big beer threatened to pull ads" and "Big story there. **Brewmasters goes--or our ads do.**" What?

Is the show canceled? And did Big Beer have anything to do with it? Not officially, but Beer News says that the last episode of *Brew Masters* is rumored to coincide with the opening of **Eataly's La Birreria** rooftop beer garden. Which, according to Eater NY, happens in mid-May. There has not been word of a second season of the show.

But then beer writer Andy Crouch tweeted: "Discovery confirms to me cancellation of @dogfishbeer Brew Masters. Blames poor audience reception." The show's ratings were solid — around one million viewers per episode — even though it bounced around the schedule (it moved from Sunday nights to Monday nights without much fanfare). As to why Discovery programmed a beer show against Sunday Night Football and then Monday Night Football, that's for them to explain.

We reached out to the show's production company Zero Point Zero for confirmation about any of this and were told, "No comment."

Zero Point Zero also produces Bourdain's *No Reservations*, so we suppose it's conceivable that he could've overheard something. Sam Calagione wouldn't comment on the tweets, but told Beer News he's a fan of *No Reservations* and that he's currently "focused on the goodness inside the bottle instead of the weirdness outside the bottle." Yeah, we'd need a cold beer if we were him, too.

© Eater

What Happened?

I knew Big Beer could be ruthless in trying to marginalize brewers they perceive as competition, but I learned that lesson firsthand with *Brew Masters*.

To this day, people walk up to me at beer events to tell me how much they loved the show. What initially attracted the producers and the network to Dogfish Head is also what I think attracted beer drinkers to Dogfish Head. We weren't brewing for the status quo. And we recognized that no matter whether we owned 5, 10, or 20 percent of the market share, the average beer drinker would probably never try our beers. We were "off-centered." We were not going to appeal to the majority. That said, we were able to carve out a very healthy, growing niche by creating beers that appeal to a small but increasing and engaged beer-drinking population—those who prefer more flavor, more diversity, more complexity, and more food compatibility in their beer. Those are the folks we've grown with; and there are a lot more of them today than there were back when we began, when we were the smallest craft brewery in the country.

And as we've grown, we've become even more experimental, more creative, and embraced more risk on the production and research and development (R&D) side than when we were smaller. Of course, we do still—to some limited degree—face a perception issue, where maybe for those at the epicenter of the beer community—the super-hard-core, dyed-in-the-wool beer geeks, as we call ourselves—Dogfish itself as a brewery isn't a new thing. There are always new, exciting little breweries, and everyone always wants to talk about what's new. But what has kept our company very relevant over the years is the recognition for pushing the boundaries of what beer can be. And, we believe, this journey has now been accelerated with this show.

BEER & WHISKEY BROTHERS

Keep in good spirits and keep the good spirits in ya.

You are here: Home » Was Brewmasters Killed by "Big Beer"?

March 30, 2011 | Jim | 112 Comments

Was Brewmasters Killed by "Big Beer"?

If you recall, we were the ones who said definitively that the Discovery show Brewmasters was dead. There were a lot of folks who said we were wrong, but we had it on good authority that the show was done. Now we have it on even better authority.

I just happened to run into Sam Calagione this morning at Eataly in NYC, in (of course) the beer aisle. He was there to announce that the construction of the Dogfish Head brew pub in Eataly is wrapping up and they'll be up and brewing in the coming weeks. It should be open in early June, so mark that on your calendars. He also helped me pick out an Italian beer after I told him about my problem wrapping my head around them. He suggested a Baladin Nora, which I dutifully purchased.

Sam confirmed that no new footage was going to taped for Brewmasters, and that he hopes the Eataly episode (which has been filmed but not aired) will still air in June when the brewpub is open for business. I hope so too, because I enjoyed the show and want Dogfish's venture to be a success. At any rate, the show is gone and not coming back after that.

But here's the thing that REALLY kills me -- timing is a bitch. Not two hours after I saw Sam, I was reading Anthony Bourdain's Twitter feed (@NoRexervations), which had two powerful and slightly cryptic tweets:

> **NoReservations** Anthony Bourdain
> @TheAtlanticLIFE Big story there. Brewmasters goes--or our ads do.
> 20 hours ago
>
> **NoReservations** Anthony Bourdain
> @TheAtlanticLIFE See what happened to Dogfish/Discovery deal. Big beer threatened to pull ads.
> 20 hours ago

Mr. Bourdain tells it like it is and knows a thing or two about how the TV world works, so if he says it, I believe it. I know we've had a lot of "big beer" news here lately (maybe too much), but I think this is worth sharing because it's entirely plausible. While I doubt Sam would have affirmed anything when we spoke, I would have loved to see the look on his face when I asked him about it. Instead the timing was off and I'm left to imagine how that moment would've gone.

Anyway, I hope The Atlantic takes Mr. Bourdain's suggestion seriously and digs into the story, because I bet there's something juicy there. This certainly calls for an expose, because this (alleged) hurdle will have to be removed if we ever want to see beer on TV again. And if you're like me, that's something you definitely want.

Update: Our pals over at BeerNews.org point out that Brewmasters and Anthony Bourdain: No Reservations share the same production company, which puts Mr. Tony in a position to know a think or two about this. Good catch guys!

Rabble Rousing Update: Looks like The Atlantic will be digging into things – Go get 'em!!:

> **TheAtlanticLIFE** TheAtlantic/Life
> @NoReservations @Beerandwhiskey Thanks for the story tip, Big Beer is all over the place these days. We'll look into that.
> 7 minutes ago Favorite Retweet Reply

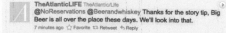

Happy Ending Update (9/26/11): Sam tells us that he's cooking something up with production company Zero-Point-Zero (the producers of Brew Masters) for the iPad.

Grain to Glass (7% ABV)

Grain to Glass was a collaboration between Dogfish Head and a small surfboard company called Grain Surfboards which is close to my childhood vacation home in Maine. Grain Surfboards hand-build their boards out of sustainably harvested Maine-grown cedar. For Grain to Glass, we used the shavings from the surfboard shaping process as an ingredient in the brewing process.

For the brewing process, we tested 90 Minute IPA, Indian Brown, and Raison D'Etre. Using Raison D'Etre as the base, we began the brew. During the brewing process, the wort is sparingly hopped with Warrior and Vanguard hops. The grains added to the mash include Pils, Wheat, Munich, Coffee, and Crystal. But it's the "grain" added post-fermentation that makes this beer so unique. The addition of cedar chips adds pungent, resiny, herbal notes to the finished product. The result is a brown ale that has a deeper shade of red than our Raison D'Etre, because it is also brewed with beet sugars.

© Grain Surfboards

The Steampunk Tree House

In 2010, some of the folks at Dogfish Head stumbled across images of a large art installation resembling a life-sized tree with treehouse. The sculpture was striking in both its size and in the intricacy of the details of it. The Steampunk Tree House was made from repurposed wood, steel, and clockwork parts.

We were so intrigued by the piece that we reached out to the artists to get more information about the it. Conceived and created by Oakland, California–based artist, Sean Orlando and the Five Ton Crane arts group, the interactive large-scale project debuted at the Burning Man event in Black Rock City, Nevada, in late August 2007. When we learned they were looking for a permanent home for their sculpture we knew it was meant to be! Two off-centered crews coming together.

According to lead artist Sean Orlando, "The Steampunk Tree House was made to explore the relationship between our rapidly changing natural world and the persistent human drive to connect with it and one another. It is our second nature."

Orlando and the Five Ton crew arrived at the Milton brewery in June of 2010 for the installation. They were kind enough to give us a good deal on the treehouse, selling it to us for $1! We did have to pay shipping, which was significantly more than the sale price. We had a great time getting to know them and watching their magic happen. On June 25th, we smashed a bottle of Life & Limb against the door and officially made Dogfish the new home of The Steampunk Tree House.

The Steampunk Tree House can be viewed and enjoyed by visiting the brewery. Access to the interior of the tree house is limited to our Dogfish coworkers as we use the space to share ideas in a creative environment; in essence, it is our off-centered safety tree.

Wanna know more?

Dimensions:

- Total height: 40' tall
- Trunk height: 20'
- Trunk diameter: 2' (5' total trunk diameter with outer skin)
- Total spread of branches: 40' diameter
- Main structural support branches diameter: 15'
- Treehouse component off the ground: 20'
- House dimensions: 15' hexagonal/12' tall

"Do anything,
but let it
produce joy."
—Walt Whitman,
Leaves of Grass

Change is in the air. At the brewery, change meant a 12,500 square foot expansion in the summer of 2009 and the addition of six 600-barrel external Ziemann+Bauer fermentation tanks from Germany. Oh, and if you didn't notice it, in June 2010 we also added The Steampunk Tree House, our off-centered, retro-futuristic sculpture.

Noble Rot

(9% ABV)

You would not think a beer with the word "rot" in it would be a big seller, but this was one beer that people really fell in love with. The name Noble Rot comes from the process of brewing this beer. It's a saison style base beer, and it gets its complexity and fermentable sugars from two unique wine grapes that we source from our friends at Alexandria Nicole Cellars in Prosser, Washington. The first addition is unfermented grape juice known as "must" from Viognier grapes that have been infected while still on the vine—intentionally infected—with a benevolent fungus called botrytis. "Noble rot" is what botrytis infection is called, hence the name of the beer. This process reduces the water content in the grapes while magnifying their sweetness and complexity. The second addition of juice into this saison-style beer comes from Pinot Gris and must intensified by a process called "dropping fruit": when large clusters of grapes are clipped away from the vine to amplify the quality and intensity of the grapes that are left behind. For Noble Rot we met the absolute legal limit of what a beer could be because, at least in this era, the U.S. federal government mandates that beer has to at least have 50.1 percent of its fermentable sugars come from grains. So Noble Rot was brewed with 50.1 percent of the fermentable sugars coming from barley and 49.9 percent coming from the botrytis-infected Viognier grapes and the Pinot Gris must. It was brewed with pilsner and wheat malt, and fermented with a distinct Belgian yeast strain. It has a spicy white wine–like body and a dry, tart finish. In subsequent batches we took to aging this beer in our 10,000 gallon oak tanks.

Oak-Aged Noble Rot
(9% ABV)

When grapes are harvested off of small vineyards in Germany and Washington state, where this grape variety is grown robustly, even today the people harvesting will have giant sacks or buckets for the regular Viognier grapes, and then they'll usually have a little fanny pack on their back. When they find the ones that have the noble rot, the botrytis infection, those go in the fanny pack, which gives you a visual of just how special and rare these grapes are. They make the beer beautifully complex.

After the first addition in Noble Rot of botrytis-infected Viognier grapes, there's a second addition. This one's using Pinot Gris grapes that have intensified fruitiness and sweetness through a process where certain grapes within a cluster are clipped away to amplify the quality and distinction of those grapes that remain in a smaller but bolder grape cluster.

This multiphase fermentation starts with adding the wheat, the barley, and the base saison, then adding the Viognier grapes infected with botrytis and then, finally, introducing the Pinot Gris grapes specially amplified in flavor through the dropping fruit process. We then age Nobel Rot in one of our giant 300-barrel oak tanks for an entire year to make this hazy, beautiful, complex, spicy beverage that has the body and complexity of a white wine, but a dry, sort of earthy character of a saison-style beer.

Tweason'ale (6% ABV)

Tweason'ale was Dogfish Head's first-ever foray into the world of gluten-free beers. We hadn't introduced a new four-pack of 12-ounce beer for almost half a decade before we brewed Tweason'ale. For this brew we replaced the classic barley foundation that you find in traditional beers with a very mild sorghum base. The hints of molasses and pit fruit that come through in the beer are balanced by vibrant strawberry notes and a unique complexity that comes with the addition of a malty buckwheat honey. The beer consists of sorghum, strawberries, and buckwheat honey. Knowing that lots of people are looking for a gluten-free option for beer, we thought it would be a great idea to brew a gluten-free beer but bring our off-centered tradition of utilizing culinary ingredients into the process.

This was a very hands-on endeavor. We pressed the strawberries by hand and it looked like a literal blood bath.

There was a great *New York Times* online article which included beautiful, animated photography of us brewing Tweason'ale, which showed what looked like a murder scene because we were all covered with strawberry juice that made it look like it was blood all over our hands and our clothes. The apple press couldn't have been any bigger than a mop bucket in our early batches brewing this beer down at the brewpub—it was like a home apple press that we used to squish all these strawberries for Tweason'ale.

Our love story started at first sight last spring...
by summer bee and berry were having a fling...
Tweason'ale
A graphic novella in four parts.
Come fall they had wed and shared their first kiss...
In winter they got cozy and, well, you get the gist.

Savor Flowers (10% ABV)

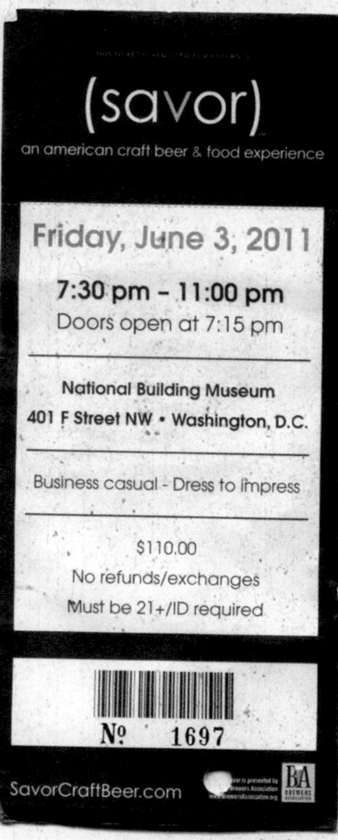

We brewed Savor Flowers in collaboration with our good friends at Boston Beer, and none other than their founder, Jim Koch. Jim is truly one of the patriarchs of the craft beer movement. Savor is the name of an event that the Brewer's Association, the trade group that represents the vast majority of America's indie craft breweries, puts on annually in Washington, D.C., to celebrate how well world-class food goes with world-class beer. Both Jim Koch and I were on the board of directors of the Brewer's Association at the time, and we knew both of our breweries were going to be attending and pouring our beers at Savor. Jim asked if I would like to collaborate on a beer with Boston Beer for Savor. It really warmed my heart because Sam Adams, which is made by Boston Beer, was one of the first beers I ever stole from my dad, and Sam Adams and Boston Beer had never before done a collaboration with an American craft brewery. Jim and I wanted this to be like a piece of installation artwork that we would unveil at Savor, meaning we wanted to brew this beer one time in one place for one event only, to make it extra special.

Jim had the great idea of kind of going back in time on how artists or journalists or politicians would collaborate on projects: they would mail each other letters and often have to wait weeks between correspondence to iterate on a collaborative project. So for this collaboration, we forced ourselves, even though we could have done this by email or phone, to only communicate about the creative iteration of the recipe by handwriting letters and sending them in the mail to each other. We thought it would be appropriate, considering the way Sam Adams would have had to communicate with the other founding fathers of America about formalizing the Revolution.

The idea came together by letters back and forth between Delaware and Boston. We'd decided on a beer driven by an often-forgotten ingredient that is volumetrically the biggest ingredient in beer: water. Brewers usually treat their water with salts or different natural compounds to make it better for brewing, but they don't usually look at water to be a source of flavor contribution to the beer. Since Dogfish Head owned a distillery, not just a brewery, we thought it would be cool to distill rosewater in our facility

8 CELEBRATOR BEER NEWS JUNE/JULY 2011

Photo by John Holl

Jim Koch and Sam Calagione toast the success of their collaboration.

SAVOR FLOWERS
A COLLABORATIVE BEER

By John Holl

Sure, it would have been easier and faster and just made more sense for the two men to exchange e-mails. But when Jim Koch and Sam Calagione teamed up to brew a collaboration beer for this year's SAVOR, they cleared time in their schedules, pulled out a sheet of company stationery and wrote each other letters. Actual letters. Then they sealed them in envelopes, affixed stamps to the envelopes, sent them off and waited for a response.

> “Ah, good conversation—
> there’s nothing like it, is
> there? The air of ideas is
> the only air worth breathing.”
> —Edith Wharton,
> *The Age of Innocence*

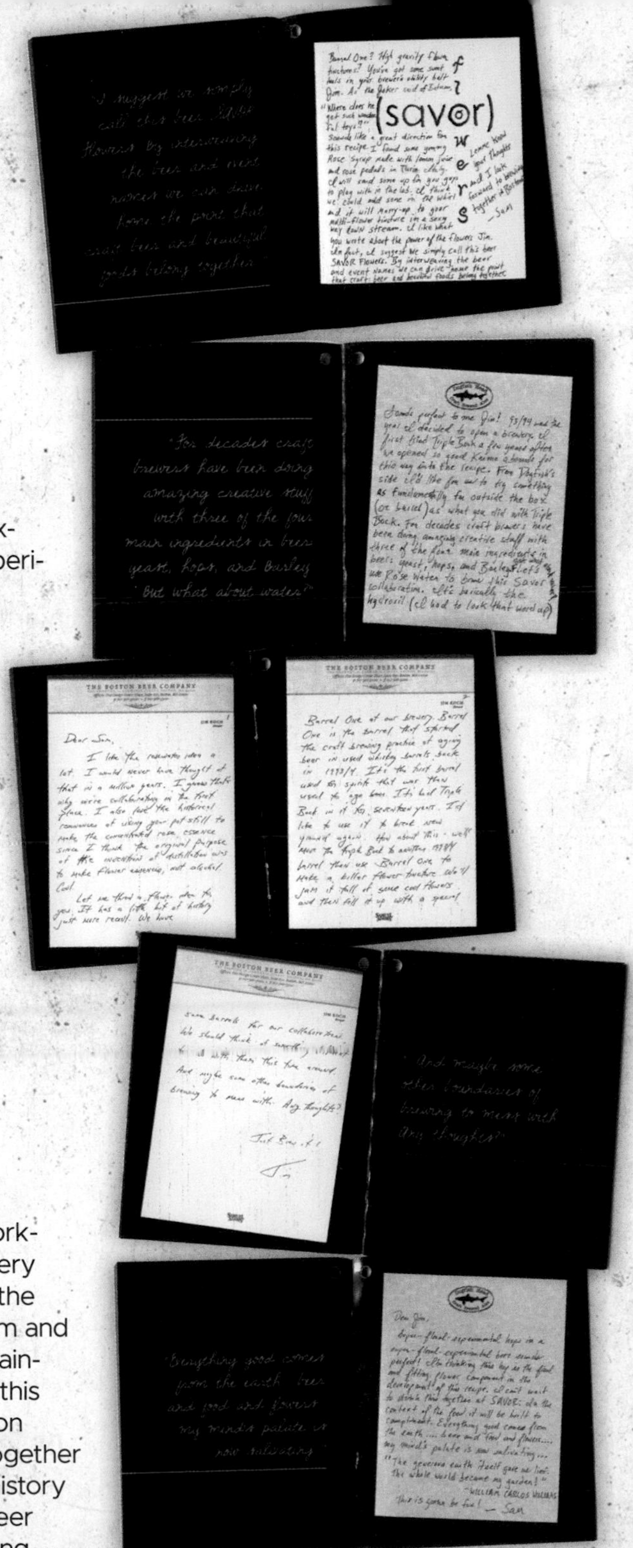

and then bucket it up and truck it up to Boston and replace the normal water for the brew with rosewater we made in our distillery.

That rosewater idea inspired us to continue to explore the idea of brewing with flowers. After experimenting with a wide range of edible flowers, we landed on a mix of dried lavender, hibiscus, jasmine, and rosebuds mixed in during the brewing process to further enhance the beer’s botanical qualities. Jim also found this hop variety on his annual hop selection trip to Bavaria that was only known as number 369 and grown for its amped up floral notes. He obtained it and we added that to the recipe to layer in another level of complexity to the beer. The Savor Flowers was aged in barrel one, which was the same bourbon barrel Jim used to age the premier batch of the first extreme strong beer called Sam Adams Triple Bock way back in 1993.

It kind of started with this distilling process and ended back in the spirits barrel to bring it full circle.

We unveiled the beer in big, beautiful, cobalt, cork-finished bottles at Savor in Washington, D.C. Every bottle had a small booklet that was tethered to the neck of the bottle that contained every letter Jim and I wrote to each other to create this recipe. I certainly wouldn’t have guessed way back in 2011 that this awesome collaboration with Jim Koch and Boston Beer would be only a small step that we took together before the most existential collaboration in the history of Dogfish Head: our merger with the Boston Beer company in 2019. Even though I’d known Jim long before we collaborated on Savor Flowers—we’d go visit each other at our booths at different festivals around the country when we were there together—it was really during that brew of Savor Flowers at the Sam Adams brewery up in Boston that I got to know other Boston Beer coworkers, not just Jim Koch. I was impressed with each and every one of them, the passion and the talent they brought to their jobs, and how they listened to each other, treated each other, and worked carefully with each other, which I think subconsciously made an impact on me and made me ever more excited to contemplate the merger many years later.

Birra Etrusca Bronze

(8.5% ABV)

Birra Etrusca Bronze was an ancient ale that was a collaboration between Birra del Borgo Brewery from the outskirts of Rome, and Baladin Brewery from outside of Turin, Italy. Brewers Teo Musso of Baladin and Leo DeVencenzo of Birra del Borgo and I all love brewing beers with culinary ingredients and thought it would be fun to brew an ancient Italian beer together. The Etruscan civilization was the civilization that preceded the Roman civilization in roughly the same area in Italy, and while Italy's most known and proud for its winemaking heritage, the Etruscans clearly had a taste for ale. As we did the research on the ancient ingredients that ended up informing our beer recipe, we decided that the backbone of the recipe should come from two-row malted barley and an heirloom Italian wheat. The specialty ingredients in this recipe included hazelnut flour, pomegranate, Italian chestnut honey, Delaware wildflower honey, and clover honey. A handful of whole flower hops were added, but the bulk of the bitterness in the beer actually came from gentian root, and the sarsaparilla-like myrrh resin that is found on trees in Ethiopia. We also learned that Etruscans when baking or making beverages did so on or in either of three materials: bronze, wood, or terracotta (i.e., pottery).

We decided that we would each brew different versions of Birra Etrusca Bronze at our three breweries, and each use one of those different materials in our beers. For the Dogfish version we brewed and fermented it and aged it in stainless steel, but we submerged strips of bronze into that beer which interacted with the yeast. Birra del Borgo aged their version of the beer in giant terracotta pottery vats, and Baladin Brewery aged their version of the beer in wooden wine barrels that were previously filled with the native wines of the region outside of Turin where the Baladin Brewery is located.

From left to right: Teo from Baladin, fermented beverage expert Dr. Pat, Leonardo from Birra Del Borgo, and Sam sample some potential ingredients for a brew.

BIRRA
ETRUSCA
BRONZE
1 Pint 9.4 fl. oz. | 8.5% Alc. by Vol.

Firefly Ale (5% ABV)

This beer was made to celebrate the Firefly Music Festival in Dover, Delaware, which Dogfish Head is proud to have been the annual craft beer sponsor for, every year of its existence. (It started in the year 2012.) When Firefly reached out and asked us to make the official Firefly Ale, I thought it would be really fun to use this beer as a platform to bring back the age-old argument of which country invented punk rock—because both British music historians and American music historians take credit for the creation of punk rock. The English argue that it comes out of the pub rock tradition, bands like Ian Dury and the Blockheads, and Americans might cite Velvet Underground as the precursors of punk.... I believe they're both right. Probably the most recognized dichotomy is that in England the Sex Pistols invented punk rock and in America the Ramones invented punk rock. This duality gave us the inspiration we needed. For Firefly Ale and the Firefly Music Festival we would brew a beer that had equal ingredient contributions from England and from the United States. We wanted it to be a sessionable, easy-drinking pale ale since the festival goes on day and night: so, a real sipper that could be enjoyed throughout a day and evening to accompany listening to great music. Firefly is an English-style pale ale brewed with Maris Otter barley and English heritage hops because the Sex Pistols invented punk rock (depending on who you talk to). To add a fruity and citrus aroma there's a late addition to this beer of American calypso hops because the Ramones invented punk rock (depending on who you talk to). We continue to brew this beer annually and evolve the recipe for Firefly to release at the annual festival every year. We have an onsite tent where music lovers can come and talk about who they think invented punk music, partake in an array of our beers, and take a breather between the performances on stage.

Dogfish Head
Craft Brewed Ales
FIREFLY
Ale
#fireflyale

American Beauty (6.5% ABV)

In 2013 we brewed our first-ever iteration of the American Beauty beer. The inspiration behind the collaboration was that Dogfish and Grateful Dead each had amazing fan groups to thank for the longevity and growth of our mutual existence. To celebrate that fan-centric brand building, Dogfish Head and the members of the Grateful Dead decided we should create this recipe with the help of our fan base. Through Dead.net, the powerful online home of the band, and dogfish.com, we announced the contest where we invited Deadheads and Dogfishheads alike to submit suggestions for what ingredients we should use to brew the beer. We started by having the members of the band themselves choose the base beer. They chose a big old pale ale brewed with 100 percent American ingredients and the name American Beauty, after the iconic album by the Dead.

We shared the basic beer concept with Deadheads and Dogfish Head lovers online: whoever submits the best idea for the recipe, along with a story of why their particular ingredient is so perfect for this concept, would be flown to Delaware to brew the beer with us. Thousands of ideas were submitted through our websites, some of them legal and some of them not, but there was one story in particular that really stood out, and it was from a guy who suggested we use granola as an ingredient in the beer. He told the story of growing up really poor and one of his earliest memories was walking around before a Grateful Dead show with his parents when he was a little boy and eating granola together in the parking lot. The next thing he remembered about that day was his dad putting him on his shoulders, walking him over to the fence, and his mom standing on the other side inside the concert venue. The father passed the son over the top of the fence because they could only afford one ticket to go to the Grateful Dead show. The dad sacrificed himself and gave the ticket to his wife and then made sure his son would also see the show. We really loved the story of this family, their free-spiritedness and creativity, and the drive of his parents to make sure their son got to see the show. We invited the now-grown man and his dad to come to Delaware to brew the first beer of American Beauty with us.

When we first brewed this beer, we called it a psychedelic pale ale brewed with granola, honey, and all-American hops. Dogfish sourced this honey and almond-infused granola that gave the beer American Beauty, its sweet and toasty notes.

The Grateful Dead collaboration is one of the most lively collaborations we've had, in that we've created numerous iterations of this collaboration over multiple years.

Collector's Can
DOGFISH HEAD
AND THE
GRATEFUL
DEAD
PRESENT
AMERICAN·BEAUTY
1 PINT 3.25 FL. OZ. | 6.5% ALC. BY VOL.

Kvasir (10% ABV)

This was another wonderful collaboration that we created with our friend Dr. Patrick McGovern, the biomolecular archeologist at the University of Pennsylvania. The name Kvasir refers to a figure from Nordic mythology, but it has also become known as a method of fermenting the juice of ripe berries. The recipe for Kvasir was developed with the help of chemical, botanical, and pollen evidence taken from a 3500-year-old Danish drinking vessel. The vessel was made of birch bark and was found in the tomb of a leather-clad woman that Dr. Pat says was probably an upper-class dancer or priestess. We got to visit the incredibly well-preserved remains of this woman which were housed in a museum in Scandinavia. Beside her in the tomb was discovered the remains of a birch bucket. We analyzed the bucket and were able to reimagine the ingredients used back then in brewing, which included wheat, lingonberries, cranberries, Myrica gale, yarrow, honey, and birch syrup. The base for Kvasir is a toasty red winter wheat, and the bog-grown lingonberries and cranberries deliver a pungent tartness to this beer. The design on the front of this beer is an artistic recreation of what the woman may have looked like. Yet another ancient ale we were proud to brew with Dr. Pat.

Dogfish Head
An Ancient Ale brewed with
cranberry, birch syrup,
cranberry juice and herbs
10% Alc. by Vol. • 1 Pint 9.4 fl. oz.

Sixty-One (6.5% ABV)

Sixty-One was born at the crossroads of serendipity, experimentation, and brotherhood. I was hanging out at Half Full restaurant—one of my favorite restaurants where I live—and waiting for my two buddies coming out for dinner. Two of us ordered pints of 60 Minute IPA, and we ordered Scott his regular—a glass of Pinot Noir. Scott ended up calling to say that he wasn't going to be able to make it. We made a toast to Scott and took sips of our 60 Minute IPAs and, for whatever reason, we decided it would be fun to take that glass of Pinot Noir ordered for Scott and dump equal parts of it into our pints of 60 Minute. We sent him a photo of us smiling and laughing to let him know we poured his drink into ours, and that his drink didn't go to waste. When we tasted the 60 Minute–Pinot Noir blend, it was delicious. I thought right there, "Man, I've got to figure out a way to brew a beer that is a combination of these flavors," and so the work began.

In 2012 we started trialing recipes. What was weird, though, was we learned that while the Pinot Noir grape in the IPA base worked well, when we started trialing other red wine grape varieties we found that there were many grapes even better suited for the recipe. It was actually Syrah grapes that produced the best flavor and ended up being the grape we used in Sixty-One. The beer gets its name because it's exactly the 60 Minute IPA ingredients plus one additional ingredient, which is Syrah grape must. Regular 60 Minute is exactly 6.0 percent alcohol, but by adding the Syrah grape must into the fermenter during the fermentation process and letting the yeast eat the sugars from the grape must, the traditional 60 Minute IPA increases from 6 percent ABV up a half percentage point to 6.5 percent ABV.

The label for this beer originally was from a watercolor I painted myself. It is a twist on a traditional watercolor. Rather than using water to hydrate the paint, I mixed the green pigment with beer to hydrate it and paint with it, and then I mixed the red pigment from the label with wine since Sixty-One is a beer/wine hybrid.

Dogfish Head
Sixty-One
The continually-hopped
India Pale Ale
brewed with Syrah
grape must.
12 fl. oz.
6.5% alc. by vol.

Piercing Pils (6.0% ABV)

We've brewed a lot of different hybrid beers since we opened in 1995. The first beer-wine hybrid distributed was Raison D'Etre. Midas Touch, a beer-mead hybrid, we first brewed in 1999. We did our first perry-pilsner hybrid called Piercing Pils in the year 2013. Perry is a cider but instead of using apple as in traditional cider, the fermentable sugars come from pears. Traditionally pilsners are really simple, crisp, light, straightforward recipes. We wanted to take that sort of crisp, light, refreshing pilsner tradition and put our off-centered culinary spin on it. We decided to do a version of a pilsner that had pears in it called Piercing Pils, as a play on words, because the goal was to make the pears sing, in a pilsner beer, which is otherwise a very traditional style of German lager. To accentuate the aromatic quality of the pears, in addition to pureed pear juice, we also found a white pear tea that had both tea in it and also dried shaved pear flesh slices to accentuate the aromatics. Both the juice and the tea were added to the boil kettle during the whirlpool to maximize the flavor and aromatic contributions. We loved this fruit because the complexity of it pierced right through the spicy traditional Czech Saaz hops beautifully, and it added a gentle acidity to this pale lager that made for a crisp, refreshing, sessionable sipper beer. We added a little bit of Amarillo hops to Piercing Pils as well, perhaps less traditional in a pilsner, but it's sort of got a citrusy, fruity aromatic character to it that we again thought worked really well with the pears.

In 1982 premium light beer grew to 5.45 million barrels, and that was probably its biggest year of growth. If you look at the craft beer movement, the year of the most growth in terms of volume was 2014. The best growth for imports was in 2006, but it was definitely craft's biggest year in 2014, so this beer, the Piercing Pils that we were doing, and beers around 2013–2014, were in the era of explosive growth. Even in these heady years of growth, however, Dogfish Head was susceptible to making occasional missteps because we were so adventurous with what we were brewing for recipes, even in a world that was becoming more acclimated to creative ingredients in beers from small breweries coast to coast.

Pilsners are traditionally drunk on hot summer days because they are very light, refreshing beers, but we thought we'd be counterintuitive and off-centered and release our pilsner in the heart of the winter. We did a crisp 6 percent alcohol pilsner and we modified the very traditional style by adding both pears and a pear-flavored tea to it. Piercing Pils was a really fun beer. A lot of people say we should bring it back, but honestly it was not the best seller in that era—I believe because we were selling it in the winter. Pilsners in general: it seems that consumers don't want to see a lot of culinary ingredient innovation in lagers the way they're more willing to have them come through in sours, wild beers, and ales. This beer *did* give us the excuse to have a pretty sweet pear-eating pie contest at the tasting room in Milton. That was a win for sure.

Wendy Domurat

On-Premise Market Channel Manager
Start Date: 2008

Wendy is Dogfish Head's longest-standing sales coworker. Like many of our OG coworkers, she never applied to work at Dogfish Head because she was too busy selling our beer for Kunda wholesalers. She made her way down to Milton for a tour of the brewery as a "thank you" for all she had done in 2007 at Kunda for us. Linking up with Sam, Nick Benz, and a few others, the thank-you tour was no joke: World Wide Stouts, some peanut butter vodka mixed with chicory stout ... you know, some of the usual suspects when celebrating someone we love. Predictably, Wendy had a wicked hangover the next morning (a big sorry to the CVS parking lot on this one). We are glad it rained quickly after Wendy came down, but all's well that ends well! Besides the hangover, Wendy got a new job (and family) working directly with Dogfish Head. A true warrior and a true professional, Wendy sets the bar about as high as you can get when it comes to Dogfish Head culture, craft beer, sales, and knowing how to lean into an all-night, beer-infused ramble through the City of Brotherly Love. This gal knows Philly.

Wendy celebrated 13 years with Dogfish this past January. Selling good liquid as a salesperson is a bonus, but for Wendy, the people and the culture of Dogfish Head give her motivation every day to get out and represent us in the market. And she is damn good at it, too. Seeing people's faces when they taste a 60 Minute IPA or a Seaquench Ale for the first time keeps her present and reminds her that she is exactly where she wants to be; there is nowhere else she would rather go. While the beer inspires, the people take it beyond anywhere we could have imagined. Wendy is without a doubt one of these people for us.

Sam and Wendy

When Wendy started in 2008, there were five people on the sales team. Five. She covered New Jersey, Delaware, Pennsylvania, and Maryland. As Dogfish grew, her region got smaller and the responsibilities changed as systems shifted. Wendy adapted with the job and her impact was rock-steady. Today, she is the On-Premise Market Channel manager—Philly style.

Wendy is also the only person to almost die at the Dogfish Inn. That's right. It is not all fun and games here all the time, and no, she was not partying that night. She was in town for a sales meeting and ended up staying in the SWEET above the cottage. She was at the brewpub and got an overwhelming desire to go back to the Inn and watch *Law and Order*. Seems normal enough. Wendy returned to the Inn and the sickness ensued. That *Law and Order* music paired well with how she was feeling. Turns out, it was the norovirus. No joke there. Don't mess with the norovirus. The Inn crowd kept a

Coworker Profile

close eye on Wendy, making sure she was keeping the fluids going, and a close friend, Angie Hawn, rolled by with provisions as well. It was like a scene from *Train Spotting* without the drugs. She came around slowly and made a full recovery, thank God!

Sipping on Busch Light pounder back in high school at her friend's dad's basement bar has given way to some far superior liquid. Bitches Brew, hands down, is her go-to when it comes to the beers we have produced. Storied and smooth sipping, Wendy loves it. A beer glass becomes a chalice when filled with Bitches Brew. And, without Wendy, we may have never gotten rid of Black and Red, which, when talking to any coworker who was around when it came out, was the worst beer we ever made. She was able to figure out a way to move some sixtels of it and help us move on to new brews.

Over the course of her years at Dogfish Head, Wendy remembers one experience in San Francisco in particular during the Craft Beer Conference. She was in town on vacation with friends, and they hit up Toronado Pub: a must for all beer enthusiasts visiting the Bay Area. With CBC happening in town, this was the place to be. Wendy wanted some Blind Pig from Russian River, and sure enough, a gentleman from Cantillon recognized Wendy and pulled her into the back room. Out of nowhere, a high five almost smacked Wendy in the face. She got her hand up in time and was able to save face. Who else would be on the other side of that high five but Sam Calagione. Mariah was there as well, and they took Wendy under their wing for the evening. At that time, CBC was very tight with security and badges, but Sam and Mariah took Wendy to the opening party at an aquarium. She'll never forget it.

Sam and Mariah don't see Wendy as "someone who works for them." They see her as a coworker and peer—someone who pushes the needle every day to make Dogfish Head better. That night, they introduced her to tons of big names in the industry and were celebrating all of what makes Dogfish so unique and memorable: Wendy and all of Dogfish Head's coworkers. That transcendental respect starts with Sam and Mariah because they know everyone plays a vital part, and they take the time to celebrate each individual. In turn, everyone has learned to do the same, so putting the "we" before the "I" is easy.

Wendy and the sales team at Dogfish drive so much for us. This tribe is held together by their shared experiences, dedication to the brand, and deep loyalty to each other. Wendy has been a major part of the glue that holds our sales coworkers together and helps keep the focus on what is best for all of us at Dogfish—not just what will drive numbers for her region. Having this dedication to each other keeps our edges sharp, and disrupting the status quo, and the sales team grounds us at Dogfish Head. For years, Wendy has always focused on the next big opportunity. Wendy has led the charge and continues to every day. Not only is she a consummate team player, but she can also pull an all-nighter like nobody else we have ever met.

If you were on a deserted island and could have one album to listen to and an unlimited supply of one beer, what would it be?

Beer: Sierra Nevada Pale Ale (Slightly Mighty is a close second)
Album: Beastie Boys, *Paul's Boutique*

Chapter 7

Take Your Pants Off

(aka Andrew Gets the Inn Job)

As told by Andrew Greeley himself.

It was a Friday morning in the spring of 2014. I was getting the shop at the Milton Brewery ready for the weekend, putting all the merchandise away and stacking cases of 60 Minute IPA. Most days there is a nice lull between the merch and beer deliveries and the doors opening at 11:00 AM, when we get to make sure everything is ready for the day's events.

For people who work in hospitality, there's always a special energy in the air on Fridays, but if you work at Dogfish Head, Fridays are a particularly special day. On Fridays at Dogfish Head, all coworkers look forward to the Friday celebration, Beer:30. This is when the taps open up for all coworkers for an hour and a half on Friday evenings and we get to celebrate the literal fruits of our labor.

I had never really worked in hospitality until I got here, but I spent a lot of time at schools in admissions. In my former life I had spent 15 years working in independent schools, coaching lacrosse, soccer, wrestling, basketball. Working in independent schools is kind of like working at Dogfish. You never know what they're going to throw at you. Maybe it's running a hotel.

I initially started at Dogfish Head in 2012, working as a part-time tour guide. Mark Carter and Kristen Barth hired me for a full-time position in the summer of 2012. I was at first conducting tours and then took on the role of tour supervisor/manager in the summer of 2013. By 2014, I had been working in the Tasting Room for about two years.

On this particular day, it was about 10:30 in the morning. All the beer had been stacked on the pallets with care with the hope that some fans soon would be there.
Just then, Mariah walked into the shop.
"Hey Andrew," she called out. "Can you come up to the conference room? I want to talk with you about something."
"Sure! I'll be right up," I replied.

Andrew in 2012 pouring samples in the tasting room

"We're in the brewhouse conference room," she said and headed through the door.
"Why on earth does Mariah want to talk to me ... and who is the 'we' up in the brewhouse conference room?" I asked myself.

The conference room is on the second floor of the brewery with a large rectangular table that spans the room. At one end of the room is an epic collection of bottles of almost every beer we have ever brewed. At the other end is a magnetic wall. On the wall hang photos of all the coworkers at Dogfish Head. At the back of the conference room is a wall of windows that looks out over Brewhouse 1, our 100-barrel bottling system.

Not sure what to expect, I headed up the stairs and opened the door to the conference room.

Sitting at the table alongside Sam and Mariah was Dogfish Head CEO Nick Benz.

"Well this is either really good, or really bad," I thought, "... but this really can't be good."

Just then, Mariah stood up, walked over to the window, and hit a switch. Curtains started to lower, closing the view between the conference room, cubicles on one side, and the brewhouse on the other, so that no one could see into the room. The light in the gap below the curtain got smaller and smaller as an uneasy feeling in the pit of my stomach began to grow.

As we watched the curtain come down, Nick was the first to break the silence: "Take your pants off!" he ordered. I was immediately put at ease. If there was ever an opportunity to bring levity to a situation, Nick Benz would be ready with a joke or perfectly timed remark. But as much as he loved joking around, Nick is also an extremely professional businessman. He is smart as hell and his mind is in permanent overdrive. But he is also a tremendous human being when the chips are down. If I were getting the ax, he would not have made a joke of it.

Mariah and Sam laughed along with Nick and asked me to take a seat.

Mariah began, "As you know, we will be opening the Dogfish Head Inn in Lewes and the opening is being planned for June. We've been interviewing for a while now but have not yet found the right person for the position of Innkeeper."

I was aware that there were candidates interviewing for the position. I had even participated in the interview process with applicants, providing feedback on them, and passing those notes on to HR. Oddly enough, that very morning I had been thinking about the Inn and wondering who was going to get the job. I was about to find out.

Nick chimed in, "Now, this is just a conversation. We wanted to get your thoughts on this, but please keep this between us."

"Of course," I nodded.

Sam went next. "We have gone through a number of applicants, and you have met a few of them as well. They have all been great—solid people for sure, and fully capable of running the Inn, but nobody has stood out and wowed us. With that said, your name keeps coming up in conversation."

Mariah could see I was a bit dumbfounded, so she explained, "We love what you have done down in the Tasting Room. And remember, this is just a conversation ... but, the way you make people feel when they walk into the Tasting Room is so welcoming. You have a team that really loves you. Mark and many others think you are a strong leader. We think you are, as well. Frankly, we are wondering if you would be open to the possibility of maybe being the Innkeeper?"

Sam continued, "While everyone we interviewed up to this point has been capable of running a hotel, they just were not a fit for Dogfish. While all that other stuff is important, there are some things that we just can't teach. That is the part that makes Dogfish so special. You have that, Andrew. We know how you feel about Dogfish Head. You are super passionate in everything you do here," Sam said. "But this is JUST a conversation!" he tacked on at the end there, with a laugh.

I had gotten that point loud and clear.

I was also truly blown away. I was honored. I had no hotel experience and had only been at Dogfish Head for a couple of years.

I responded, "I am truly honored, and I don't know what to think. I have no hotel experience. I am still learning. The closest thing I have to experience was working in a boarding school for a couple years as a teacher and dorm parent for 80 high school students."

Mariah replied, "Well, that's more experience than we have!"

She continued—and I'll never forget this—she said, "Andrew, when we opened the pub in Rehoboth in 1995, we had no restaurant experience. When we opened the brewery, we had no brewery experience. Right now, we have no hotel experience. We will learn together, we will make mistakes together, but we will do this together."

I thought of the stainless-steel pint I received when I started at Dogfish Head, as part of my welcome packet. On it was a chain block-and-tackle hoisting up the shark and shield with the words, "Together We are Heavy."

Sam jumped in, "We don't want your answer right now. Can you meet me tomorrow morning at the Inn and I can show you our plans and our vision for the place?"

Sam and I made plans to meet the next morning, and I headed back down to finish my shift. As I left the conference room, I thought about Mariah's comments about the Tasting Room. I had recognized from my first days there that Dogfish Head was all about culture. The goal of the team at Dogfish Head is to create an amazing experience for the people who come here. It's not about the stuff, necessarily. Yeah, the beers Dogfish Head is known for are going to draw people in, but it's the feelings that people get from the coworkers at Dogfish Head; it's the energy that Sam has when people meet him; it's the energy that the tour guides have, that the servers down at the pub like Olivia, Courtney, and Ashlee have, that create the Dogfish Head experience. All of them, they love what they do, and it comes through in every interaction guests have with them. That same feeling of deep joy for everything we do is what I was trying to cultivate in the Tasting Room.

I couldn't help but feel excited, but I also didn't let anybody know about the opportunity presented to me. I tend to jump in with both feet before testing the water, but I knew I had to hold space, so I just started thinking through what this might look like. Sam had written on his steering wheel of his midlife-crisis Dodge Challenger Super Bee, "Go Slowly, Go Thoughtfully." Good advice to this day.

Still, I thought to myself, "There's no way I could say no to this."

The next morning, I met up with Sam in front of what would become the Dogfish Inn. Initially built in the 1970s, the property was formerly called the Vesuvio Motel and was an old roadside inn that had fallen into disrepair. It was second-generation owned, and the gentleman who owned it had grown up there, watched his parents run the inn when he was a child, and then raised his own kids there.

Sam and Mariah had purchased it back in 2013, and the renovations were under way. The buildings had been gutted, and the day I met Sam to talk about his vision, there were three different crews working on various projects, from installing windows and doors to putting in new floors to replacing the roof. We walked over to the smaller building to the left of the larger structure that was still stripped down to studs. As we made our way into the building, Sam began to explain his vision for the Inn. He described the Inn as being a "Base Camp" for beer enthusiasts and adventure seekers visiting Delaware.

Original Vesuvio Motel, 2013

"When people visit one of our restaurants," he explained, "they spend a few hours with us. When they come to Milton to do a tour and have lunch, they may spend a little more time with us. The Inn gives us the opportunity to spend a day or two ... or more ... with our fans, coworkers, and partners." This kind of brand experience was unheard of on a beer brand front.

He also spoke of plans to invite distributors and coworkers who traveled to the area to stay there. The plan would be to invite them in during the off-season months and they would have a retreat of sorts and get to really interact with our brand and coworkers.

Sam explained how the experience of creating the original Dogfish Head 360-degree package we initially launched in 2005 had really planted the seed for this idea. In it, Dogfish Head partnered with a hotel owner in town who offered an off-centered room at The Inn at Canal Square named "The Brewmaster's Suite" so guests could have a unique immersive experience with Dogfish Head and Coastal Delaware.

Treat All Of Your Senses To...
The Dogfish Head 360° EXPERIENCE

"Who would have thought the most civilized hotel bedroom in the U.S. could be called The Dogfish Brewmaster's Suite? Had I stayed more than one night, I would have been in severe danger of learning to relax."
- Michael Jackson, "The Beer Hunter"

The 360° Experience will invigorate all of your senses. You will SEE Coastal Delaware's true beauty while kayaking and boating along its scenic waterways. You will HEAR live, original music from rising artists. You will FEEL the deluxe comfort and charm of a premier, waterfront inn. You will SMELL the aroma of fresh hops and barley and learn about the art of brewing while touring Dogfish Head's Milton brewery. And finally, you will TASTE the purity and distinction of the region's finest ales coupled with wood-fired cuisine in a fun, relaxed atmosphere.

(See flip side for package details)

Two Day Weekend Package Includes:

- A guided tour of the Dogfish Head Brewery in Milton
- Two nights accommodations in the Brewmaster's Suite at The Inn at Canal Square in the Heart of Historic Lewes
- Dogfish Head soap, shampoo, accessories and a cold six pack in the fridge
- A Saturday evening boat tour aboard the S.S. Dogfish from The Inn at Canal Square to The Dogfish Head Brewings & Eats BrewPub in Rehoboth
- Transportation back to The Inn at Canal Square
- A $50.00 gift certificate to the Dogfish Head Brewings & Eats BrewPub

April 29, 2005 to October 31, 2005
Package Price $575.00
Inquire about reduced Weekday Packages
One of three Quest Kayak Adventure trips may be added for a special rate. Please ask the reservationist for more information.
RESERVE YOUR PACKAGE TODAY
by calling The Inn at Canal Square at 302.644.3377 and reference the Dogfish Head 360° Experience Package.

I had been coordinating some of the 360-degree packages and had a good sense of the experiences people were looking to have on those trips. This only reaffirmed all I was feeling about taking on the Innkeeper role.

Sam's vision of the place and how it was all coming together was inspiring. He explained that in the lobby there would be a thoughtfully curated collection of books available to guests called the City Light Library. There would be a cauldron in the outdoor area that would entice guests to sit around its fire, guests would be welcomed with a proprietary coffee blend each morning, each room would display the artwork, and on and on.

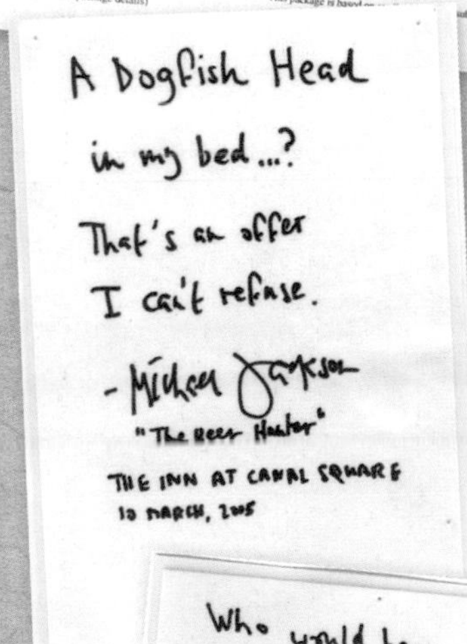
A Dogfish Head
in my bed...?
That's an offer
I can't refuse.
- Michael Jackson
"The Beer Hunter"
THE INN AT CANAL SQUARE
10 MARCH, 2005

To walk the Inn grounds that day was to be walking through the middle of the process of creating something from nothing. Sam and I parted ways and I felt completely stoked. It is rare to come across people who galvanize and motivate you like Sam and Mariah do. They turn fiction to nonfiction through the process of creation, hard work, and inspiration. Sam and Mariah also constantly push all of us at Dogfish to do something new. It can be hard. But we like to do hard things, because that is where growth happens. I remember vividly the words that came out of his mouth as we looked out at the Lewes and Rehoboth Canal. "I hope you will come on this journey with us."

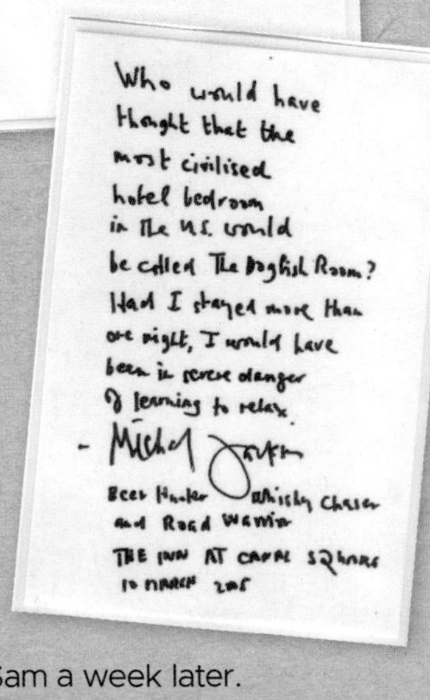
Who would have
thought that the
most civilised
hotel bedroom
in the U.S. would
be called The Dogfish Room?
Had I stayed more than
one night, I would have
been in severe danger
of learning to relax.
- Michael Jackson
Beer Hunter Whisky Chaser
and Road Warrior
THE INN AT CANAL SQUARE
10 MARCH 2005

After giving me about a week to think about it, Nick reached out to me. I knew that while the transition to the Inn would mean long hours and lots of work at first, it would also help create a better life for my family in the long run. That spring my son Ben had just been born and my daughter Molly was eight. I had to think about what this change would mean for them. I knew that running the Inn was an opportunity that would never come my way again and that the universe was putting it in front of me for a reason.

I enthusiastically accepted the role with a bone-rattling high five to Sam a week later. It was May 7th and I had just committed to Sam, Mariah, and Nick Benz that I would leave my position and a team I truly loved working with in the Tasting Room in the Milton Brewery to come on board as the off-centered Innkeeper at the Dogfish Inn.

Traffic to the Tasting Room at the Milton Brewery had been ramping up significantly and I was having a difficult time balancing running the team in the Tasting Room while figuring out how on earth I was going to run an Inn with no team, no housekeeping, and no experience. I even recall someone telling me, "You can't run the Inn! People go to college for those types of careers!" Aargh ... the words of encouragement from a pessimist. Don't ever listen to them and you will be just fine in this adventure called life!

What exactly is an Innkeeper I kept thinking to myself? For me, the title Innkeeper evokes visions of a gruff character with long hair and an unkempt beard, exuding a faint odor of beer and likely carrying a lantern warning people, "A storm is a-coming!" I had at least three of these characteristics nailed, but I don't think that was why I was asked to take on the responsibility.

I was checking my email in what was my makeshift office down in the Tasting Room—that meant I was sitting on a case box of Burton Baton with my computer set up on case boxes of Midas Touch for the desk. Now that is a cubical if there ever was one.

There was an email from Sam at the top of my inbox, so I quickly opened it. It was addressed to Ryan Schwamberger who at the time was running Dogfish Head Brewings & Eats in Rehoboth, and me. Ryan is still there today and is a hospitality Jedi to end them all. In the email was a link to a *Wall Street Journal* essay Sam wanted us to read about omotenashi. (No. This is not a strange ingredient we want to put in a beer.) The article was titled, "Japan's Red-Carpet Service" by Oliver Strand.

It was a killer article.

From: Calagione, Sam
To: Schwamberger, Ryan; Greeley, Andrew
Sent: Wednesday, May 7, 2014
Re: omotenashi

Hello y'all
check out this article from WSJ below – I am sharing this because I think you each get this philosophy of omotenashi and are on the front lines of guest experience – how it overlaps with our ideal of hospitality and dovetails with our purpose statement and the exploration of goodness– please read it and share it in any way you see fit - also Ryan and Andrew - please carve/paint the word in calligrafitti somewhere subtle on your desks in Rehoboth Pub and Lewes inn as a subtle reminder as you teach and lead our co-workers how important this ideal of omotenashi = goodness is best.
– sam

THE EXCHANGE

ESSAY

JAPAN'S RED-CARPET SERVICE

From a department store's elaborate welcoming rituals to a hotel's nearly uncanny sense of its guests' needs, one writer explores how the Land of the Rising Sun has perfected hospitality culture.

BY OLIVER STRAND ILLUSTRATION BY PATRIK SVENSSON

The article explored the service culture of Japan, which it describes as "polished and comprehensive," but what really stood out was the concept of truly meeting guests where they are, and that by working in hospitality, we are not providing some handbook experience to the guest; we are experiencing their very unique and individual experience with them. Our brand of hospitality at Dogfish Head is about being present with each individual, so when they experience their first sip of 60 Minute, it is like it is our first sip as well. By being part of the wonder and awe of it all, it not only maintains it, but it grows it exponentially.

Beyond the concept of omotenashi, the article also highlighted the difference between shareholder capitalism and stakeholder capitalism in the world. In the shareholder world it is all about the company and the almighty dollar for that company. Stakeholder is different. Stakeholder capitalism is about investing in the people who work for a company. It spoke to the importance of having coworkers who are invested in the success of the business because they are invested in what the company is about. By investing in the people who do the trench work every day, we end up taking what is a team and making them a tribe.

What Sam referenced in the email as our ideal of hospitality and our mission statement refers to the Emerson quote emblazoned on the walls of all of the properties—the same one that has been distilled down to "Off-Centered Goodness for Off-Centered People."

The Emerson quote is the purpose statement of the Inn as well. It has been present in our ideas since the day Dogfish Head was a work of fiction in the form of a business plan.

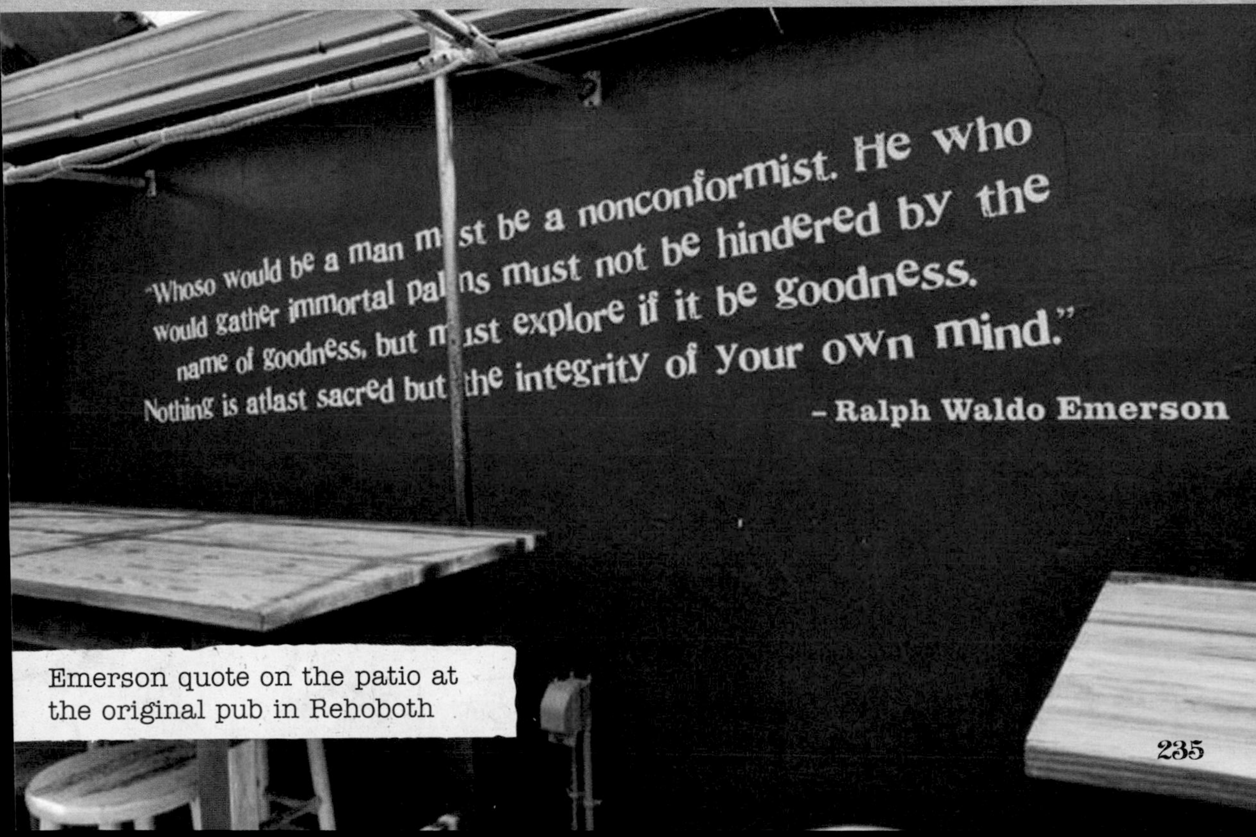

"Whoso would be a man must be a nonconformist. He who
would gather immortal palms must not be hindered by the
name of goodness, but must explore if it be goodness.
Nothing is atlast sacred but the integrity of your own mind."
– Ralph Waldo Emerson

Emerson quote on the patio at the original pub in Rehoboth

Sam could not have sent this article at a more perfect time. While the Inn was quickly coming together from a construction standpoint, I was scrambling to get everything else together for the opening, which was less than two months away. We were on a ridiculously tight timeline to get the Inn fully up and running. I knew we would hit our deadline, but this article reinforced what I already knew. The architecture and interior design firm that Sam and Mariah had brought in, Studio Tack, now known as Post Company, would ensure the space was consistent with the Dogfish Head brand. And there were countless others involved in designing the various elements and details of the Inn that would make it an experience exceptional. However, it would be the people we hired to staff the Inn who were going to influence the experiences of our guests and ultimately be responsible for creating that omotenashi experience.

I was in the process of interviewing candidates who would become the coworkers at the Inn, and was working with Annie in HR, bless her soul, to find the perfect candidates. We were looking to hire two Innmates ... yeah, it sounds like jail. Someone said it sounded like being on a boat ... but no matter which way you spin it, it sounds like jail. We also needed to bring on an assistant Innkeeper.

You can build the most amazing facility in the world, located in the most beautiful destination in the world, and serve the best food in the world, but if the people working in those spaces suck ... so will the places. When it comes down to creating an experience, the people will always make a far more memorable impact than anything else. Why is this? Well, Maya Angelou pretty much nailed it when she said, "People may not remember exactly what you did, or what you said, but they will always remember how you made them feel."

The phrase, "Give a Fuck," is written on the wall in the office at the Inn as well. What does this really mean? It means: care about what you do and take pride in it no matter how small the task may be, even if the task is cleaning a toilet or folding a towel. If we put our heart into what we do, it shows in the final product. The moment we stop putting our souls into our work is the moment we stop being off-centered and stop living up to the word of Emerson.

As for the request Sam had made to calligrafitti, the term omotenashi on the Inn walls, and keeping the essay and its ideas of omotenashi at the center of the Inn experience, I have shared and continue to share it with coworkers. It has been passed along to folks working in the Tasting Room in Milton, in Brewings & Eats, and in Chesapeake & Maine. It is also shared with anyone who works at the Inn. When Inn coworkers read the article, they are asked to explain how it applies to what we do at the Inn and at Dogfish Head. No matter how many times we ask the question, coworkers manage to identify another unique connection between the article and the Inn that we hadn't considered before. Because of this, we never stop looking at what we do or thinking about how it impacts our guests. The real benefit is that we never stop learning how to improve the experience of our guests.

Two responses from the article from two different coworkers follow.

"It's taking a read of people and intuitively knowing that they want to get to their room and lay down after the drive they had; it's putting a message on someone's door in silly plastic letters because their boyfriend/girlfriend/wife/husband wanted to surprise them. The fine-tuned anticipation of someone's happiness when we do something out of the ordinary for them. Every tiny action we engage in that we do for guests at the Inn has a ripple effect on how they view our company."
—Jean Greathouse, Innmate and Fun Enthusiast

"Just the other weekend, we had some folks in the SWEET who were here for a birthday. Since we had a note about it in their folio, I brought it up while they were hanging around in the lobby on Friday after an evening bar-hopping in Lewes. The four of them told me that there wasn't much planned, just enjoying the weekend—then the wife of the birthday boy whispered to me about how they had a large surprise party planned the following night. When I checked in with them again on Sunday, she was happy to tell me about how it all went, and I was happy to hear about it. I love that I have the inclination to care about and interact honestly with our guests."
—Cara Digby, Assistant Innkeeper and Detroit tough

We hired Cara Digby for the role of Assistant Innkeeper, and Cara is still cranking with me at the Inn today. When I first talked to Cara, she was working at Brewings & Eats at the time and came highly recommended by Ryan Schwamberger. Cara had been serving at the pub and had no hotel experience. What stood out to me about her was that she cared about people. When folks came through to the pub, she could talk beer all day with them, but she was more interested in them being taken care of. This was exactly what the article was speaking to and one of the main reasons I am grateful to have her with me at the Inn to this day. It is also the reason why folks returning in the summer know her by name. Now I must say, she is from Detroit, so don't go messing with Digs … she will let you know … but her heart is tremendous.

Welcome to Lewes.
Mother Nature,
do this.

The coworkers at Dogfish Head absolutely love Dogfish Head and this motivates all of us to bring our best selves to work with us and to represent the company as if we are representing our family.

To this day the essay is still present and making an impact at the Inn and Dogfish Head, but it was a key moment in helping me get focused when we were sprinting to the get the Inn open. It still reminds me that being present with guests will leave more of a lasting impression than anything else I can do. People really do make all the difference.

The Inn

The Inn is located on the Lewes Canal, part of the Intracoastal Waterway, and within walking distance to Lewes Beach. North of here the canal connects to the Delaware Bay. If you head south down the canal, it will take you all the way through Rehoboth to the town of Dewey, into Rehoboth Bay, and to Indian River Bay. By boat, you can get all the way down the waterway to the Indian River inlet. Boating, kayaking, and paddle-boarding are common along the canal.

Many of the guests who stay at the Inn ask, “Does Sam ever come by?” If it’s early in the morning, there’s been more than one occasion where I have seen him out there on his SUP from the Inn windows and could say, “There he goes heading down the canal.”

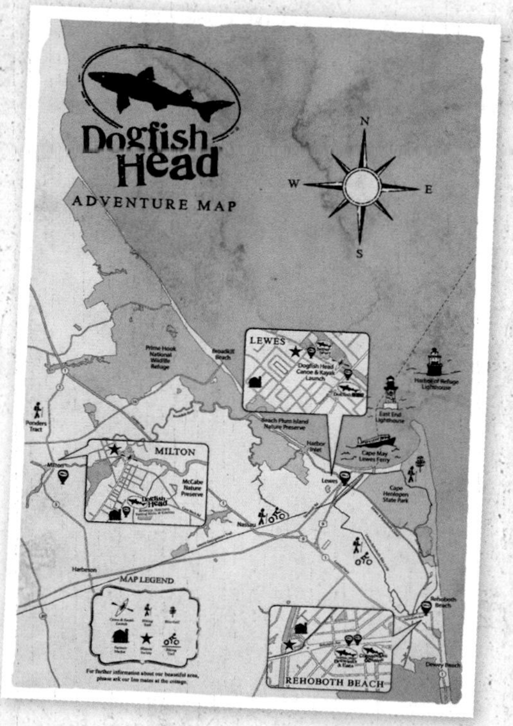

The Inn is right around the corner from downtown Lewes—so when people stay at the Inn, they can walk or bike to food, dining, and shopping. The Inn is about five miles from Dogfish Head Brewing & Eats and from our restaurant Chesapeake & Maine. Many guests grab a bike, ride downtown for dinner, and then loop back up. A lot of guests in the summer will disappear on the bike at 10 o'clock in the morning and then get back here to get ready for dinner.

There are two separate buildings on the Inn property. There is also an additional rental property two blocks from here, which we call the Super SWEET that is a free-standing house with all the amenities. The Inn evokes the feeling of the traditional two-story seaside motel. On the main structure it's all outdoor entrances. We have 15 rooms here, and then there's a suite in the cottage above the office. There are eight single king rooms and seven double queen rooms. It's sort of base camp for anyone coming to the area. Explore the outdoors. Explore everything Dogfish has to offer. Explore everything Coastal Delaware has to offer.

We refer to the three locations where Dogfish has sites as the Beer-muda Triangle in Delaware: the three points being the Inn, the Milton brewery, and the restaurants in Rehoboth. I like to think that for guests visiting from outside the local area, the Inn functions as the central hub of their experience. People are constantly coming in and out to visit various destinations, but they spend most of their time here. You go to the brewery, and you're not going to spend more than four or five hours there. You go to the pub, maybe one or two hours. The Inn provides visitors a chance to really engage with the brand and really engage with the people and the locations.

The Cape May-Lewes Ferry terminal is about a mile from the Inn, right over the drawbridge from us here. Next to the ferry terminal there's another spot called Grain on the Rocks, and they serve a ton of our canned beers as well as some beer-infused menu items.

Bunyan's Lunchbox was the Dogfish Head food truck that first landed at the Milton brewery in 2012. We served beer-infused food from it until we built the kitchen there. After that, the Lunchbox got a paint job and ended up down by the ferry terminal, where visitors using the ferry service can grab a beer on their way in or out of town. The Lunchbox has good food, tons of Dogfish beer, and it's a hangout space, with cornhole boards, benches, live music, a firepit, and a super-chill vibe.

Detail

One of the things that is so special about the Inn is the attention to detail, this idea of it being very Wes Anderson-esque ... you have Dogfish Inn pencils perfectly positioned on every single table. Everything is curated and laid out. We wanted to do it right, so we were very detail-oriented with all aspects of the design.

"Everything matters. Everything impacts your experience where you are, whether it be the sound, the lights, the colors, the smells, the smallest details—everything matters."

The People

One thing all the coworkers have in common is that we feel we are keepers of culture—the culture of Dogfish Head and the culture of Coastal Delaware.

When you sit down and you talk to someone at the distillery, like our distiller Alison Ruark, or you talk to one of the brewers standing at the bar, like Seth Limanek, or you talk to someone from the lab, like Ryan Mazur or Janelle Mazur who are standing at the bar talking to guests—it's real. There's a deep connection

Welcome to Lewes.
Mother Nature, let's do this.

that happens when our coworkers interact with our guests, and it is one thing I love about Dogfish. It is so fundamental to the brand and people's experience of it.

When people come back to the Inn, they look for our housekeepers, like Pat Dowdell, who take deep pride in everything they do and have huge personalities as well. They engage in conversations with guests all the time, and that's what we want. Those details matter. I say to them often, "Aim small, miss small." If we want everything to be dialed in, we have to sweat the small stuff. We need to watch every detail, and if we're doing that, everything's going to line up. If you're aiming, and you're shooting a bow and arrow, and you're trying to hit the hay bale, and that's all you're trying to hit, you might miss the hay bale. But if you aim at a plate on the hay bale, you might miss the plate, but you're going to hit the hay bale. If you aim at a quarter on a plate, you might miss the quarter, but you're going to hit the plate. The same concept applies to how we focus on the details in running the Inn.

When people walk into the Inn, they talk about the smell. We hand-make a cabin spray we use on the property. That spray has Palo Santo essential oils and a little bit of orange. It also has some spruce, with a nice woodsy, clean smell to it. To get the essential oils to blend with the other ingredients requires alcohol, so we add some Analog Vodka from the distillery in Milton. That detail makes an impact. We have people come back to the Inn, and they say, "It smells the same. What is that smell?" The fact that people remember the smell of the place is the kind of impact we want to have on our guests.

The more focused we can get on what we are trying to do, the better we'll be. That focus comes from the Emerson quote. That focus comes from all the things that we talk about that make us great. It comes from us knowing that our guest engagement makes a difference. All those little details, if each of us is focusing on different details, it's going to go well.

Local sourcing

Basecamp Blend coffee complementary in rooms

When we create personalized experiences for our guests' special occasions, we put together packages with other local businesses to create experiences unique to Lewes. We have a Romantic Chemistry Package named after our beer. In that package we use chocolates from the locally owned chocolate shop less than a block away, and we order flowers from Flowers on Savannah, a local flower shop.

In the cottage, we offer guests a blend of coffee as unique as the Dogfish Head brews. The coffee is a cousin of our Chicory Stout beer. The coffee beans we use are locally roasted at Notting Hill Coffee just down the street. Before the beans are ground and brewed we add roasted chicory and malted barley—a dark Munich malt—procured from the brewery. Chicory is a very common ingredient in New Orleans cuisine, but its culinary use goes all the way back to early French cuisine. It adds sort of a molasses-y, earthy note to the brew. The coffee beans are blended with barley, then ground and brewed, creating a very distinct flavor to the coffee.

In each room, we provide a pour-over coffee setup that comes with an 8 oz. bag of Basecamp Blend. We have worked with Rise Up Coffee Roasters on many projects including our Booze for Breakfast coffee liqueur. Rise Up, much like Dogfish Head, was born on Delmarva and is a people-, mission-, and process-focused company, tapped into the local vibe—so it made perfect sense to use them for a coffee blend at the Inn. For the Basecamp Blend, Rise Up roasts beans from multiple locales, taking inspiration from our beer, Pangea, where we pulled ingredients from all seven continents. It comes with a pour-over carafe and all the necessary tools you would need to brew the perfect cup in the comfort of your own room.

When we were a much smaller brewery, we tried to locally source all of the ingredients we used. One of our first beers, Chicory Stout, was a prime example of that. The coffee for that beer comes from a roaster right here in Lewes. We use their coffee for our Chicory Stout Coffee that we sell at the Inn. It is like the coffee cousin of the beer we make. On top of this we have collaborated with Rise Up Coffee Roasters. They have done a Basecamp Blend for us as well. We have brewed beers and spirits with them along with the coffee. The Inn

and the concept behind the Inn is all about being part of the community. We are always looking to source everything that we can locally as well as partnering, patronizing, or collaborating with other businesses and brands in town. It helps us to engage with the various events or opportunities in town and helps give guests a complete Coastal Delaware experience.

Explore

The Inn is an off-centered hotel. You look at traditional hotel business models or at people who've gone to school for hospitality, and most are taught that the goal is to monetize your property—get people to your place and keep them there. Get your guests to spend their money at your place. At the Inn, we encourage people to enjoy nature through our partners and to patronize other businesses. We want them to get up to the brewery, to the pub, to Chesapeake & Maine, but we also want them to get out. That is the off-centered way. Get outside of your comfort zone. Do things you hadn't planned or hadn't tried before! Go see the state park. Go have dinner at Matt DiSabatino's restaurants Kindle or Half Full. Go over to Heirloom and have an unbelievable meal there. The diversity of restaurants, to me, is like the diversity of our beer portfolio, and the more diversity there is to it, the richer the experience is going to be for our guests.

One of the biggest ways we choose to support Lewes and encourage guests to experience and support the local businesses is that we do not serve beer at the Inn. Often, people will arrive and are like, "What? Are you kidding me? There's no beer here?" Some people conclude, "Well, maybe it's illegal." We have changed legislation multiple times in Delaware, but we decided that we didn't want to serve or sell beer at the Inn. And because of all the great bars, restaurants, liquor stores, and breweries in the area, by the time people check out, they can get all the beer they need. This is really is a base camp for them to get out and explore. If we put taps in the cottage here, it'd be overrun in the summer. And guests might prefer to stay at the Inn versus going to explore the area.

Not selling beer on the premises gives guests the space to relax and enjoy the Inn and the down time between busy days. The other part of it is, and Sam says it all the time, the rising tide floats all ships. Lewes and this community have supported Dogfish Head from the day Brewings & Eats first opened in 1995.

Being able to draw a bigger circle—not just trying to keep them here, but establishing Southern Delaware as a destination—is our goal. If they're craft beer visitors who stay at the Inn but want to tour other local breweries, we'll point them in the direction of people that we've done collaborations with, like Dewey Beer Company and Burley Oak down in Berlin, or Revelation in Rehoboth.

On the Fourth of July there was a ride from the Inn celebrating independent craft beer and the independent craft beer seal. We had just completed a collaboration with Revelation Craft Brewing in South Rehoboth, so Sam, Mariah, and about 40 people rolled out of here on bikes and headed to Revelation. From there, everybody headed to Brewings & Eats, and then eventually they made their way back to the Inn. It was a pretty cool event on the Fourth of July, all about supporting other local folks, promoting craft beer, and celebrating independence.

Local

By 1997 our first brewery in Lewes had opened its doors, and just down the street from us was a liquor store called R&L Liquors. It is ranked one of the best liquor stores in the state of Delaware, and Tom in there is just a huge Dogfish fan. The team at R&L remembers Sam walking in there with a case of beer many years ago and asking them if they would sell his beer, and so they became one of the first liquor stores to sell our beer back in the day. Not having beer for sale at the Inn is a nod to R&L and their support all those years ago as well. We want people to go to the liquor store here and meet Tom.

With the restaurants in town, same story. They've supported us ever since we opened. Matt DiSabatino is the owner of the restaurant Striper Bites, which is located in the backyard right next to us. In the backyard, literally. Matt and Sam are great friends and share their love of our town. We are working on a fireside food delivery program with them. When people come in for early check-in, and we don't have the rooms ready yet, we'll send them over to Striper Bites. Big Fish Restaurant Group, also good friends of ours, now runs Striper Bites and the program continues with them. There are just so many amazing food options in town. These are just a few places that Sam, Mariah, and all of us love, and we want people to experience the community that has supported us all along.

The cottage

To the left of the main building, there is a cottage. This space is a comfortable spot for guests to hang out. There are a lot of different spaces in here: a big farm table, which acts as a sort of dining area. Across the room we have a couch and seating area around a fireplace and a turntable with a vinyl collection. Guests will come in in the morning, hang out, drink coffee. Sometimes they'll head into town, grab some food, bring it back here and

Welcome to L
Mother Nature let 's

have breakfast. We have an Innactivity drawer packed full of games for guests to play. We have everything from Cards Against Humanity to Scrabble. We have also ended up in here with many impromptu beer tastings initiated by guests. The space brings people together.

"Whoso would be a man must be a nonconformist. He who would gather immortal palms must not be hindered by the name of goodness, but must explore if it be goodness. Nothing is atlast sacred but the integrity of your own mind."
- Ralph Waldo Emerson

The Emerson quote that is emblazed on the walls at all our properties is on the inside of the key box behind the front desk at the Inn. We put it there so guests and our coworkers can see it every time it is opened. It is a reminder of what guides us.

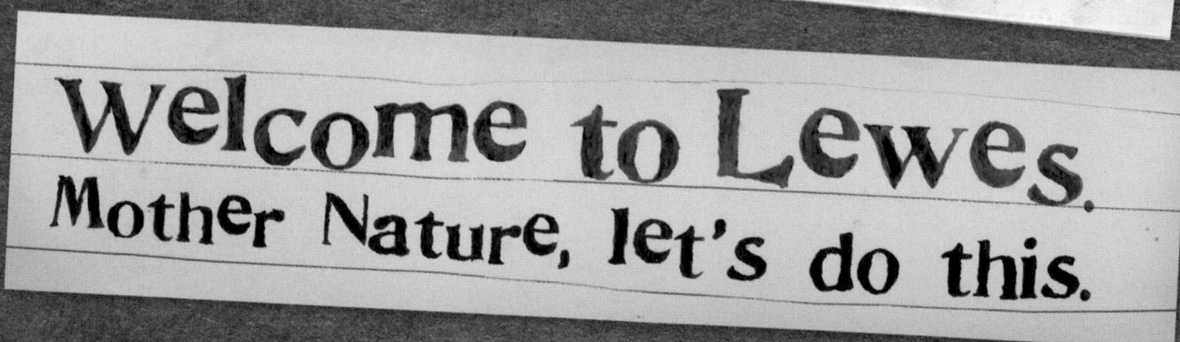
Welcome to Lewes.
Mother Nature, let's do this.

Above the fireplace is a saying that's kind of our shout-out to how we want people to experience their time with us. It is like a rally cry to get our guests out exploring the natural wonders of Coastal Delaware. "Welcome to Lewes. Mother Nature, let's do this." Sam and his son, Sammy Jr., painted it before we opened. I remember sitting in here and watching them paint it. The rhyme is also a hint at how to pronounce Lewes because it's not how it looks. There's a uniquely different way to pronounce it.

The City Lights Library

In the cottage there is the City Lights Library. Just before we opened, Sam traveled to San Francisco. Being a book lover, he took a trip to the famous City Lights Bookstore and the Vesuvio Café. The Vesuvio Café is where famous authors like Allen Ginsberg, Jack Kerouac, and Neal Cassady would write, hang out, drink some beers, read their poetry, and stick it to the man, and shout that "Fuck the Status Quo" all over the place. Sam had just bought the

"You don't have anything—
if you don't have the stories."
—Leslie Marmon Silko, *Ceremony*

Vesuvio Motel, so seeing the Vesuvio Café, he felt there was no way this was simply a coincidence. While in City Lights, Sam explained to the staff that we were opening an Inn, and they agreed to work with us to curate a library of the 50 quintessential American novels for our cottage.

Lawrence Ferlinghetti, who started City Lights back in 1953, participated in the curation. He was a poet, painter, and activist, but he also attended Northfield Mount Hermon, Sam and Mariah's alma mater. Ferlinghetti originally published Allen Ginsberg's, *Howl*. There's not necessarily a lot of really light beach reads. We've got some heavier books in here, like Bukowski's *Tale of Ordinary Madness*. We have *Infinite Jest*, which we challenge folks to read in one day, Walt Whitman's *Leaves of Grass*, the *Autobiography of Malcom X*, Sam's favorite, *Moby-Dick*, and a bunch more guests can borrow. If you open them up, inside it's just like a classic library book. We don't have the Dewey Decimal System; it's only 50 books, but each has a little checkout card, and guests take these, go back to their room, and read them, or take them down to the beach, or sit on the patio and read them around the fire—and then they can return them. Guests can also buy them. Our best sellers are *Catcher in the Rye* and *Moby-Dick*.

There's a chapter in *Moby-Dick* about chowder, and that's where Sam got the idea to make the chowder we used to sell in Bunyan's Lunchbox and at retail. It was a hardtack chowder made with heavy cream and some Palo Santo beer in it. (*Moby-Dick* has more of a legacy than the chowder, and we are okay with that.)

In the Cottage are two huge metal boards, and on the boards we point people in the right direction and give them options on how to explore Costal Delaware. We also have lists of all the tours and events that guests can book. The different tours include the Brewery tour, Quick Sip, Grain to Glass, Randall Jr., Distillery tour, and the Brew Pub. We also have a schedule of what is happening at the restaurants, the hours, the live music at the pub, and our Delmarva Spotlight where we have local artists playing at Chesapeake & Maine and Brewings & Eats.

One of the benefits of staying at the Inn is that we are able to book tables at our other properties. While Brewings & Eats and Chesapeake & Maine don't take reservations, we can add guests to the waiting list, so they can stay on the Inn property and we can let them know when their table is ready. Another part of being a guest of the Dogfish Inn is that your key fob will get you a cocktail flight or a beer flight and an appetizer for half price.

Record section

In the cottage we have a vinyl record player and we now have a pretty good record collection. Originally, we received 25 albums that were donated to us from our buddy, Steve Fallon, who runs the local independent record store, Gidget's Gadgets Retro Emporium in Rehoboth. He owns two record shops and used to operate a lot of cool clubs, including the famous Maxwell's in Hoboken. He gave us our first 25 vinyl records to get us started.

Since that time our collection has more than doubled. We have guests who come back and bring us albums to add to our library. One guest brought us a rare Blondie album to add to our collection. Cara has also raided her parents' collection to add some rare finds to the collection. There are no TVs in the cottage, and that was on purpose.

There is an outside fire pit and inside fireplace at the Inn that are popular gathering spaces for guests. The fire pit is what is referred to as a cowboy cauldron, and with this fire pit, the bowl itself weighs over 50 pounds. It takes two people to lift it up due to its size. We have a fire almost every night. This is where the fireside chats happen with Sam. We've had fireside chats as big as 120 people out here, so we've packed this space for sure.

When we light the fire in the evenings people gather around it on the circle of benches, with beers they brought from home or picked up at the brewery or pub, and share their stories about what they did that day. We have seen some real friendships kindled around this fire, which is why we wanted to have it in our yard. The purpose is to connect guests with not only Dogfish Head but also with each other as well. The community grows more and more every year.

On Saturdays when Sam is available he'll come sit for an hour and do fireside chats with guests. Everyone brings beer since we don't serve it at the Inn. We do promote the consumption of it, and fireside is one of the best spots to have a pint or two with Sam after a long day exploring Delaware.

Many home brewers will bring their creations with them to the Inn and give them to us. They end up in our fridge and we share them at team meetings.

Some nights we have impromptu concerts. Anything goes. But the best thing about this is it's a place to end your day. People go out on their adventures all day long. Some of them are just doing the brewery circuit. Others spend the day down by the water. Some of them are going fishing. People are doing tons of different activities. At the end of the day they all come back here and share their adventures with one another.

We have a huge farm table out in the yard by the fire pit. The middle of that table opens up, and we can fill it with ice and beer. In the back corner we have raised garden beds where we grow tomatoes, jalapenos, cucumbers that we use in our infused waters, basil, and whatever else we want to plant for the summer. Cara runs point on it and adds to it every year.

We have guests who come here so frequently they have bought places in Lewes, and they still come and hang out at the fire pit, but now as honorary guests. We have guests who make friends with other guests around the fire pit and they end up leaving together and linking up with each other in Philly or DC. They come back and plan vacations with each other. It is pretty amazing to watch the connections people make around the fire. Where did they meet? Dogfish Inn.

"Keep a little fire burning; however small, however hidden."
—Cormac McCarthy, *The Road*

The rooms

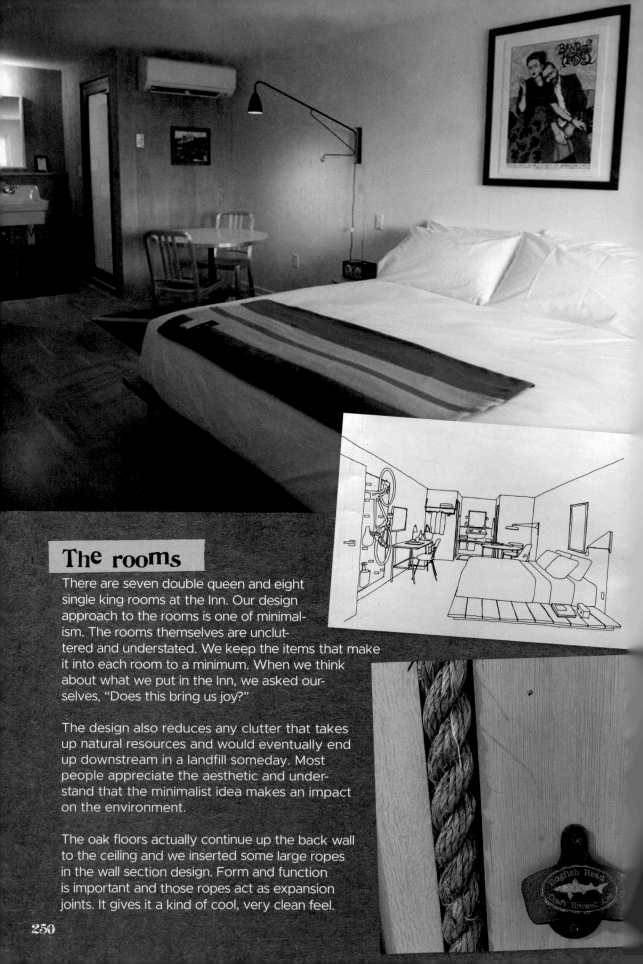

There are seven double queen and eight single king rooms at the Inn. Our design approach to the rooms is one of minimalism. The rooms themselves are uncluttered and understated. We keep the items that make it into each room to a minimum. When we think about what we put in the Inn, we asked ourselves, "Does this bring us joy?"

The design also reduces any clutter that takes up natural resources and would eventually end up downstream in a landfill someday. Most people appreciate the aesthetic and understand that the minimalist idea makes an impact on the environment.

The oak floors actually continue up the back wall to the ceiling and we inserted some large ropes in the wall section design. Form and function is important and those ropes act as expansion joints. It gives it a kind of cool, very clean feel.

The furnishings

Studio Tack, now known as the Post Company, curated the elements in each room. There is a digital handbook that provides background on everything in the rooms, from the barstools sitting by the windows, to the table, the chairs, and the bed platforms. The desks are handmade in Lancaster, Pennsylvania. The minimalist clothes rack was made by FORT, a Los Angeles–based company that leverages reclaimed materials to create beautiful pieces of custom furniture. People are constantly ordering the same furnishings for their homes, as they first experienced here at the Inn.

Initially, Sam thought it would be more aligned with a rustic, coastal getaway to not have TVs in the rooms. Mariah stepped in and pointed out what life might be like for a family here on a rainy summer day and that TVs might be a good idea. It was a good call on her part. However, come summer time, we don't have rooms full of people watching their TVs. By the time midday hits at the Inn it is quiet around here, which is how we wanted it to be. Guests are out on their adventures. They're up at the brewery on a tour. They're down on the beach hanging out. They're doing what they want to do, and we are not necessarily the venue. We're where they come to recharge after their exploration.

The art

Each room has a hand-painted rendition of the *Lightship Overfalls*. Lightships were originally used by the United States Lighthouse Service as floating lighthouses in the early 1900s. The *Lightship Overfalls*, located next to the Lewes Ferry terminal, is one of maybe 17 lightships left in this country. Many of them are gone, but the Lightship Overfalls remains and is distinctive to Lewes. It's a beautiful, floating piece of history and floating museum. A local artist named Steve Rogers hand-painted 16 different versions of the *Lightship Overfalls*. Hanging in each room is a unique original painting of the *Overfalls*, adding a little piece of Lewes flair to the space. We do love our home town.

The *Overfalls* prints also have custom frames done by One Man Gathers Studio, run by New Jersey organic gardener, chicken raiser, composter, rainwater collector, and food preserver Matt Myers. He specializes in giving old wood a second chance. Myers began working with Dogfish in 2013, providing 200 frames for Dogfish Head's eclectic art collection glued to the ceiling of its Milton tasting room. Myers framed Steve Rogers' *Lightship Overfalls* paintings with wood he salvaged from an 1840s barn in Warren County, NJ.

In addition to the Steve Rogers paintings we also have curated, signed, and numbered concert poster prints from all the artists we have worked with on our beer labels over the years. These artists include Tara McPherson, David Plunkert, Marc Spusta, Jim Mazza, and Jermaine Rogers. In one room you may find a Primus poster; in another you may find a David Bowie poster. We have actually had guests request rooms based on the art in the room. "Is the David Bowie room open? I liked that room!" We can make that happen for you....

There are beach chairs in each room. You go to hotels, you get a nice robe but you don't know who's worn it. We skipped the robe and went with beach chairs by Lawn Chair USA. Lawn Chair USA created a custom webbing and arm color combination of their classic, low-back beach chair for us at the Inn. We also have some Apolis Market Bags in the rooms for guest use, also for sale in the cottage. We partnered with Apolis on their iconic Market Bags for a special edition that has the functionality and ease to carry some beers and a blanket down to the beach.

There are Woolrich blankets in each room. We initially partnered with Woolrich to make our Pennsylvania Tuxedo beer, and when we opened the Inn, they designed these co-branded blankets for us. Each room includes a blanket that guests can use during their stay. People often bring them down to the outdoor fire pit or take the blankets down to the beach. It's just a great, all-around blanket. Woolrich was a family-owned company from the pre-Civil War era with much about their brand that kind of lined up with us. We had a strong partnership with them.

The Growlers

In every room there is a 32-ounce growler that guests can use to bring beer back to the Inn. The growler allows them to carry even small-batch beers that are only available on tap at the brew pub or brewery that might not be available in bottles or cans. People often come back with growlers containing different small-batch beers that they've bought. They'll sit around the property, share different beers, and talk about their adventures, which is exactly what we want to have happen here.

The bathroom

Everything has a story.... There is handmade, handcut Dogfish Head beer soap in each room. The soap is made from the hops and barley used in our 60 Minute IPA.

We have the Malin+Goetz toiletries, and this stuff is legit. In the bathrooms we have art from the same crew that did the concert posters in the bedrooms, but in here it is the actual beer labels they created for us. In one room you may find a Mazza concert poster on the wall and a Jermaine Rogers beer label print in the bathroom. Even the toilet paper has a story. We work with toilet paper company Who Gives a Crap, which launched out of Australia in 2012. Regular toilet paper is made from trees, so it's devastating to forests. Cara discovered a company that manufactures toilet paper from bamboo: it's super-soft, but also sustainably harvested. Fifty percent of all their profits go to helping build toilets in third-world countries, so you can feel good about using this paper when you flush. The TP is without a doubt as close as we will get to our guests—and it turns out we do give a crap!

In each room, there's a wall-mounted Dogfish Head bottle opener. About a week before we opened, Sam and I went through every room and picked the best spots for those openers, which are often near the showers. You can wake up, grab a cold beer, jump in the shower.

Respect our mother

In every room there is a sign that states, "Respect our Mother," to remind guests that we like to keep it as green as we possibly can. Many hotels have adopted this program. We'll make your bed every day, take care of you every day, but if you want your linens clean, we'll do it every three days, and that just helps cut back on water usage.

Hotels and restaurants produce tons of garbage, but we try to cut back on as much garbage as we can. The Inn has a basic recycling program. While we do recycle, we need to reduce first, and we need to reuse second, and then we can recycle, because recycle still heads downstream. It is no accident that "Reduce, Reuse, and Recycle" are listed in that order. We hear you loud and clear here at the Inn. The more we can divert from heading downstream, the better off we are. The toilet paper's a good example of us making a simple choice to reduce our footprint, and the tissues come from the same company. We give each guest a bar of soap, but nobody uses it up in two days so we have a bag in the room in case guests want take it home with them. Tons of toilet paper gets left here and we don't use every roll to the very end. We want people

to have a fresh roll, but we're not going to throw that roll away. We will stockpile in the back some with our ripped-up linens, some of our sheets that might have some stains on them, and old lost-and-found items. We take it to Casa San Francisco Center, which is a nonprofit based in Milton, Delaware. Everything that the Inn doesn't use gets donated to them. Guests will leave stuff behind like sweaters, sweat-shirts, flip-flops. We reach out to guests whenever we find anything, but if they say, "Keep it. I don't want it. I bought the flip-flops while I was down there," then it'll go to Casa San Francisco and find a whole new life with someone else. If we can't reuse it, we will find someone who can. Sure, it does make some work for us, but it is worth it when we understand why we are doing it.

In the showers we use Speakman shower heads. Speakman is a Delaware company, and the shower heads we have are high-pressure, low-flow. Speakman has designed these high-pressure showerheads that cut water usage 40 percent.

The map

In each room there's a functional map. The quote from the Cottage fireplace is also included on the back of the map: "Welcome to Lewes. Mother Nature, let's do this!" Cara Digby also hand painted a watercolor of the map and it hangs in the cottage. On it you can see a bike loop that helps people orient themselves before they ride to the pub or the state park. She also created a more detailed map of downtown Lewes on the information boards out of electrical tape. It's a functioning map, and the idea is it's an adventure map, providing various bike paths that you can take. Primehook National Wildlife Refuge is on here, Cape Henlopen State Park, and the McCabe Nature Preserve, which is where coworkers have volunteered time, helping build trails and cleaning up. McCabe Preserve is about four minutes from the brewery.

The bikes

The Inn provides bikes for guest use. For these we did a collaboration with our buds at Priority Bikes out of Brooklyn, NY, founded by Dave Weiner who started the company in 2014 with crowdfunding. We carry their Coast beach cruiser, which has a super light aluminum frame and belt drive system, and holds up to salt, sand, and water like no other beach cruiser you will find. Guests can ride a 15-mile loop between the Inn, Cape Henlopen State Park, and our two restaurants in Rehoboth. All of the bike fix stations on the loop were supplied by Beer and Benevolence and Dogfish Head. Mark Carter, our coworker, helped get them installed and maintains them. This means that if you need air in your tire and you hit up a station in the state park, we not only put you back on your bike, but we also stash a pump out on the trail to make sure you don't get stranded.

One of the businesses we work closely with is Quest Kayak, owned by Matt Carter, the younger brother of Mark Carter. Matt rents stand-up paddleboards and kayaks. He does a dolphin kayak tour. He offers a history paddle. There's a kayak tour where they go up Delaware Bay to an old shipwreck that they go check out at low tide. Another service that he provides that we have utilized not just for our guests but also for our own internal brewery events are his beach parties. Matt will get all the fire permits if you want to have a fire down on the beach, and get you set up for a whole beach party—tables and chairs, umbrellas, paddleboards, and cornhole boards. You just walk down to the beach and it's ready to go, and it's great fun.

The comment cards

We talk about Analog Beer for the digital age. The guests' comment cards are analog. People leave reviews on Yelp and on TripAdvisor, and we have tons of reviews on both those sites. But if you look at our comment card box, we have hundreds and hundreds of different cards from people coming to the Inn. People are so much more apt to leave a handwritten note to us than they are to do an online review. So we love that people engage in that way. The comment cards are the exemplification of a job well done and confirmation that people really connect with what we do here. When guests leave those comment cards—we don't do it for everyone—but the odds of us replying to your comment card with a postcard saying thanks for coming to stay with us is pretty high. The ones that I love the most talk about all the different places they went, but the ones that really stand out to me are the ones that talk about the continuity between the restaurants, the brewery, and the Inn. These comment cards are speaking to how engaged the coworkers at Dogfish are—at the Inn, at Brewings & Eats, at Chesapeake & Maine, and up in Milton. The sense of community across all the locations is something that makes a huge impact on the people who visit, and that is core to who we are. We also often receive great ideas about ways to improve the Inn, and come wintertime we'll go through them and implement the ones we feel will make the experience of the Inn better. We're constantly trying to fine-tune and tweak things where we can.

I often reflect on what Mariah said to me that day in the office when they first offered me the Innkeeper job. "Together" is the key word in all we have done at the Inn. True to Sam and Mariah's form, together is how it has gone. Nick has moved on from Dogfish Head, but he helped teach me a great deal about running a business. Steve McLaine now oversees what I do at the Inn, and I learn more and more from him every day.

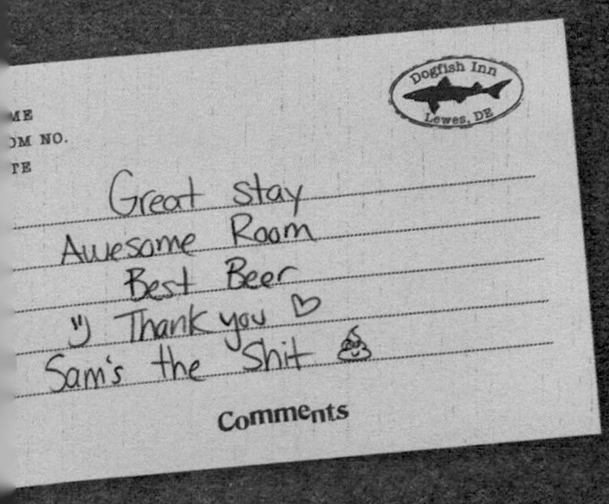

People often talk about the "culture" of Dogfish Head. It can't be pinned down in one statement. The Emerson quote is as close as we can get to it, but there are so many facets to who we are. The Inn is a representation of almost all of them … besides the fact that we don't offer beer here. We are about so much more than beer and you can really feel, understand, and experience that at the Inn: which was the vision all along. This is a culture of lifelong learners.

Pennsylvania Tuxedo

(8.5% ABV)

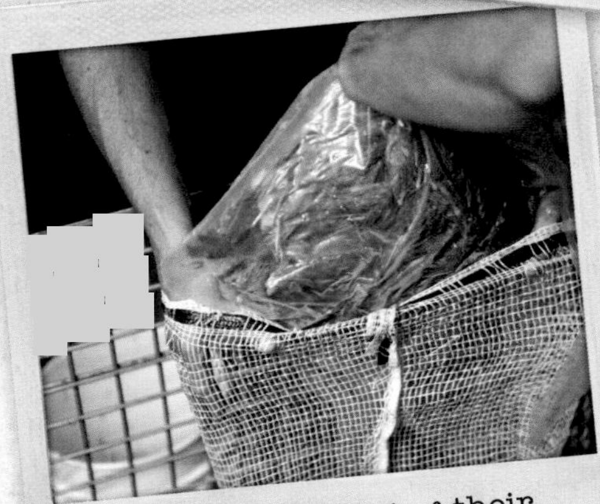

Spruce tips making their way to the brew

The same year we opened the Inn, we began a new beer collaboration. In 2014, we released a super-fun beer—and a wonderful collaboration—our Pennsylvania Tuxedo.

I often go to the website Alibris to search for books. The site specializes in obscure books, sometimes first editions that are rare and valuable, and sometimes random, rough, one-off books. On the site I'd found a journal from the patriarch of the Woolrich family. Based in Pennsylvania, Woolrich is the oldest outdoor clothing company in America. In fact, the Woolrich company manufactured blankets for soldiers during the Civil War. In the journal that I bought, the patriarch of the family talked about setting up his mill on a farm in North Central Pennsylvania. He chose the land because it had a fast-moving river next to it that he could use to power his wool mill. On top of this, it was great farming land, and on it he grew wheat and rye as crops. In his journal he told a story about raising a barn, and he had some friends over to help him build it. He made them all home brew that had spruce in it, and they all got drunk together. He even described nearly falling off the rafters of this barn while he was building it. Good to know they were getting after it and taking risks.

Reading that story really captivated my imagination. I googled the Woolrich company and found out the business was still owned and run by family members—seventh-and eighth-generation family members—Nick Brayton and Joshua Rich. I reached out to them and said, "Hey! I read about the founder of the company and how he grew and milled these grains, wheat and rye, and used spruce to brew beer. How about we work together and come up with a modern craft beer recipe celebrating the legacy of Woolrich? Let's co-design some outdoorsy clothing to go with it, because Dogfish Head as a brand is very outdoorsy and nautically oriented."

We kind of took the best of the outdoorsy-ness of Woolrich and the best of the seaside outdoorsy-ness of Dogfish and combined them in this collaborative project. One of the creations that came out of this collaboration is the wool blanket we provide for guests at the Inn. The name of the beer, Pennsylvania Tuxedo, refers to the wearing of the signature Woolrich check. Some readers may have heard of Canadian tuxedos (or some other region), which is when you wear a denim jacket and denim pants at the same time. A Pennsylvania tuxedo is when you see the hunters dressed head-to-toe in the black-and-red iconic Woolrich check. Through many decades of trial and error they designed that pattern with those colors intentionally, because when you're cleaning a kill, and you wipe the knife against yourself, the viscera and blood dries on your clothing but it fits in well with the red and black of the check and doesn't look dirty. Form and function is a must.

Pennsylvania Tuxedo is a rye and wheat-infused pale ale with spruce tips. Getting the spruce tips for the recipe was a true labor of love. The family members check the woods around the Woolrich wool facility in Northern PA, in the early spring, to see if the fresh spruce shoots are sprouting on the trees. They're very different from the hard needles of spruce that are on the tree year-round. The new shoots are almost like a salad green: soft, leafy shoots. Once these tips sprouted, the family would have their coworkers leave the mill for a day and go out and forage in the forest around Woolrich, Pennsylvania, filling giant bags with spruce tips that would then be shipped down to our brewery so we could make the beer. Instead of a fresh hop beer, we would do a fresh spruce tip beer, calling it Pennsylvania Tuxedo. We brewed that every year from 2014 through 2018. People really dug it, but we've put it on hiatus for now. Someday it may come back.

CLASSICS

SINCE 1830

WOOLRICH MEN'S

TROUT RUN

FLANNEL SHIRT

Men's Trout Run Flannel Shirt

C. Our Trout Run Flannel Shirt is a wardrobe staple that can chase the chills of an early spring morning without unnecessary bulk. Traditional button-down collar lined in comfortable cotton twill. Button-through patch pocket with pen slot. Lightweight 100% cotton 5 oz. flannel. Imported. S-XXL. Classic fit.

SCC6280 $55

WOOLRICH & DOGFISH HEAD — A UNIQUE PARTNERSHIP

In 2014, Woolrich and Dogfish Head Brewery initiated a working partnership that produced a limited-edition ale named "Pennsylvania Tuxedo," brewed with spruce tips collected from trees growing in Woolrich, PA, and a line of clothing and accessories incorporating the signature Dogfish Head logo and colors.

Josh Rich, Executive Vice President, Woolrich

Sam Calagione, Founder & President, Dogfish Head Brewery

B | green

Rosabi (7.6 ABV)

In 2014 we brewed another beautiful beer called Rosabi. We have a long history of collaborating on projects with musicians that we love. Some of them with well-known artists like Miles Davis or Pearl Jam were super fun, but the collaborations with indie bands and musicians have been equally rewarding and exciting.

I fell in love with the music of an electronica musician named Julianna Barwick who was born in the South but moved to New York City. Her first album, *The Magic Place,* was released in 2011, and I listened to it a bunch. I reached out to her through her record label and asked her if she'd consider collaborating on a project. This turned into a very extensive collaboration.

I met her in New York and asked her what her favorite flavors in a beer were, what her favorite ingredients in the culinary world were, and what were her favorite dishes to eat—with the plan to triangulate the flavors in her answers. She explained she liked bitter more than sweet, she loved sushi, and she loved spicy foods, so we designed a beer to Julianna's palate called Rosabi. It was like a rosé beer before rosé beers were cool, because this was 2014. We made it with wasabi and red rice because her absolute favorite dish is sushi. We wanted to make a beer that had sort of the wasabi kick to it, subtle but there, to pair perfectly with wonderful fresh sushi.

The other cool part of this collaboration was the music that was created. Julianna's music is known for having looping vocals along with a synthesizer that she plays. Her songs are lush and orchestral-sounding, but when she is recording tracks, it is usually just her in a room in a recording studio looping her voice to create layers and depth and then playing a synth. I thought it'd be fun if we recorded a bunch of sounds from our brewery and sent her the audio files and asked her to create original songs that incorporated recordings of the equipment at our facility making the Rosabi beer. The IT gurus here at Dogfish placed microphones on certain pieces of equipment. They mic'd up the grain mill as it crushed the grain, as well as the boiling kettle, the bubbling fermenters, and the bottling line. We recorded the sounds of the machines during our production and sent her those raw files. She took those sounds and created a four-song EP called *Rosabi EP*. It got a 7.6 score on Pitchfork and we lovingly hand-inserted these 10-inch EPs into every single case of Rosabi that we sent out. It was a super-fun project with Julianna Barwick. We've remained friends. We swap music for beer every year, and we're really proud of that collaboration.

In 2013 when we christened our beautiful new cathedral-like 200-barrel brewhouse in Milton, Delaware, we invited Julianna to coastal Delaware, where she helped brew a test batch of Rosabi with us. Even more, the night before we brewed together she actually put on a performance and did a private concert just for our coworkers.

Julianna Barwick
ROSABI EP
1 PURE 2 MEET YOU AT MIDNIGHT
© 2014 Julianna Barwick
THANKS
i would love to thank sam for the invitation and the honor of working together with him and his brewers to create rosabi, and to all of the people at dogfish for such a warm and friendly reception when i played there. it has been a true dream and a great learning experience the entire way through and i can't imagine a better, more excited group of people to work with to make it all happen. i'll never forget it! thank you all so much! – Julianna
Very kind sister Julianna, my Dogfish co-workers and I have enjoyed working with you on this project immensely. Thanks for the ongoing inspiration! – Sam

Beer Thousand (10% ABV)

Back when we were a 12-gallon brewery, I used to listen to the album *Bee Thousand* by Guided By Voices on a cassette player. I used to flip that cassette, so I would be listening to that one amazing album all day long. One of the highlights of my life was how this whole beer collaboration played out.

Robert Pollard and the rest of the band came down to spend time with us in Milton. I remember Robert walking up to our bottling line, the day we were bottling 750 mil bottles of Bitches Brew, our collaboration with Miles Davis. Robert walked up to the line, grabbed a bottle—which is super-dangerous, because the bottling line is moving really, really fast—pulled out an opener, and cracked it open. This is a 750 mil bottle, the size of a champagne bottle, and he started chugging this 10 percent alcohol, inky stout an hour and a half before he was going to be onstage. I was like "Wow. This is going to be quite a night." It was a pretty cool sort of baton-passing moment to think of one legendary innovator, Miles Davis, going down the throat of another legendary innovator, Robert Pollard. The Beer Thousand collaboration was designed to celebrate the 20th anniversary of the Guided By Voices classic album, *Bee Thousand*, so we brewed a bracingly hoppy, strong, 10 ABV beer called Beer Thousand instead of "Bee Thousand." It was an imperial lager that had 10 grains and 10 hops varieties and clocked in at 10 percent ABV, so 10 times 10 times 10 equals Beer Thousand.

The band played at the Milton Theatre, a 100-year-old theater right here in downtown Milton that had been semi-refurbished. The paint was in shitty shape throughout, and I remember it had only held plays and poetry readings, really mellow things, until Guided By Voices played there in 2014. They plugged in, started their set, and there were hundreds and hundreds of us

"There is nothing like puking with somebody to make you into old friends."
—Sylvia Plath, *The Bell Jar*

Guided By Voices at the Milton Theatre

in the room. I think it was the first time Guided By Voices ever played in Delaware, and as they went into their first song with a heavy bass and loud guitars and drums, the vibrations from the amplification of the equipment made all these little flecks of paint come off the ceiling. For the remainder of the hour-and-a-half performance it felt like you were in a room that was snowing, while Guided By Voices played and literally stripped the paint off the walls with their amazing punk rock. The Beer Thousand collaboration with them was an amazingly proud moment for us as lovers of indie rock in the indie craft beer community.

Beer for Breakfast (7.5% ABV)

Dogfish had brewed what we believed was the first distributed coffee stout in America made with crushed coffee, chicory, and licorice root called Chicory Stout, so Beer for Breakfast was sort of an "everything but the kitchen sink" version of a coffee stout. It was tricked out with all kinds of breakfast ingredients, including Guatemalan Antigua cold-pressed coffee, maple syrup harvested from my family's farm in Western Mass, and the quintessential Delaware breakfast touch, Rapa Scrapple, was sort of the secret ingredient in the beer. For those of you uninitiated, outside of the Mid-Atlantic area—which is sort of the scrapple belt of America—scrapple is all the stuff from a pig that doesn't make the test to get into hotdogs, so it's a pretty interesting breakfast meat. It comes in a gray-colored loaf you slice and fry in a cast-iron pan. We worked with a local company called Rapa Scrapple and had them make an extra-lean version of scrapple with the same herbs and blend of spices that they put in it so that we could brew with the scrapple. You can't use traditional bacon—not that most people would try to brew with bacon—but bacon or even traditional scrapple has a high content of animal fats and oils in it. When you brew with substances that are rich in oils and fats you don't get a good fermentation because the yeast that's trying to grow gets stuck to the microscopic globules of fat and oil. That slick oil also kills the head retention on a beer, so a beer can't have a nice foamy head if it's made with oily substances ... like bacon or scrapple. We put the scrapple in with our mash. We also added applewood-smoked barley, kiln coffee malt, flaked oats, roasted barley, caramel malt, molasses, milk sugars, brown sugar, and roasted chicory, which all laid the foundation for this breakfast-themed concoction. At 7.5% ABV, Beer for Breakfast was very popular. Who knows? Someday it may come back.

Dogfish Head's scrapple beer scores big

PATRICIA TALORICO
THE NEWS JOURNAL

Scrapple, the regional breakfast meat made with hog organs, isn't for everyone.

And depending on your taste preference, scrapple beer is either the greatest thing ever, or the grossest.

While haters are going to hate on a complex offal-infused stout that's as black as the Grinch's soul, the eager and the curious who packed Dogfish Head Brewing & Eats Friday, Dec. 5, to sample the world premiere of Beer for Breakfast knew what they were getting into.

The lure of scrapple beer was hard to resist and the limited, brewpub exclusive scored big.

So big, the six kegs, each made with four pounds of scrapple, were going much faster than anticipated. While it was on tap in Rehoboth on Monday, the beer wasn't expected to last long.

"People better get here fast," said Dogfish Head founder Sam Calagione, somewhat surprised by the popularity of the dark beer that has a "smoky meatiness."

"We didn't make enough of it."

Take that, scrapple haters.

Scrapple beer was so well-received at Friday's standing room only, two-hour happy hour, Rehoboth brewer Ben Potts and Calagione said it won't be a one-and-done novelty. They plan to make Beer for Breakfast again for the Rehoboth Avenue brewpub in January for tasting by early February. The beer also will be available at Boston's Extreme Beer Fest in March 2015.

As soon as the kegs of scrapple beer were tapped, a porky aroma filled the first-floor dining room. The odor might have been the draft beer, but it was more likely from the free scrapple pizzas, scrapple sliders and scrapple tacos coming from the kitchen to accompany the drink.

Dogfish Head fans, who tend to be devout, are well-acquainted with Calagione's passion for pushing the envelope and using what was once considered non-traditional ingredients, like coffee, apricots, licorice, and, yes, now scrapple, in the beers he has been making professionally for the past 20 years.

JASON MINTO/THE NEWS JOURNAL

Sam Calagione speaks at the Dogfish Head unveiling of its beer for breakfast on Dec. 5, made from Rapa Scrapple.

Enthusiasts came from as far away as Virginia and North Carolina to sip the breakfast-themed stout brewed with 25 pounds of locally made RAPA Scrapple. The beer's ABV (alcohol by volume) was high and clocked in at a tipsy-inducing 10 percent.

Tom Greenwood had only tasted scrapple once before, but the Lewes resident was enthusiastic about the beer.

"This is a wonderful product. I like the richness and the color. And I love the hint of saltiness," he said. "I'm not a vegetarian, so I was very intrigued by the concept of putting scrapple in beer. I wish they had it in a bottle."

Noah Baerveldt, formerly of Louisville, Kentucky, also was a fan. The Dogfish Head bartender, who moved to Delaware eight years ago, said the stout was "ama[illegible] what really strikes me. You really get that creamy, thick body texture."

While he said the coffee in the stout was "really nice," it was harder to distinguish the flavor of scrapple. "There's hints of it in the finish," Baerveldt said.

Delaware is the Scrapple Capital of the World. RAPA Scrapple, based in Bridgeville since 1926, is its largest producer. It also makes Habbersett and Greensboro scrapple brands.

RAPA Original Scrapple is made with pork stock, snouts, hearts, flour, cornmeal and spices. But its strongest components are pig's liver and sage, said RAPA general manager Donna Seefried. Drive through the tiny Sussex County town most weekdays beginning around 4 a.m. and take a deep whiff. That distinctive aroma means the factory has started [illegible]ple in its [illegible] [illegible]rapple just for Dogfish Head that was a leaner version of its original recipe.

I wasn't sure what to expect from the first sip, but I couldn't detect any liver flavor and would not have guessed Beer for Breakfast was made with scrapple. There was no oily residue from the meat in the glass. Past experience with other Dogfish Head beers made with fatty ingredients, such as pine nuts and olives, has taught the DFH brewers how to avoid any unpalatable oiliness.

Potts, who grew up in Pennsyvlania, never tasted scrapple before he began brewing with it. He said the Dogfish Head staff tested several cooking techniques to get the best flavor and texture.

"We boiled some scrapple, we broiled scrapple, we baked scrapple. In the end, we went with baking scrapple and then we added it in the mash. It turned out well," Potts said, admiring the beer's rich, creamy head.

"The scrapple really comes through as an umami earthy roastiness towards the end of the taste," Calagione said.

RAPA's Seefried said, after tasting the beer, she also picked up nuanced scrapple flavors.

The beer has a pitch black hue, and, to me, the overwhelming aroma and taste, in an appealing and earnest, get-out-of-bed-now! command, was coffee. The dark roast is made by the [illegible]S Bean Factory in St. Paul, Minnesota.

Would I sip scrapple beer again? Yes. It was hearty, heavy and drinkable with hints of smoke – the barley was smoked over applewood that came from Fifer Orchards in Wyoming – and a touch of sweetness – it has Massachusetts maple syrup as well as lactose, or milk sugar.

It would go well with savory dishes, especially, and most obviously, eggs. Still, the liquid version of scrapple is an acquired taste, and it is perhaps best consumed and savored, during cold weather months, in smaller snifters rather than a full pint glass.

Calagione didn't grow up eating scrapple in his Massachusetts hometown, but he was introduced to it by his wife Mariah, a Delaware native. He's now a scrapple enthusiast.

WEDNESDAY [illegible]

DELMARVANOW.COM | 39

FOR IMMEDIATE RELEASE
Contact: Justin Williams
justin@dogfish.com
(302) 684-1000, ext. 267

Dogfish Head Craft Brewed Ales

Dogfish Head's Beer for Breakfast brewed with 25 pounds of scrapple

Draft-only breakfast stout to debut at special Dec. 5 Happy Hour

Back in 1994, when Sam Calagione was working on a business plan for a nontraditional brewery, one of the homebrew recipes he tested was a breakfast-themed stout. A few months later, Chicory Stout — brewed with organic Mexican coffee, licorice root and chicory — helped launch Dogfish on our off-centered path.

Now, 20 years later, the itch for a breakfast beer is there again, and we're going big.

We added 25 pounds of Delaware's own Rapa Scrapple to Beer for Breakfast.

Dogfish Head Beer for Breakfast

RAPA ★★Scrapple★★ Our Original

"It's been wonderful to see dozens of breakfast-themed beers come to market since we first did ours," says Sam. "I thought it would be a great time to flex our creative muscles and try to brew a beer that has the most diverse group of ingredients referencing the meal and its name. It's sort of an 'everything-but-the-breakfast-nook' stout."

The nods to breakfast run deep:

- Maple syrup harvested from the trees at Northfield Mount Hermon, the high school in western Massachusetts where Sam met his wife, Mariah.
- Barley smoked over applewood from Delaware's Fifer Orchards, for that applewood, bacon-y aroma.
- Lactose, or milk sugar.
- For the quintessential Delaware touch, 25 pounds of a super-lean version of Rapa Scrapple's famous recipe. Rapa, the world's largest producer of scrapple, was started by brothers Ralph and Paul Adams in Bridgeville, Del., just down the road from Dogfish.
- Last but not least, a special blend from The Bean Factory in St. Paul, Minn. The coffee, added cold press post-fermentation, is a nod to one of Sam's all-time favorite bands,

Dogfish Head
BEER FOR
BREAKFAST
STOUT
12 fl. oz.
7.4% Alc. by Vol.

Connie Park

Big Fish Admin
Start Date: 2009

People come to our sites in Delaware every day of the year with the hope of catching a glimpse of Sam and maybe, just maybe, getting an autographed picture. Imagine if you could work directly, one-on-one, with Sam, Mariah, and all the other top leaders at Dogfish Head. Sounds sweet, right? It is. And for Connie Park, this is a reality. Connie holds the title of Big Fish Admin, but that is not to say it has been boring by any stretch of the imagination. Her role and title is one that, very much like Dogfish Head, is constantly evolving. Basically, whatever anybody needs, Connie will take care of it. She is really the glue holding the executive squad together. Sometimes she just deals with the needs of Sam, but one thing is for sure: one day at Dogfish Head is never the same as the next.

Not a fanboy when she originally applied in the fall of 2008, Connie needed a job after her high school sweetheart and now husband Dave landed a position in Salisbury, MD. Connie was working at an investment firm at the time. She saw a job description for Brewceptionist and had never heard of this "Dogfish Head." Dave urged her to apply, so she did. When Connie showed up for the interview, the place was gross compared to the corporate world she had been in, but the first thing that went through her mind was, "This place is cool." She was feeling the vibe.

Connie on the far right with the Dogfish Head GABF team

The interview went well, but she didn't get the job. Big Mama beat her out! You can read that story in Big Mama's profile. Like most folks after their first brush with the Dogfish world, she wasn't going to take no for an answer, so she started to stalk Cindy in HR and applied for every position that was posted. Cindy called Connie in the spring of 2009 and had a job for her. Executive assistant. Connie locked it up, and the 10-year evolution of the position began.

What is the "glue" that makes it not only work at Dogfish, but also allows Connie to support Sam and Mariah on such a profound level? What is the absolute best part about working side-by-side with Sam and Mariah? The trust. "There is give and take, a trust that has been built over time. I know that they know that they can depend on me and trust me, and they value that. I am not in the business of recognition." Trust is far more valuable to her. Sam and Mariah both know they can trust that Connie will always be there no matter what. She is key in holding it all together.

Working from a place of authenticity, Connie never seeks credit for all she has done. The engagement in the work, the relationships, and the trust are more than enough to sustain her. This example sets her apart, and, in turn, helps set Dogfish Head and its culture apart as well. It begins with the people.

Trust is easy when everything is running smoothly. When difficulty, friction, and conflict come about, that is when trust is tested. Hard days unite us. The hardest day for her was the Boston Beer merger announcement. Due to the nature of the situation, very few people knew about it and Connie was in the inner circle. This was bigger than just business, though. It was about people, and Connie knows better than anyone what Dogfish Head and all its people mean to Sam and Mariah. The logistics

Coworker Profile

of this day alone were challenging, but there was no way to know how the community would react. Knowing how much Sam and Mariah love the people of Dogfish Head, and being one of the few that knew, Connie remembers the weight of that day. Communication had to be spot-on. Having Connie in the mix ensured that happened.

If you have attended Analog-A-Go-Go, WOCAAW, or the Dogfish Dash, it is more than likely Connie was either checking you in at the entry tent or giving you your runner's packet for the Dash. These are the days when she is reminded that life at Dogfish Head is truly special. "Our job is so full of entire days where what we do would never happen anywhere else," she observes. This past year, she was in the Lewes Christmas Parade with her husband Dave. After the parade, they landed at Dogfish Inn. The fire pit was surrounded by coworkers, guests at the Inn, and friends from town all mingled together. Everyone laughing, celebrating, and genuinely enjoying each other's company. Connie loves to find that moment of pause and be present in these situations. In these moments, she can see and feel the "why" behind all we do.

This may come as a shock, but Sam can be impulsive at times. On any given day, Connie may find herself ordering anything from fake blood, to kilts, wigs, fake mustaches, an entire food truck shaped like a lunch box, eclectic artwork (you can see much of it hanging at Chesapeake and Maine today), antique dive suit and helmet, and on and on. This doesn't include ANY of the beer ingredients she has ordered over the years. When she reflects on working with Sam, she says, "I never have an end-of-year review . . . because I have my end-of-year review all year long."

One of Connie's fondest memories from her time at Dogfish is getting to attend GABF. "Everybody here works just as hard as the person next to them. Choosing who gets to go to this event is impossible. I feel like we all work our asses off here, but we can't send everybody." Connie, being who she is, never felt like she should go. Instead, she spent her time organizing trips for the people who were lucky enough to go. This particular GABF event was attended by other longstanding coworkers who poured their heart and soul into what they do at Dogfish Head. It was on this trip that she came to find her fondest beer of ours: Liquid Truth Serum. Fitting for Connie to love this beer with how much trust is put into her.

If you were on a deserted island and could have one album to listen to and an unlimited supply of one beer, what would it be?

Beer: Slightly Mighty
Album: The Eagles, *Their Greatest Hits*

Change is the one thing we can really rely on in the world of Dogfish Head, and it comes fast and furious some days. We can't innovate if we can't be agile. When you look at the leaders at Dogfish Head—from Sam to Mariah to other leaders—there must be something holding it all together. It's Connie. Connie is the glue person, and the glue person takes a good team and makes them great. Reflecting on her time working with Sam, Connie notes "There are those days when it feels like everything is going wrong, and then sure enough, something else goes wrong. The perfect storm kind of days. It is on those days that I look at Sam and he really is the calm in the storm. He sees us through it." Connie is that calm in the storm for all of us, helping to see us through whatever may come next.

Chapter 8

Enjoy the Journey

In 2015, just before I turned 46, my grandmother Jessie passed away at the glorious age of 96. She had run a small business with her husband, Sam, and had been a great inspiration to me. As I thought about her life, I figured if my grandmother lived to the age of 96, then it was certainly reasonable to assume I could live to be, say, 92—if I started taking better care of myself, stopped stressing out so much, and stopped trying to do so many things so quickly.

So I decided to treat my 46th birthday as my definitive midlife moment—the unofficial halfway mark of my journey along this mortal coil—and celebrate this existential milestone memorably with gusto. I traded in my sensible used Volvo sedan for my 500-horsepower Super Bee. This wasn't just any muscle car. It was the newer iteration of my boyhood dream car that I have thought about since the late 1970s when I was a six-year-old doodling the earlier model upon my grade school textbooks.

Sitting in the driver's seat of my new used muscle car, paintbrush in hand, the sound of the throaty engine music to my ears, I began painting the words "Go Slowly, Go Thoughtfully" in bright red acrylic paint on the center of my steering wheel.

I bought the car on my 46th birthday and within just two months had to bring it in for service twice. The mechanic explained that the car's "bigass engine" (mechanic's term originally, now mine as well) needed more time to warm up than normal, much smaller engines do; I couldn't just jam the car into drive and peel out.

Hence, the "go slowly" reminder. And the "go thoughtfully" part is to remind me not to check my phone for any reason while driving. To focus on the present, the task at hand, and to enjoy the journey.

My 500-Horsepower Super Bee

"Go slowly, go thoughtfully."

This reminder, to go slowly and go thoughtfully, emblazoned on that steering wheel, had also become the mantra for the thoroughly enjoyable, illuminating, and challenging personal and vocational midlife crossroads I found myself navigating at the time. Like that engine, I was beginning to warm up to the notion that I can't move as quickly or take as many risks with myself or my company as we did a couple of decades ago when we were both much younger.

Celebrating the Epiphany

Within a few weeks of my 46th birthday, Dogfish Head celebrated a milestone as well: our 20th anniversary as the first brewpub in the first state. I figured if I were going to treat 46 as a halfway point in my personal life, it would also make sense (at least to me) to treat the 20th anniversary of the company I founded as the halfway mark of my role within this company. Thus, I reasoned, Dogfish Head would be the only company I would ever work for. Why? Because I love what I do and I love the people I have gotten to know as coworkers and beer lovers throughout the two decades of my entrepreneurial journey. But I also realized that to be the most beneficial to the company, my role at Dogfish Head over the next 20 years needed to be different than the type of work I did during the first 20 years. In a word, I needed to evolve. The work priorities and habits I had relied on in those first 20 years could not sustainably remain the same for the next 20.

To commemorate, capture, and internalize this epiphany, I decided I would get a tattoo....

Joining the Fans

Like the famous line spoken by Blanche DuBois in the play *A Streetcar Named Desire*, I have always depended on the kindness of strangers. At the heart of Dogfish Head's exploration of goodness is our off-centered version of the golden rule—always aspire to do for others as you would want others to do for you. With the help of hundreds of amazing, talented coworkers past and present, and the support of many tens of thousands of fans, we have succeeded in building a company focused on producing the types of beers, spirits, food, events, and spaces that we envisioned other creative, adventurous, rebellious people would want to experience, engage with, and rally around.

And rally they have. Dogfish started out as the smallest brewing operation in America and is now the 13th-largest craft brewery out of over 4,000. Throughout the years I have met, personally thanked, and high-fived tens of thousands of hardcore Dogfish fans who have acted as our evangelists, introducing their friends to our beers, and helping us grow. Some of these evangelists are so passionate about Dogfish Head that they literally bled for us, tattooing various regions of their bodies with our brand to make it part of their permanent selves.

When people would show me their tats or ask to take photos with me as they flashed their tattoos to the camera, I felt both pride and gratitude. Over time, though, as I met more and more of these bold and inked Dogfish evangelists, a third emotion would creep in—guilt. If these people cared enough about what Dogfish Head stood for to literally brand themselves, the least I could do was to join them in solidarity. After all, I first sketched the Dogfish shark-and-broken-shield logo nearly 22 years ago when writing my business plan, and I had been thinking about it and obsessing about its place in the world pretty much every day since.

So, in 2015, I was a 46-year-old entrepreneur with a new tattoo and a used muscle car who sometimes peeled out at stop signs but didn't break speed limits as often as he used to when he drove the more sensible Volvo. To her immense credit, my erratic driving habits embarrassed my wife, Mariah, more than the muscle car or the tattoo. I had also taken to wearing a mullet wig on the rare occasions she'd accompany me in that car, under the pretense that I thought she might be less mortified if pedestrians and other drivers in our small town didn't recognize the crazy driver she was riding with was her husband. It goes without saying that Mariah's sense of humor and patience with my shenanigans, starting when we began dating in high school in the mid-eighties, remains unflappable.

Admittedly my tat is less ornate and bold than some others I've admired, but it's pretty much identical to the sketch I first drew 22 years ago. "But it's facing the wrong way," I can almost hear you saying, if you are familiar with our logo. Nope. The image of my tattoo did not get reversed in the design phase of this book. I purposely decided to have the shark in the shield face outward on my forearm instead of inward, as it would were it a faithful representation of our company logo.

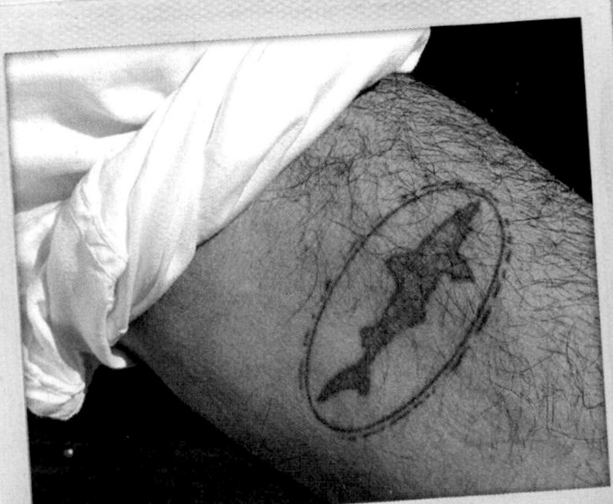

Sam's tattoo

Off-centered

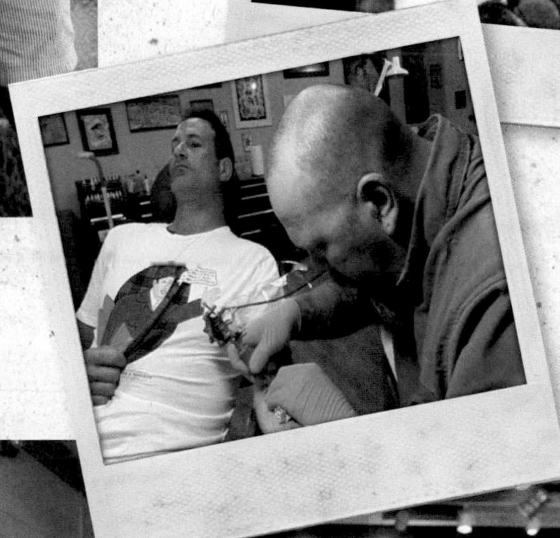

Dogfish Head
Craft Brewed Ales

Proceed slowly, go thoughtfully

So ... this is how getting a tattoo, the second notable moment in my most-excellent-midlife-crossroads, tied so directly to the first notable moment of buying that used muscle car. To use a vehicular analogy, when Dogfish first opened, we were sorta like a 50cc dirt bike—simple, nimble, thrilling, and powered by a very small engine. Instead of horsepower, if you look at our payroll the year we opened, we originally ran on about 20 manpower. We could bet the farm at every turn and make split-second spontaneous decisions and whimsical choices. We all could keep aware and in tune with each change of direction because all of us experienced these zigs and zags together in the same single building, the brewpub in Rehoboth Beach, where we brewed and sold our beers and cooked and sold our food.

Dogfish Head started out as the physical embodiment of my imagination. The small team in charge of the brand in our earliest days could act this way at Dogfish when it was tiny because its potential existed more in our heads than in the marketplace. You can risk a lot more when you have very little in totality to put at risk.

As we got bigger, we needed to grow more slowly. And we needed to go more thoughtfully. I used to thrill in taking unplanned risks, abruptly zigging the handlebars of my dirt bike to the left when everyone (both inside and outside the company) would expect me to turn to the right. I would get a thrill when the almost-out-of-gas dashboard light would come on and my adrenaline would pump as I sped down the road without knowing if I would make it to the next fuel stop; none of that mattered because I so zealously enjoyed the risk-soaked ride.

By 2015, this company, which began pretty much as a figment of my imagination, had grown into our company—230 coworkers and counting. And our company needed to run a lot more like a very powerful, very intricate muscle car than a frisky little dirt bike. This is no longer necessary. It's also no longer what is best for Dogfish Head if it is to continue growing—slowly and thoughtfully—in a direction that is best for the company and that allows Dogfish to have a life that is longer than my own (remember, I am pretty sure I am only going to be around for exactly 46 more years).

I am trying to look up and look out for the best ideas instead of looking too much within—which gets me back to my midlife tattoo. As I mentioned, the shark-and-shield logo on my arm faces out. If I did the tattoo accurate to our logo, it would face in. It's facing out to remind me that I must do so as well.

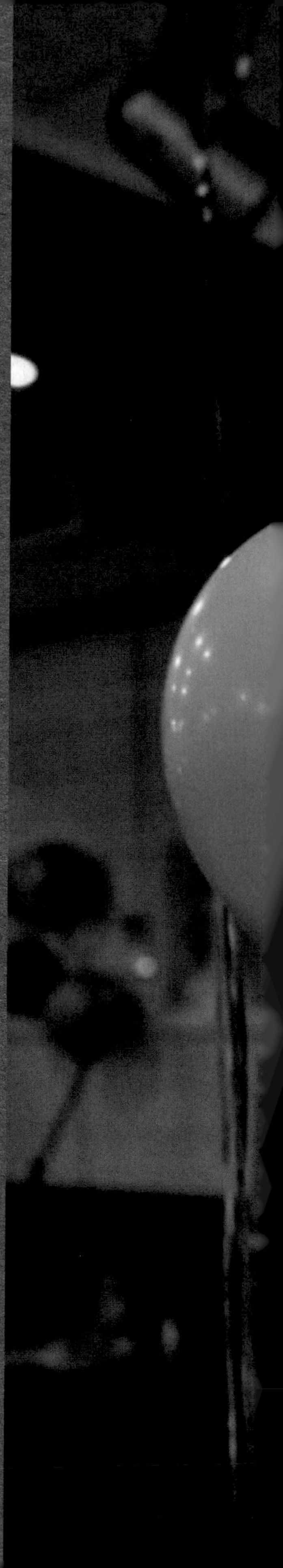

“The best teacher is experience and not through someone’s distorted point of view.”
— Jack Kerouac, *On the Road*

HIGHER MATH

Higher Math
(17% ABV)

In 2015, in celebration our 20th anniversary year of Dogfish Head, we thought it'd be fun to brew a really big, huge beer that would age so well that it would taste great 20 years after our 20th anniversary. We were hoping to hit 20 percent alcohol, but the yeast strains did not cooperate with us or our plan. The name Higher Math was meant to be an homage to my original homebrew that I made in New York City. For that beer, I saw some overly ripe cherries as I walked by a bodega, bought them cheap, and squished them into a pale ale recipe. That first beer was one of the inspirations for the recipe for Higher Math. Since it was a tribute to that first beer, the recipe was for a strong golden ale fermented with sour cherry juice and cocoa nibs. It was meant to clock in at 20 percent ABV, but it actually only fermented to 17 percent ABV.

The cocoa nibs and the sweetness from the unfermented sugars along with the cherries combine to create a perfect dessert beer, almost like a cognac. With notes of stewed cherries and pineapples, along with late notes of cocoa and a nice lingering sweetness and sort of notable warmth from the alcohol, it makes for a perfect cold-weather winter dessert beer. If you open a 12-ounce bottle we recommend you split it between two snifters or red wine glasses because it's so complex.

"We shall not cease from exploration
And the end of all our exploring
Will be to arrive where we started
And know the place for the first time."
—T.S. Eliot, *Four Quartets*

Sick Cider (6.5% ABV)

In 2015 we also brewed our first pure cider. Since we wrote the legislation in Delaware ourselves for the microbrewery statute I was, I guess, smart enough in the moment to give us the latitude where I defined within the state that if you have a microbrewery license you can ferment from apples and fruit, not just from barley. So I knew we had the legal right to make cider in our brewery. In 2015 we finally got around to doing our own off-centered take on a cider. Up to this point we had only done a hybrid with Positive Contact. We decided to name our first cider, Sick Cider. It was basically an unfiltered, very rustic cider made with five types of Delaware-grown apples, including Fuji, Roman, Stayman, Red Delicious, and Golden Delicious. This cider was 100 percent barrel fermented with a culture of funky and wild Brettanomyces yeast, and this dry, tart, refreshing cider was aged for a full year in spent red wine barrels before we released it to the public. People really dug our Sick Cider, and we ended up using some of it in a distilled spirit called Esprit Malade from our distillery.

We've pressed a lot of fruit in our apple presses at Dogfish, but it took us until 2015 to do our first full-on pure cider.

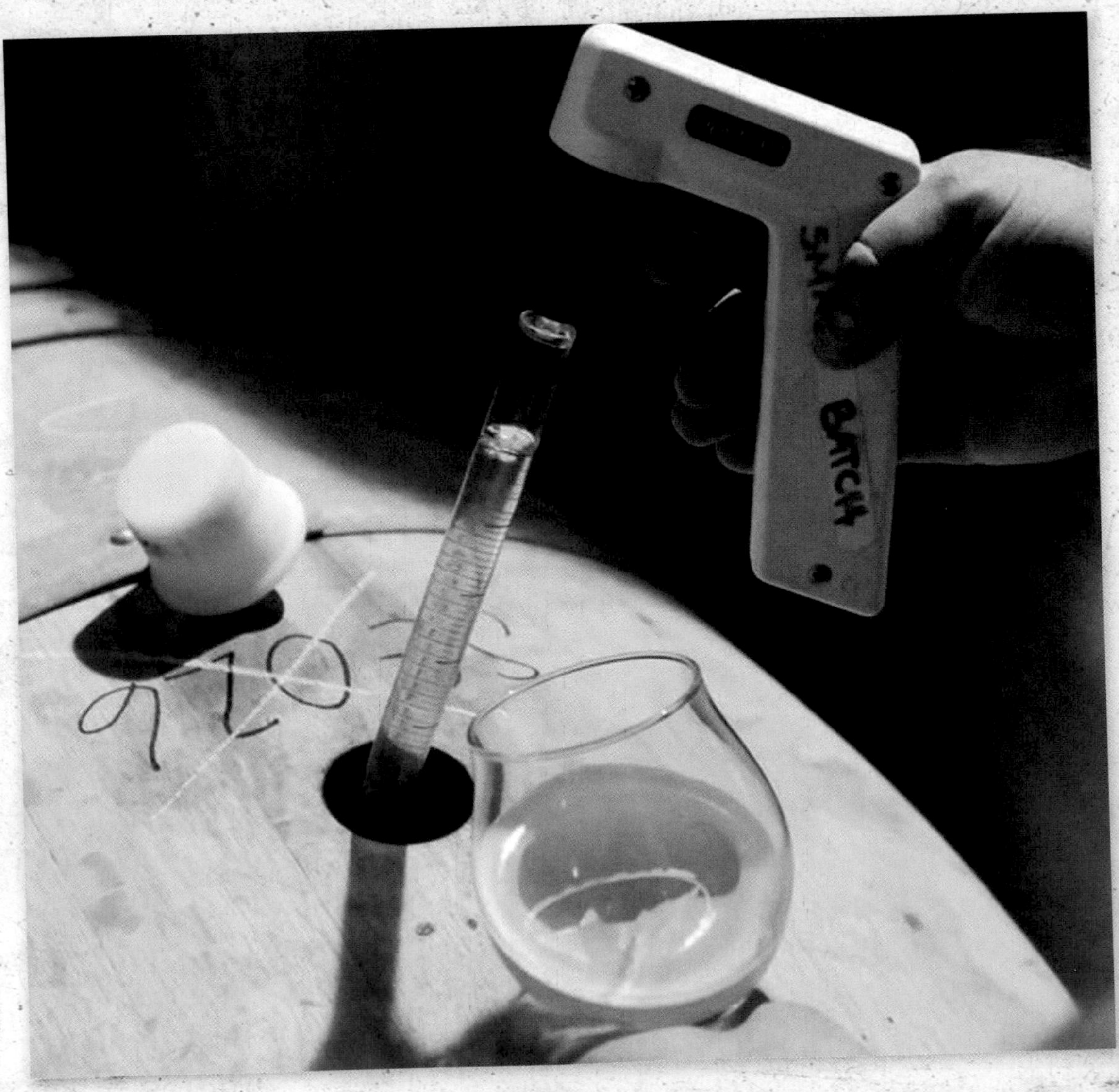

Liquid Truth Serum
(7% ABV)

This is a fun beer. When we used to conduct our interviews at Dogfish Head, after a long day of interviewing a potential coworker as a candidate, we ended the day by taking the best candidate out for drinks. And we called that component of the interview process the Liquid Truth Serum phase.

At Dogfish Head our community and culture are *so* important to us—and we are the keepers of it. Going out for dinner and a few drinks helps us and the candidate understand each other more fully. Now don't go getting us wrong here. People are not required to drink, but damn if some candidates didn't really lean into the pints. And you'd be surprised, or maybe not, how many potential coworkers flame out during the Liquid Truth Serum phase of the interview process.

That's kind of how we figure out if folks fit in with our culture or not. It's so inherent to our culture, which is, "Hey, not only do I enjoy working hard side-by-side each day with my coworkers, but they are people I like to go hang out with and have a few drinks with."

So to kind of capture and celebrate that tradition, we came up with a beer called Liquid Truth Serum. Also called that because the myth is that beers only pick up measurable bitterness, what we call as brewers IBUs (International Bitterness Units), during the boil. It was thought for a long time that a beer could only pick up IBUs if the hops were boiled in the beer because that temperature band of boiling and above is where it was thought IBUs were captured. The truth, we discovered, was very different. We did a lot of trial-and-error brews to see if we added an inordinate amount of hops in different temperature beers, below boiling (between 170 and 205 degrees), you could then get a ton of hop character and complexity, but keep the bitterness contained by never adding any hops to the boil. We also decided to incorporate four different states of hops: whole leaf, liquefied, pelletized, and powdered. Liquid Truth Serum is a wonderful beer that we still make today.

Just remember that when you go out to dinner and have a few cocktails on a job interview ... you are still on the interview.

16 oz.
myth: IBUs
(hop bitterness)
can only be achieved in the boil.
truth: 4 different hop additions added in the whirlpool make this beer truthfully hoppy without being deceptively bitter.
Dogfish Head
Liquid Truth Serum IPA
INDIA PALE ALE
12 FL. OZ | 7% ALC. BY VOL.

The Dogfish Head Distillery

Dogfish Head was the second craft brewery in the United States to open a craft spirits distillery. The spirits industry, much like the beer industry, is dominated by giant corporate brands. The difference between two brands of gin from two different big corporate distilleries has less to do with their flavor or their ingredients and more to do with their image, packaging, and marketing.

In the same way that we established our own versions of off-centered beers, we decided we would create a line of off-centered spirits. The spirits industry is a complementary industry where we felt we could get in early on the scratch-made, small-batch spirits movement and be an innovator. So, in 2002 we commissioned the "Frankenstill," our first 200-gallon pot still. We decided to begin by building a small craft distillery within our existing brewpub in Rehoboth. It, like much of our early brewing equipment, was built out of scrap metal. I was back at one of the auctions again looking for brewing equipment and saw the bottom of a grain silo for sale and I thought, "Hey ... that looks like a still." So I bought it and we started our journey down the spirits path.

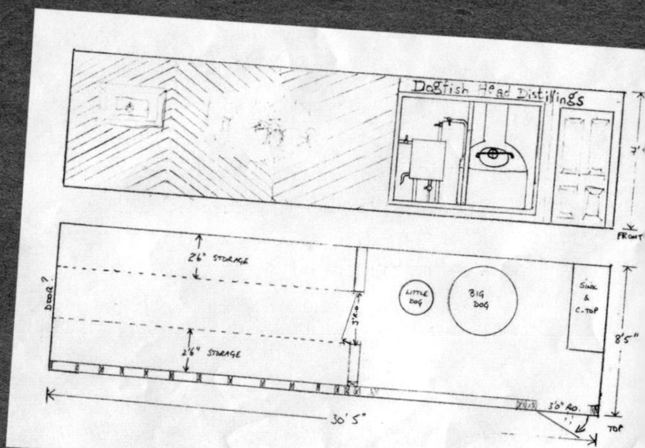

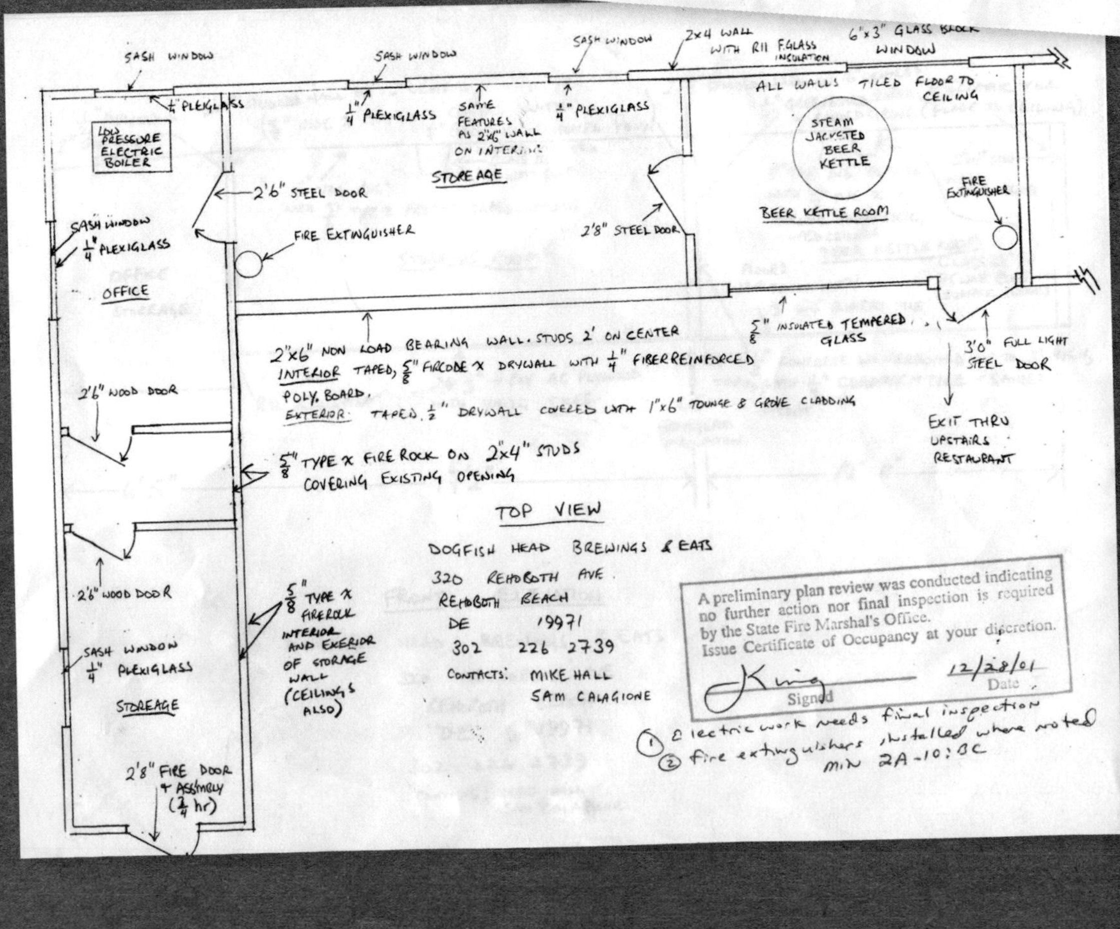

Alison in the Rehoboth Distillery

I had some friends who were huge fans of World Wide Stout at the time, who were also engineers, come design a pot still using the reclaimed stainless steel grain silo—in exchange for a full trunk of World Wide Stout. Our coworker at the time, Mike Hall, and our friend Doug Griffith pitched in and Frankenstill was born.

Just as we had to change the laws in Delaware to open the first brewery, we also had to change the laws to be able to distill in Rehoboth.

Labeling Brown Honey Rum at the Pub

The still was installed on the second floor of our original Dogfish Head Brewings & Eats. The distillery was visible to the restaurant through a big plate-glass window facing the dining room.

We worked on recipes, concepts for our spirits, packaging and buying, and helping to design the distilling equipment.

The first spirits we distilled were our off-centered rums back in 2002. Our rums have always been made from scratch using nontraditional ingredients like honey, orange, and coriander. We also had a Blue Hen Vodka and a Brown Honey Rum.

Since creating rum requires using cane sugar during the fermentation process, we used Grade A fancy molasses as our sugar source. We prefer to use molasses rather than cane juice or refined sugar because the end result is a richer flavor, better suited for aging.

We also made our Blue Hen vodka with infused flavors that varied by the season and my whim. And Jin (as in gin), distilled with botanicals, including juniper berries, cucumbers, and whole-leaf hops. I'm pretty sure our Jin was the first hop-forward spirit commercially brewed in America.

Unlike our scratch-made rums, when we first began distilling gins and vodkas we skipped a step in the distilling process because we didn't have enough space for all of the necessary equipment. Rather than start at the first stage, like many other distillers, we bought grain neutral spirits in 55-gallon drums for our gin and vodka, and then added flavors and bottled it.

Original distillery bottling process

I was never excited enough to promote these spirits outside our walls because, while we enjoyed being able to experiment by adding different ingredients to our spirits, we started with an existing product rather than starting from scratch. This meant our early spirits were not as authentically homemade as our beer, rum, and food.

But we were somewhat physically restricted from creating other scratch-made spirits or growing the distillery business because the initial distillery was small and housed in a small upstairs room within the restaurant's dining room space that wouldn't allow for expansion.

We began the work of relocating our spirits production to a new state-of-the-art distillery located in the heart of our Milton brewing campus, allowing us to tap into all the same awesome malt suppliers, brewing expertise, equipment, and warehousing space that supports our off-centered ales.

Small-batch distilled spirits have emerged as a growing market, attracting the same kind of passionate loyalty as craft beer. We decided to expand the distillery outside of the restaurant and bring in a team to focus on distilling.

Reimagining the distillery

In 2015, we decided it was the right time to build a full-scale distillery. Moving our spirits' production to a full-scale distillery meant we would no longer need to rely on using grain-neutral spirits as the starting point. We could create craft spirits that were more aligned with the Dogfish Head brand and the quality our customers had come to expect from us. We could ferment and distill the spirits from scratch. And by making everything 100 percent from scratch, we could use all real ingredients starting in their rawest form and never add bulk spirits or flavorings.

But a full-scale distillery also meant we would no longer fit in the small space on the second floor of the brewpub in Rehoboth, currently occupied by our beloved Frankenstill. So we began plans to build the new distillery in the heart of the Milton brewery.

There we could still benefit from the endless culinary influences and inspirations from the Rehoboth brewpub, but we would now also have access to the world-class ingredient suppliers, technologies, testing labs, brewing equipment, and infrastructure used by the Milton brewery. All of it. The same equipment that makes our beers stand out and stand up in front of our fans would now be fundamental to the distillery.

When we began the planning for the new distillery, we had 13 years of R&D under our belts, we had a thick recipe book that documented the various craft spirits we had honed

Graham looking in on the first run

over the years, and we had our location. Now all we needed was someone to run it.

Enter James Montero. Right around that time, James had interviewed with the Dogfish team for a different role. James had been working in marketing and innovation for a large company for about ten years and explained that he was actually working on a business plan to start his own distillery. Sam explained to James, "We are ramping up the Dogfish Distillery. Would you like to come on and help develop the brand and the positioning or sort of, you know, reinterpret the brand positioning with a focus on marketing?"

There it was. A moment of serendipity. James was all in. And with James in place as the manager of the distillery, it was time to get down to business.

Sam and James headed to Vendome Copper & Brass, a metal fabrication company located in Louisville, Kentucky, to check on the new equipment for the distillery. Vendome Copper & Brass is a family business that has spanned four generations. Sam had chosen them to fabricate the new distillery because they share many of the same values of Dogfish Head. They use extremely high-quality, responsibly sourced materials; their dedication to craftsmanship and attention to detail is unmatched; and they have built an enduring company by taking care of coworkers. Because of these reasons and many more, we really connected with Vendome Copper & Brass. So Sam chose them to fabricate the next iteration of Dogfish Head distilling.

At the heart of the distilling operation are two 500-gallon copper stripping stills and a 250-gallon copper vodka column. With this new, larger equipment installed, Dogfish Head suddenly had a bigger canvas and a much bigger tool chest to work with—and it was exciting. We could start playing with more levers and really refine the flavors and experience of the spirits we delivered to our customers.

"You can make spirits from almost any type of raw material and we have chosen to start with the same ingredients that go into our beer. In our process, everything starts in its rawest form, from scratch, and we use the best ingredients available. We use a batch distillation approach through each stage—it's a bit more work than other approaches, but it allows us to closely monitor and control each step of the distillation process."
—James Montero, General Manager, Dogfish Head Distilling, Co.

Barrel Honey Rum

(40% ABV)

While we've distilled many variations of off-centered rums over the years, the hands-down local favorite has been our Brown Honey Rum, which is subtly sweet and a smooth sipping rum.

Our Barrel Honey Rum is an evolution of this original favorite, distilled in a manner that celebrates the unique Dogfish Head ingredients and process.

The process begins in the Brewhouse, right alongside our off-centered ales. In the distillery, Head Distiller Graham Hamblett runs the wash through our 500-gallon copper pot still. The alcohol is stripped, and out comes 80-proof low wine. He then runs the low wine through its spirit run on the same pot still, cutting out the heads and tails to capture the hearts, the cleanest part of the spirit. On the way to the cellars we add our proprietary "Doggie" yeast—we chose this because the yeast imparts fruity esters, which add a ripe banana character. The rum is proofed down to barrel strength (~110 proof) and we age it in new #3 char American Oak Barrels.

Once the distiller determines the spirit is ready, we dump the barrels into a tank to proof down with water to bottle strength (80 proof), add a touch of honey, and then bottle.

We launched the new distillery business with a brand-new take on vodka. Vodka is an awesome challenge because, by definition, it's supposed to be odorless and flavorless or have very subtle fruit flavors. So how do we make a spirit that is off-centered when it is supposed to be odorless and flavorless? Our creative approach is to use a flavor-forward blend of beer brewer's grains to make our wash (the pre-distilled fermentable liquid that is the base for our vodka and gin), which gives it a rich earthy sweetness in the taste. By fermenting the wash for our vodka with our proprietary Doggie ale yeast, the aroma of the vodka will have subtle fruit and pepper notes. This delicate sweetness will make it distinctive from odorless and flavorless competitors.

If I were taking the lead on our 2.0 distillery project, I would have likely been inclined to launch this new business with something intensely flavorful and exotic, but we decided it would be best to first create a more approachable product, and launch with a more off-centered take on the conventional spirit classes of vodka and gin, and then release some more experimental spirits a year or so later. Walk before we run and put our storytelling powers around how great these from-scratch spirits taste instead of around stories of spirits so exotic they wouldn't fit into categories like vodka and gin.

When we first began distilling from-scratch vodkas, the vodka space was much like beer in the mid-1990s, when Dogfish Head got its start. The beer industry was dominated by a few conglomerates, liquid void of character and authenticity. We set out to make a vodka that captured the core of Dogfish Head, so it's made with 100 percent brewer's malt and our proprietary Doggie yeast. Everything is scratch-made, like it used to be, as the name suggests, during a simpler time.

"One of America's most inventive breweries also makes a worthy sipping vodka." —*Paste* magazine

Analog Vodka (40% ABV)

This is not your average vodka: made from a base of malted barley that we mill in house, right alongside our off-centered ales. After the starches in the grain are converted to sugars, the worst is sent to the cellars, where our proprietary Doggie ale yeast converts the sugars to an alcohol target of 7.6 percent.

In the distillery, we run the wash through our American-made, 500-gallon copper pot still. The alcohol is stripped and out comes 80-proof low wine. Then we run the low wine through our 25-foot-tall, 20-plate vodka column, cutting out the heads and tails to capture the hearts, the cleanest part of the spirit. Reverse-osmosis water is added to the 190-proof hearts, and after light filtering, it's time to bottle.

Clean and crisp with subtle grainy sweetness, you'll find hints of pear and cherry that make for a smooth finish.

Sonic Archeology (25% ABV)

We are not just a brewery with an addiction to music, we are also a distillery with an addiction to music. With the new distillery up and running, we came up with the idea of creating and packaging a ready-made cocktail: using spirits from the distillery that would harken back to what was going on in the music scene when cocktails first gained popularity over straight spirits.

James initially came up with the idea that the cocktail should be inspired by what was happening in the country around that time.The 1920s saw the convergence of several genres of American music. As radios gained popularity as a standard feature in American households, radio stations became more commercial, more focused on entertainment, and started broadcasting music. People began hearing new kinds of music from different regions of the country. Suddenly music that had only existed in little pockets of the country was being heard in households everywhere. Recording companies would send talent scouts to different parts of the country to record sounds that had previously never been recorded or even heard beyond local regions—like banjo, bluegrass, gospel, Hawaiian, and so many others. This fusion of music genres eventually gave birth and had a huge influence on the distinguishing sound of American Rock 'n Roll.

In 1919 the Eighteenth Amendment to the Constitution led to the prohibition of alcohol in the United States. Strict laws making the production, transportation, and sale of alcohol illegal sparked a boom of cocktailing in bustling speakeasies throughout the country. With sales and distribution channels cut off, many spirits were bootlegged. To hide the flavor, spirits were mixed with other ingredients. They would commonly blend whiskey with brandy and grenadine.

Because the law restricted production, transport, and sale of alcohol within 12 nautical miles of the coastline, many alcohol enthusiasts would travel by boat beyond the 12-mile limit to legally drink alcohol. To make transporting the cocktails easier, passengers would blend everything in a bottle and sneak it onto the boats. The mixing of cocktails would happen before they embarked on the ride, and they would ride out on boats to the 13th mile and party.

Sonic Archeology is a liquid tribute to that blending of sounds and the blending of spirits that defined the Roaring Twenties, reimagined for today. We combined ingredients popular in most Prohibition Era cocktails—black brandy, whiskey, and a mixer. Instead of the traditional grenadine, we decided to use fresh pomegranate juice. The result is a smooth-drinking cocktail that combines the flavors of tropical fruit, lemon, and a pleasant oak.

Planning a cocktail party? You don't need to sacrifice flavor complexity for convenience. You no longer need to have all these different ingredients on hand. You don't need all the mixing equipment—the shaker, strainer, jigger, or anything like that. All you need is a glass, ice, and a bottle of Sonic Archeology and you have a ready-made, bar-quality cocktail.

Chesapeake & Maine

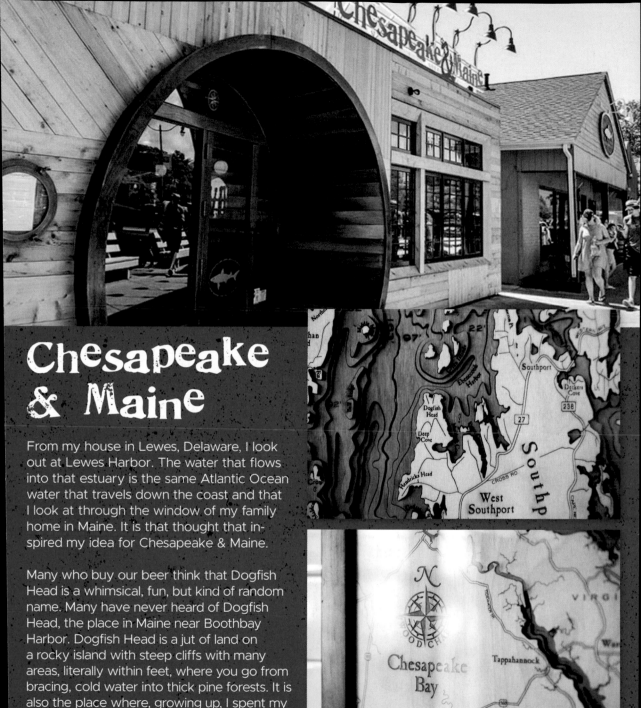

From my house in Lewes, Delaware, I look out at Lewes Harbor. The water that flows into that estuary is the same Atlantic Ocean water that travels down the coast and that I look at through the window of my family home in Maine. It is that thought that inspired my idea for Chesapeake & Maine.

Many who buy our beer think that Dogfish Head is a whimsical, fun, but kind of random name. Many have never heard of Dogfish Head, the place in Maine near Boothbay Harbor. Dogfish Head is a jut of land on a rocky island with steep cliffs with many areas, literally within feet, where you go from bracing, cold water into thick pine forests. It is also the place where, growing up, I spent my summers. There is no town on the whole island, just a store and a few restaurants. During the day the air is intensely clear and clean and smells of nature and trees and salt; at night the sky is brilliant with stars. I identify Dogfish Head as a brand with an intense and palpable immersion in the rawest forms of nature: the sea, the woods, and the wilderness.

Chesapeake & Maine would be a concept that combined our two Dogfish Head brand home geographies. My goal in conceptualizing Chesapeake & Maine was to connect these two loves of mine, to connect the origin story of Dogfish Head with the locale of our brewery. I wanted a project that allowed people coming to Coastal Delaware to also experience where I got the inspiration for Dogfish Head, the brand.

I didn't know of any restaurants that combined these two regional cuisines. It seemed like the perfect concept to complement the traditional wood-grilled food we served at our existing Rehoboth brewpub. And so, in the same way we identify unexplored combinations of flavors in beer and spirits, we identified a yet unexplored combination of ingredients and flavors that would combine those of the Maine coast with those of the Chesapeake region.

Most readers can probably imagine what awesome cuisine would be served in these areas. A lobster shack in Maine would likely include fried clams, lobster rolls, and New England white chowder. The quintessential Chesapeake crab shack might serve crab cakes, Old Bay–seasoned fries, and hush puppies. But nobody had combined these two regional cuisines with an off-centered flair under one roof. Chesapeake & Maine would be our geographically enamored seafood restaurant. Part of what we do is to commit to sourcing 100 percent of the seafood we serve at Chesapeake & Maine direct from fishermen in Maine or watermen in the Chesapeake Bay region. The seafood we source is truly world class.

When the building became available right next door to Dogfish Head Brewings & Eats, called Finbar's Pub and Grill, it was game on! In 2015 we began construction, transforming the restaurant and neighboring Irish Pub into Chesapeake & Maine.

We designed a bar that would serve as the main stage for a world-class cocktail business to highlight our emerging line of scratch-distilled spirits coming out of our Milton distillery. These partnerships brought a level of differentiation and distinction to Chesapeake & Maine.

"The voice of the sea is seductive, never ceasing, whispering, clamoring, murmuring, inviting the soul to wander in abysses of solitude."
—Kate Chopin, *The Awakening*

Smoke in the Water Oysters

Before we opened, we wanted to see if we couldn't put an off-centered spin on oysters. For this project we collaborated with our friends at Hoopers Island Oyster Aquaculture Company on the Chesapeake. The plan was to see if we could get a hop-infused raw oyster. The idea was that since oysters filter water, if we could get them to filter a bunch of hop-infused water, we would have exactly what we were looking for. A true marriage of our beers and the oyster we could serve on the half shell. It turns out, oysters do not like hops. When the hops hit the water, the oysters would snap shut and never take on any hoppy character because they were not filtering the hop-infused water. But we were not going to quit. We decided to shift gears and went with a culinary smoked sea salt. That worked! When it was all said and done the "Smoke in the Water" oysters are served raw and have an amazing smokey aroma and flavor all packing into a raw oyster. With Chesapeake & Maine being the two regions we pull from for our menu, a custom-built raw bar is the first thing guests see when they walk through the front door—and Smoke on the Water is often available.

We opened our doors to Chesapeake & Maine in March 2016, in downtown Rehoboth, Delaware, with all sorts of great menu items hailing from our namesake regions. We have Whole Maine Lobsters, a Maine Clambake, Chesapeake Bay Crab Cakes, and a Land and Sea Burger. The burger is dry-aged Roseda Farms (the same local beef we use at Brewings & Eats), along with Maine Lobster with Pico De Gallo and a house-made Chipotle Aioli. I love this one because it has local beef born in the Chesapeake region and lobster from Maine.

We reached back out to our friend and artist Jon Langford for some of the art on the wall by the bar. We have worked with him on many different projects, from beer labels to acoustic jam sessions around the firepit at the Inn. In one dining room we have a custom wallpaper of mythical nautical maps and sea monsters designed by Tony Millionaire, and in another, we have an old dive suite surrounded by copies of Sub-Mariner comic books.

The cocktail and bar program has always been a major focus for us since we opened our doors at Chesapeake & Maine. On tap we have a variety of keg-conditioned cocktails developed up in Milton and we are always pushing the envelope behind the bar to come up with new and innovative ways to utilize our line of spirits. In fact, in 2017 we were a James Beard Award semifinalist for Outstanding Bar Program.

Don't Chuck Your Shucks

With upwards of around 90 percent of the seafood consumed in the United States coming from foreign waters, it has been both a blessing and a curse for us to only source our food from the Cheapeake and Maine regions. Sustainability is at the forefront in both of these places, and we work to engage on the same fronts. We work with a local nonprofit group named Delaware Center for the Inland Bays, or CIB as we call it. CIB has a program called "Don't Chuck Your Shucks," where they collect shucked oysters from local restaurants and take these spent shells and use them on shoreline restoration projects and in oyster gardens. We have had groups of coworkers from Chesapeake & Maine volunteer to help with the program.

SeaQuench Ale (4.9% ABV)

I know we're supposed to love all our children equally, as parents, but in the history of Dogfish Head I've never hung out with one of my "children" as often as I hang out with SeaQuench Ale. Everyone's palate is different, but for me, SeaQuench Ale is the most beloved beer, personally, that we've ever made. I'm also now 50 years old, and my metabolism's slowing down, so the fact that it's relatively low in calories and carbs makes it a great option for me to drink when I'm having a few. SeaQuench Ale is also story-rich—one of our most story-rich beers we've brewed for sure.

I often speak of the Reinheitsgebot, which was the Bavarian Beer Purity Act established in the year 1516. At that time, the Bavarian government mandated that beer had to be made, and could only be made, with water, barley, and hops. (Yeast was, kind of, a given. It had yet to be understood that yeast was a single-cell living organism. This was pre-microbiology and pre–Louis Pasteur understanding, you know, of a sterile environment or what yeast and bacteria are.) So the Reinheitsgebot was established, and it really changed the landscape of beer around the world. Within a few centuries, almost all commercial beer was bowing down to the Reinheitsgebot and adhering to this very limited concept of what ingredients could go into beer. Now think about the fact that Dogfish Head brews the oldest known fermented beverage in the history of civilization—Chateau Jiahu. The physical evidence of the ingredients for beer dates back almost 10,000 years to the Jiahu province in China. In the context of the Reinheitsgebot, which is from the year 1516, today we think of "traditional beers" as beers that adhere to the Reinheitsgebot. But the Reinheitsgebot has only been around 500 years—while people have been making beer for 10,000 years! At Dogfish,

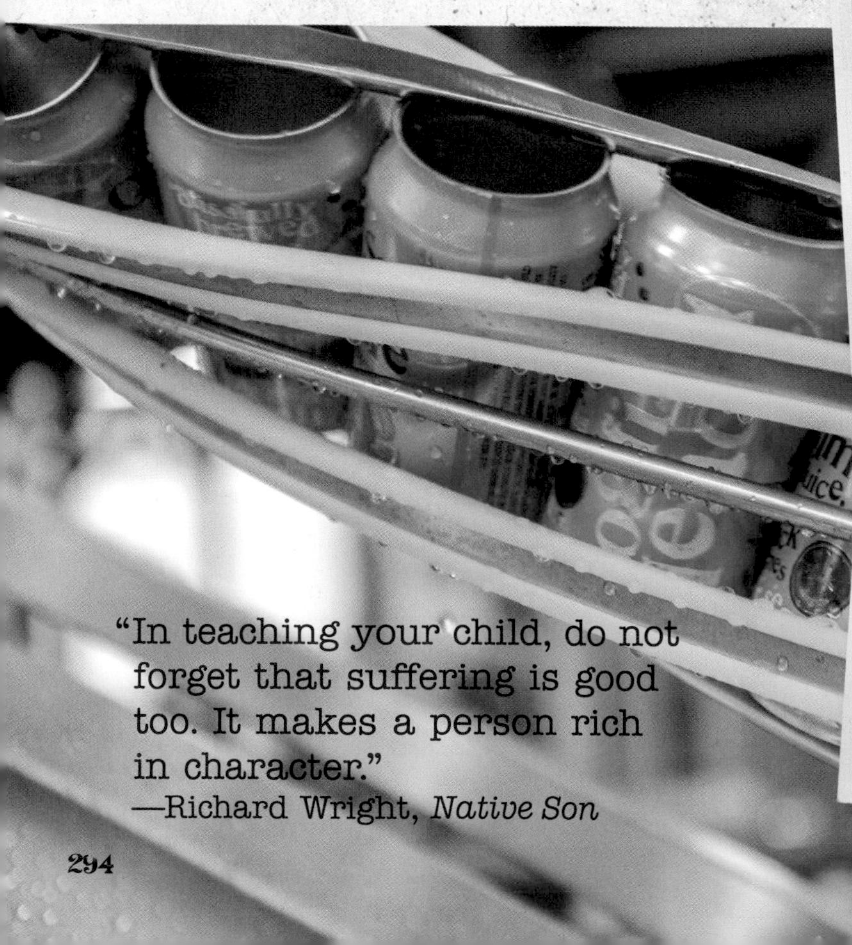

"In teaching your child, do not forget that suffering is good too. It makes a person rich in character."
—Richard Wright, *Native Son*

Bust-a-Limes

we've always considered the Reinheitsgebot to be nothing more than a relatively modern form of art censorship. To really give the middle finger and a high five to the Reinheitsgebot in its 500th anniversary year, the year 2016, I thought it'd be cool to brew a beer that, like the martial art Jiu Jitsu, uses your enemy's power against them. We wanted to brew a beer that recognized all the most celebrated, thirst-quenching German beer styles and mash them up in a way that allowed us to also bring in our culinary-ingredient Dogfish DNA that's pretty much the antithesis of the Reinheitsgebot.

Researching some of the quintessential refreshing German beer styles, Kölsch, Gose, and Berliner Weisse came up. At this time Dogfish Head was already brewing the first fruit-fermented Berliner Weisse distributed in America, called Festina Pêche, so we knew how to brew sour beers. SeaQuench Ale is three beers brewed in sequence, hence the name, SeaQuench Ale. First, we brew a Kölsch, which is a very low acidity environment, ideal for growing yeast in. We brew the Kölsch in a triple-batch fermenter, as the first third of the beer. Then on top of the Kölsch we add a thread of traditional Gose, made with sea salts from the mouth of the Chesapeake and off the coast of Maine, two locations significant to Dogfish Head. Then the third addition is a Berliner-style beer, but in that one we add crushed-up black limes and lime juice. We smash them all together to create SeaQuench Ale.

Black limes are one of the essential ingredients in SeaQuench Ale. There are beers made with lime juice and traditionally Goses were made with salt, but a breakthrough for us was finding black limes—which are basically limes that are first boiled in salt water or salt water brine, then set outside in the sun to dry until they turn into this really dark brown or black version of what used to be the green rip limes. A black lime develops a thick leathery skin since so much water has been boiled out of it there's no water left in the pot and no moisture left in the lime. Each lime is superlight in weight. What that process does is concentrate the flavor of the lime and make it really powerful in whatever dish you put it in. The limes originate in Oman and you can easily find them at Middle Eastern grocery stores and markets.

There is more to this story....
I'd gotten to know Jeff Gordon who'd been at our brewery in Milton a couple of times when he was down racing for NASCAR. His wife's Belgian, so he's into really good beer and he's a wine lover, too. Jeff and I became friendly and his race team became friendly, and one time they invited me into the pits with them. Jeff and his lead engineer were showing me his car and how every inch of his car, ergonomically, was thought through specifically for his body. I noticed a tube coming out of the inside of his driver side window and I asked, "Oh, what's that tube for, Jeff?"

He touched the tube, "That's where they pipe in my special Gatorade." And I said, "Oh, that's cool—the Gatorade company let you choose your own color of Gatorade."

And he explained, "No. Actually, they hooked me up to all these tubes and probes and monitored my body going, you know, 140 miles an hour at 120 degrees, or whatever, around the track for a few hours. They checked all of my systems and figured out exactly, for my physiological state while racing, what my body needed for liquid, and they built it for my body."

I listened to Jeff tell the story, and I said, "Holy shit. Can I talk to those scientists that you worked with?"

While I was working on the recipe for SeaQuench Ale, Jeff Gordon introduced me to the scientist who used to be the head of the Gatorade Beverage Institute, and I started sending this scientist samples of our SeaQuench Ale for analysis. As brewers, we have to be careful about what we say about our beers, because the Food and Drug Administration mandates breweries cannot make health claims. So while it's not advertised, what I will share is that we worked very closely with this beverage scientist to analyze each test batch of SeaQuench Ale on a molecular level, with the idea of optimizing the recipe so that we could say, "SeaQuench Ale is the most objectively thirst-quenching beer at a molecular level Dogfish Head has ever brewed." We would certainly never use a word like "hydrating" in marketing SeaQuench Ale. But we certainly do use the term "thirst quenching" when we talk about SeaQuench Ale. SeaQuench Ale is now the best-selling sour beer in America, and sour beer is now one of the fastest-growing styles in America.

SeaQuench Ale was the first beer to go on tap when we opened Chesapeake & Maine in 2016. The beer is the perfect complement to the restaurant's seafood menu.

Matt Barth

Learning & Development Specialist
Start Date: 2009

Matt knows his way around a cask of beer and rubber mallet.

As told by Matt Barth on *The Moth*, 2019:

It's 2009. I'm a Boatswain's Mate in the United States Coast Guard. I'm coming off a long tour of duty and going home for a couple days to see my wife and my son, Alex. He's one year old. I've got tickets to the Atlantic City Beer Festival. I'm excited about that, and life is good, you know. I'm a craft beer fan excited to come off duty.

I pick up Alex. We have a great day together catching up and everything else. I was ready to unwind after all this duty but my wife comes home late. That's not unusual. It was kind of happening over the last month or so and I had these thoughts, you know. How could I keep things together over this last little while? On duty, all these questions kept coming up. Where is she? What's going on? I had these questions and I thought, "I'm just going to ask her."

It was later toward the evening on my first day back and I threw it out there, "Is there someone else?"

"Yes. Would you like a bowl of ice cream?" she said. I'm not making this up. I don't know what I'm supposed to do or say. I mean, what did she really expect me to say? "Yeah, with sprinkles. Thanks, babe!" So that happened. She didn't want to talk about it that night and I didn't know what to do. I do know I didn't have any ice cream that night. I went to our room and tried to sleep. Alex was sleeping in his room. It was a rough night, to say the least, and I didn't get much sleep.

The next morning, I wake up, have breakfast with Alex, and she still doesn't want to talk about it—but I've got my tickets to the Atlantic City Beer Festival. I figured, "You know what? I'm going to go to the festival. I'm going to try to clear my head, and maybe when I come back we can talk about this." And I head off to AC Beerfest. I don't have a great time because so much is going through my head. I head for home, and when I arrive, everything I loved is gone. My wife is gone, my son is gone, my dog is gone ... everything. I'm left with just this empty home and all these thoughts. What just happened to my life?

The next year was what I refer to as "hell year." It was the worst time in my life. I was dealing with a messy divorce, defending myself from bogus lawsuits, and trying to take care of Alex on a Coast Guard salary. I bought a house in 2006. It's now 2009, and it's not worth anything close to what I paid for it.

I'm in the Coast Guard, though, and I want to take care of Alex, but I am required to keep going away on duty. I realize I'm going to have to leave my career. I make the decision that I must leave the Coast Guard.

I try to go back to college on the GI bill and quickly find out that trying to live off that is nearly impossible. I've got nothing. I can't make my mortgage payments. I can barely get food for Alex and me. We don't have any health insurance. Anytime you don't have health insurance, that's when things go wrong. I'm trying to fix my car and had to cut this piece of metal off and weld it in a new piece. I'm cutting it off with an angle grinder and while I'm cutting it, BOOM! A piece of metal just hits my shirt. And I look down at my chest and say "Hey! there's a hole in my shirt.... Huh? That's weird." Then it feels strange and I look down again. "There's a hole in ME!" It's looking pretty bad, so I go inside. I try to take care of it, but I can't stop the bleeding. It's bad. Alex hears the commotion and comes

Coworker Profile

over. Looking at the wound, I know that I need stitches, but I'm up to here in debt. When you're in such debt like this and just can't get things going, you tend to make these irrational decisions. I thought, "I can't go to the hospital right now. If I go to the hospital, I'm going to have to pay all these bills. I know what I need to do!" I got the sewing kit out, and as I'm pushing the dull Singer needle into my skin Alex shuffles a chair over. He's just about three at the time. He climbs up on this chair and puts his little hand on my shoulder. He says, "Everything's going to be okay, Daddy. Everything's going to be okay." Stitch after stitch after stitch after stitch, that's the way it is. And I patch myself up.

After that, I started patching up other areas of my life. My Coast Guard buddies called me up and they said, "You've been out for a little while. We've got some advice for you. We know what you want to do. You were always encouraging us when we were your crew. You'd encourage us to go do what we wanted to do. Go to the station we wanted to go to. Go to the Virgin Islands, whatever. Get through these missions. Seek out what WE want to do. Matt, it's your time now. It's your time to do what you want to do. And all you ever do is talk about Dogfish Head. You take us on tours, you drag us out there ... and you love it. You're talking about Dogfish all the time! You need to get a job at this brewery." Wow. I'll never forget that conversation. But I have doubts.

How am I going to just jump into this brewery thing? How is this going to provide for me and my son and everything else? I looked at what I could apply for and there was a part-time tour guide position open in the Milton tasting room. Part-time, seasonal, and only for a couple months. I applied and got the job, but how on Earth was this going to work? I'm making eight dollars an hour working three days a week, while trying to take care of Alex and everything else. I just had this feeling though and couldn't shake it. I knew that I could do this. This is my foot-in-the-door moment here. I worked hard. I enjoyed my time there. Had a lot of good fun working with great people, a good environment. Telling the stories, talking to customers, and taking them on tour and everything else. I was also working with a supercute coworker at the time.

The summer was coming to an end. I couldn't let this opportunity go by. I must make something of this. With two weeks left and the job coming to an end, I talked to my boss at the time, Mark Carter. We're having the conversation and he has some ideas. I'm saying I really want to stay here and make something of this. Sure enough, a week or two later, I got my first full-time job at Dogfish Head. And that was like eight years ago.
I was a lead bartender at the time. This was it. I got health insurance. I was getting paid a bit more. Things were looking up. I'm taking care of Alex and all the other things in my life started patching up.

I will keep building my career. Keep finding new ways I can educate myself and educate others. I have been growing. It's been awesome, but now I live a happy life in Coastal Delaware with my wife Kristin. Who, by the way, is that cute coworker that I met eight years ago. My son Alex is 11 years old, and Kristin is a great stepmother to him. My son Zachary, that Kristin and I have together, is 4 years old now. I wouldn't be here if it wasn't for perseverance. Perseverance is what brought me to my people. Dogfish Head is all my people. Boston Beer is all my people. I learned perseverance in the Coast Guard through tough missions and tough times and pushing through and accomplishing big things and big missions, but I also learned more about perseverance from my little boy when he was 3 years old and put his hand on my shoulder. "Everything's going to be okay, Daddy. Everything's going to be okay." Thanks, Alex. Everything is okay.

If you were on a deserted island and could have one album to listen to and an unlimited supply of one beer, what would it be?

Beer: Liquid Truth Serum
Album: The Clash, *London Calling*

Chapter 9

The New R&D Brewery

EscarGOSE

Dogfish Head, has been a consumer-oriented innovation company since the day we opened. Listening to our fans has always been deeply rooted in our DNA. In our earliest days, when we sold a pint the transaction was hand-to-hand direct to the consumer, from the room that it was brewed in. Anytime a new beer went on tap, when someone was handed a beer, they would also be given a handmade comment card and a little golf pencil. We would ask every single person, "Hey, please take one minute and give us your feedback on this beer."

The feedback made an immediate impact because we were only brewing in 12-gallon batches, and we

were brewing three times a day, five or six days a week. When you're brewing 20 times a week and you're getting that much immediate feedback from customers, you can quickly change one ingredient or one process and the next time you brew the beer, you've created a different flavor. Hopefully, when a person comes back, I would recognize them and run up with a pint and say, "Hey, remember when you said that we had too many raisins in the Raison D'Etre batch? We listened. Try the new batch. We backed off the raisins by 20 percent. Let me know what you think."

During those years it was really critical that we had that small brewing system in Rehoboth. Because that's where we would go to throw spaghetti at the wall and take some risks and create some really exotic unique recipes on a smaller system. But when word about our collaborative brewing process spread, it galvanized the beer lovers in our community to visit, to take part in our process, and become testers and ambassadors of our beers. People were really impressed that we were listening to them to such a degree—that we were asking for their feedback and then making tweaks in the recipe based on that feedback.

For a long time, we had a five-barrel brewhouse in Rehoboth. Then we actually downsized to a two-barrel brewhouse so we could do more small-batch innovations on a smaller scale. As we got busier and busier, we learned the size of two barrels was kind of like pissing into the wind. We kept running out of beer and couldn't keep the tap lines flowing. When we redid our entire Rehoboth campus in 2018, we put in a brand-new, state-of-the-art, five-barrel brewhouse with ten-barrel fermenters. Bryan Selders, one of our longest-tenured brewers who is a great innovator himself, runs it. When I get an idea for a beer, I share that by email or phone with Bryan, and the two of us together will create a recipe around that idea.

While the home brewing system of brewing small-batch projects with coworkers at the brewpub in Rehoboth was sufficient to provide beers for the taps at the brewpub, we didn't have a proper R&D system large enough to put trial recipes on tap at the brewery where the customers

7 BBL in Milton

could come in and try them to give us feedback. But by adding another R&D brewery in Milton, Mark Safarik, our brewmaster, and Dan Weber, our R&D brewer, can do even more experimenting with our beers.

That respect and collaboration that was at the core of our R&D process with beer lovers in our earliest days is alive and well today at Dogfish Head. We have 10-gallon, 5-barrel, and 7-barrel systems, in addition to our larger production breweries of 100-barrel and 200-barrel vat size, so we can innovate at all different scales. It's nice when you have small brewing systems, because you can do some really risky and exotic things without having to spend a lot on high volumes of ingredients or worry that it's going to sell through.

We haven't lost that spirit of listening. Those echoes still come across and we want them to. We still use those 10-gallon, 5-barrel, and 7-barrel systems to experiment but then we don't just share those experiments with our own sensory teams or coworkers. We actually still put those experiments on tap at our Tasting Room in Milton, that has a kitchen as well, and at our full-scale production brewpub in downtown Rehoboth, Brewings & Eats. We now have a more intricate system for collecting beer-lovers' feedback that allows us to capture input and respond. We ask consumers to give us feedback on these beers and to be part of the story of these beers. Would they buy them if they went to their markets? We collect all that data, and it's really critical to informing our innovation pipeline. As we consider what to release the following year, we're literally checking what beer lovers love the most out of our own locations and that informs our innovation process.

And while we can no longer hand every fan who drinks our beers a pint and a comment card, creating interactions that feel like the next best thing are what we want to deliver to our fans.

Beer Exploration Journal ... let's do this together!

We've always believed in the positive power of collaboration here at Dogfish Head. Whether it's a wasabi-infused pale ale brewed with musician Juliana Barwick or a limited-edition clothing capsule designed with family owned Woolrich Inc., we've worked alongside myriad partners over the years to create some of our most inventive and creative off-centered ales and projects. But there's one partner we've consistently collaborated with since we first opened the doors of our Rehoboth brewpub back in 1995, and that's you, the consumer.

From the very beginning, we've turned to our visitors and guests to gain valuable insight about our beers. Chatting with folks across the bar we've learned what they love, what they'd like to see more of, and even the occasional "please never make this again."

It's been a journey, but thanks to off-centered evangelists like you, dear reader, we've continued to push the boundaries of the craft beer world, while brewing creative ales of the highest quality. And now we want to take those conversations from across the bar one step further, giving you a greater voice in our creative process with the addition of the "Beer Exploration Journal."

Designed to give you a peek into the world of R&D at Dogfish Head, the Beer Exploration Journal not only gives you the inspiration behind upcoming beers, but a direct line of feedback to our team. A form with just six simple questions, you'll be asked to evaluate and rate new beers on tap exclusively at our Milton Tasting Room & Kitchen and Rehoboth brewpub. Everything from your thoughts on the story that inspired the beer to would you ever get this beer again—we want to hear the good, the bad, and the ugly!

Always fresh from just the other room, each beer presented as part of the Beer Exploration Journal is brewed from either our fully manual 5-barrel brewery in Rehoboth or the 7-barrel R&D system in Milton.

Our brewing and quality teams then embrace that feedback to figure out how we can tweak and reinvent a recipe for an even better experience. It's possible that a single beer could go through multiple iterations because of results from the Beer Exploration Journal, with appearances on our internal taste panel along the way until we get it juuuuust right.

So how do you get involved? First of all, start planning your next visit to see us here in Coastal Delaware! With a slew of exclusives on tap at all times, we'll need you to sample the latest—and hopefully greatest—featured Beer Exploration Journal brew in order to give us your feedback. Tough job, but we think you're up to the challenge.

Then visit www.beerexplorationjournal.com to share your thoughts. That's it! You're officially an honorary member of the team, and you can proudly say you helped bring an off-centered ale to life. It's kind of like that feeling when you knew about a band before they made it big.

Forgot your phone? No biggie. Our Milton Tasting Room & Kitchen and Off-Centered EmPOURium in downtown Rehoboth Beach both feature dedicated iPad stands where you can submit your thoughts on the featured beer of the moment.

Squall IPA (9% ABV)

Squall IPA is a continually hopped, unfiltered, bottle-conditioned Double IPA. First released in the early 2000s, we brought it back in 2016. Squall is the younger sibling to our 60, 90, and 120 Minute IPAs. Like those beers, Squall starts out as a continuously hopped IPA.

Squall is brewed using three different types of malt. Like the 60, 90, and 120 Minute IPAs, it is continuously hopped throughout the boil. It is then dry hopped with Simcoe, Amarillo, and Palisade hops. Unlike its siblings, it's not carbonated in a tank but rather, bottle conditioned.

Being bottle conditioned, the beer is naturally carbonated. Beyond the yeast added during fermentation, additional yeast and sugars are added just prior to bottling, triggering a second fermentation to occur in the bottle.

That additional yeast will also consume flavor-destroying oxygen picked up during the bottling process, allowing the bright hoppiness to shine through. This process naturally creates the CO_2 required for carbonation, which results in finer champagne-like bubbles when the beer is served and leads to a smoother mouth feel, a denser foam, and actually helps with the shelf stability of the beer. This is because the flavor-destroying oxygen trapped in the head space by the bottle cap during bottling is scavenged out of the beer by the refermentation process that comes with bottle conditioning.

Bottle conditioning is a traditional process that naturally carbonates the beer in the bottle, using additional yeast and sugar. Dogfish Head only makes one other bottle-conditioned beer and that is our 75 Minute IPA.

Once bottled we age Squall for two weeks, then it's ready to ship out the door. And while the residual yeast and sugars in the bottle help to consume any of that flavor-destroying oxygen, this is one that's meant to be consumed sooner rather than later.

The beer pours a beautiful copper color. The continual hopping, dry-hopping, and bottle conditioning give Squall a really complex flavor with bright, citrusy, and hoppy notes that

"Squall is an OG New England IPA."
—Sam Calagione

are a favorite of many, many fans. In fact, I've heard rumors that it may make a small-batch return at one of our properties in Coastal Delaware—so visit us soon!

Clocking in at 9 percent ABV, Squall is a citrus-forward IPA with floral notes of pine and grapefruit. And because it's bottle conditioned, you'll appreciate that "psst!" even more as you crack open a bottle.

Bière de Provence (8.3% ABV)

Back in 2016, looking for inspiration for our next beer, I flipped through a French cookbook when I came across a recipe for a traditional provincial chicken dish from the southeast of France. The region where this recipe originated is also that region between Belgium and France where so many great saisons and bière de garde—or "beer for keeping"—come from historically.

There was a section that explained the history of this classic French dish made with herbes de Provence. Reading the ingredient list, my mouth started watering. The herb mixture was heavy with lavender, marjoram, bayleaf, and chervil—a leafy green herb in the parsley family. The dish sounded like it would go beautifully with a warm fermented saison.

We'd been brewing saisons for about a decade, including our Noble Rot and Saison de Buff, so creating a beer with these culinary ingredients to add to our saison offerings was irresistible.

We started with two-row wheat, rye malt, and Jarrylo hops, which gave us an 8 percent base rich with rye, wheat, and barley. We began creating test batches from there by adding lavender, bayleaf, marjoram, and chervil. The beer is then fermented using a Belgian yeast strain.

The lavender, bay leaf, marjoram, and chervil gives it a floral and spicy nose, while the Belgian yeast lends a sweet and malty flavor profile to the beer. With a hazy golden appearance, and not too hoppy at just 30 BTUs, Bière de Provence is a summer beer that has a flavor just as complex as it is crisp and refreshing, with a seriously smooth finish.

If Raison D'Etre was first designed to be the ultimate partner for a wood-grilled steak, and SeaQuench Ale was a beer designed to go with beautiful fresh raw oysters from the mouth of the Chesapeake or off the shore of Maine, Bière de Provence is another culinary-inspired beer that was designed to go great with a traditional French poultry dish. For me it feels, tastes, and smells like skipping through a field of wildflowers and herbs.

"The Hills Are Alive with the Sounds of Bière de Provence"

—Sam Calagione

Siracusa Nera (10% ABV)

The favorite part of my job at Dogfish hasn't changed in 26 years. I get to spend time with two of our brewers making a beautiful beer that has dandelion root in it and pureed oranges and cinnamon bark as well. Many of the other moments I'm most proud of at Dogfish Head are in supporting the creative ideas of other people at this company who may be brewers or from any department who have an awesome idea for a beer that we can then rally around and help that person make a reality. Both Siracusa Nera and Lupu-Luau are shining examples of this.

Amanda Petro

Siracusa Nera is a wonderful recipe that was actually the creation of our coworker Amanda Petro, a brewer here at Dogfish. It was her recipe. She served it at a small-batch dinner at our pub and people really loved it. I got to try it at one of our events and said, "Well, this is beautiful beer, let's scale this up and sell it coast to coast." The beer is a combination of a traditional roasty Imperial Stout with a jammy red Syrah grape wine must. The beer is bold and complex and has notes of coffee, dark chocolate, and star anise from a blend of roasted malt with flavors of plums, cherries, and stewed fruits in a jet-black stout. That is a mouthful! When a beer is strong in alcohol—if you don't age it before you sell it—it has "pointy elbows," meaning it's sharp and the alcohol can be biting in the taste. We've learned in our time brewing plenty of high ABV beers that they can often benefit from aging on wood—because wood is porous and there's an oxygen exchange with the wood-aging process that really softens those sharp elbows that come with strong beer. Siracusa is no different: we use our giant American oak wood aging tanks to lay Siracusa Nera down for a bunch of months before we package it, and that adds some nice light, toasty, vanilla notes to the beer as well.

Lupu-Luau

(7.3% ABV)

Lupu-Luau was inspired by a coworker chef, Emily, who had the idea to build a recipe around coconut flakes that she brought to me and our brewer, Mark Safarik. It started with a conversation I was having with the two of them on Benevolence Day, the day we close all our businesses and the entire company helps build homes for Habitat for Humanity and work on trails for The Nature Conservancy. At the end of the day, we all meet up at the brewery in Milton for chili, beer, and some bocce.

This particular spring Benevolence Day was hot and sunny. My Mediterranean skin enjoyed the sun, but Emily's skin is lacking in melanin and the sun was not kind to her that day. As we were noting this, Emily spoke up and said to me, "You can say it, Sam, I am pale as f**k." Mark and I laughed and then it hit us: Let's make a beer called "Pale as F**k." We started beer-ingredient riffing with Emily and she suggested coconut right away. The moment was sort of kismet because somebody had dropped off a sample of dehydrated coconut water on my desk earlier that week. At the same time, someone had dropped off some hops at Mark Safarik's desk that smelled like coconuts. We combined Emily's idea of flaked coconut with the dehydrated coconut water and the coconut-scented hops to make this beer.

For a very short time it did hold onto its original name, but we knew that might not fly in the marketplace so eventually we changed the name to Lupu-Luau, made and distributed by Dogfish for numerous years. This is a favorite story of mine: Emily was so proud that she got to be part of bringing a beer idea to life that she got a tattoo featuring all the ingredients in the Lupu-Luau beer—to go along with her tattoo of Tom Hanks.

Romantic Chemistry

(7.2% ABV)

In 2016 we also released Romantic Chemistry, a seasonal India Pale Ale. The name and the ingredients are a play on the notion of a three-way. Intermingled in the recipe for Romantic Chemistry are the three main ingredients of mango, apricot, and hops. The beer is also dry hopped with three different hop varieties to deliver tropical fruit aromas and a hop-forward finish.

Chemistry is a big part of Dogfish and our beer geekery. There is always the quality and consistency aspect of how our beers are being produced and eventually delivered to the fans, but the main chemistry for this beer was looking at the way both the citrus and the hops shared a common chemical compound.

The name Romantic Chemistry is a nod to the fact that to make this beer required a lot of trials in the lab to create the perfect intermingling of ingredients. We have almost a dozen full-time coworkers in our quality control laboratories, committed to making sure our beer is bulletproof in terms of quality and consistency. For this beer their roles were even more critical to the brewing process.

For this beer we wanted to hone in on a naturally produced oil called myrcene that brings citrus notes forward in both the hops and the fruits we planned to use as ingredients. We chose apricot and mango, which both have high levels of myrcene oil. Myrcene oil is also found in the hops that we added to this beer, making them complementary. There is a flavor romance between the fruit and the hops in this beer and as we looked deeper there is some serious beer-geek chemistry happening here as well.

Brewing is both chemistry and alchemy—a combination of science and creativity—and so a beer like Romantic Chemistry is a perfect example of how we bring those worlds together.

CHEMISTRY
IPA
ales for off-centered

Beer To Drink Music To

(9% ABV)

We've always said at Dogfish that we're music geeks as much as we're beer geeks. It's not just Bryan Selders and me who are raging music lovers but many of our coworkers as well. When I started brewing on our first brewing system, I had a boom box in the brewery and there was always music on. I also studied the burgeoning movements of hip-hop and punk rock to inform how we would grow the Dogfish brand. We decided the Dogfish Head brand would be very DIY because we grew up watching punk bands back in the pre-internet day when they would design their own gig posters, screen print their own T-shirts, book their own tours across the country, and load up their own equipment.

You had to do everything yourself, but by doing everything yourself you could put your stamp of what your band or your brand stood for onto everything you did. That sort of DIY spirit that came from the worlds of punk rock, early hip-hop pioneers like Afrika Bambaataa, DJ Kool Herc, and so many other musicians who were building their own scene—stealing electric power from the lights on out-door basketball hoops to set up giant sound systems in different boroughs of New York to get the community dancing and rapping over the music.

> "Record Store Day just kind of kicked this all off."

Those sort of stories definitely influenced Dogfish Head's journey, so we bring our love of bands and music into the beer recipes themselves. As you can tell by now, music has been at the heart of what we do at Dogfish Head since before we opened, so it's a natural fit for a brewery that makes "analog beer for the digital age," to be the official brewery of Record Store Day. Record Store Day is this awesome holiday that was started to bring more aware-ness and support to independent record stores for their contribution to music and the artists they support. Much like America's independent craft breweries, record stores are fighting an uphill battle against larger, more powerful, and better-resourced competitors.

In the case of Dogfish Head and Sam Adams Boston Beer, we only make up 2 percent of the total beer market, versus Anheuser-Busch InBev, which owns over 50 percent market share; MillerCoors, which owns over 20 percent market share; and then there are Heineken and Corona, and all the other big players. Like Dogfish Head, Sam Adams, and other craft beers, these little indie record stores are up against Spotify and iTunes. We felt like these

indie record stores were kindred spirits, not only because we love music, but because they, too, are Davids up against Goliaths just like craft beer brands. We've been proud to be the official brewery of Record Store Day for many years at Dogfish Head. So in 2016, we decided to create a special brew to celebrate Record Store Day.

The beer, Beer To Drink Music To, is a Belgian-style, triple brewed with sweet orange peel, green cardamom, peppercorns, and vanilla. It was built to be the perfect beer to be paired with listening to music. It's a golden orange color, with notes of toffee, cardamom, cloves, and subtle notes of vanilla.

Mark Carter

Beer & Benevolence Director
Start Date: 2009

A Delaware native, the retired Marine Corp major and lifetime surfer/environmentalist is one of the most engaged people you will ever come across. The dichotomy of a super-chilled-out-surfer-vagabond and Marine Corp major is personified in Mark Carter. He is like a walking Yin-Yang. Deeply entrenched in our local community and the nonprofit world, the concept of service is more a way of life for Mark. On any given day you may find him at sunrise riding a wave at Cape Henlopen State Park, sitting on a local nonprofit board, eating a good taco, meeting with town managers to get logistics tight for a running fundraiser, tending to his chickens and organic farm, taking care of his kids, or watching a sunset on the Broadkill River with a beat-up copy of John Muir's *The Wilderness Journeys* in one hand and a pint of 60 in his other. Mark knows what is important in life.

Dogfish Head started when Mark was a junior in college at VMI. Chicory Stout and Shelter Pale Ale were the first craft beers he ever had. Being a Delaware native, he felt some pride in what this little brewery from his home state was doing. In 2009, Mark was a kayak guide and personal trainer. A tour guide spot was opening, and Mark came on to cover some shifts. An events position opened, he threw down, and that was it. Mark knew Sam and Mariah, and Dogfish Head was exciting, fun, and allowed him to feed his Dharma Bums, surf lifestyle. Today, Mark works with nonprofits while wearing his Dogfish hat. These nonprofits are working toward the greater good and it inspires him to get out of bed every day and come to work. While Major Carter has covered some bases, he went full-time Beer and Benevolence in 2015. He has sat, quite literally, at nine different desks in our Milton offices. Nine. This rolling stone gathers no moss.

Mark and Andrew pouring at GABF

He "officially" started at Dogfish in 2009, but prior to that, he had been running people on "Pints and Paddles" and some other boat trips out of Lewes. "Pints and Paddles" is a tour program Mark and his brother Matt Carter started. Quest Kayak, a company we continue to partner with today, takes folks out on kayak tours around Cape Henlopen for sunrise, out to see dolphins in Delaware Bay or the ocean, up the Broadkiller River, and even out to an old shipwreck in Delaware Bay. You then load up post-kayak paddle and head up to the brewery for a tour. Ninety minutes on the water, 90-minute tour, 90 Minute beer—that is a good day. Back in 2009, Mark would be your kayak guide, your brewery tour guide, your bartender, and likely, your spiritual counselor. The program still runs today but focuses on the Broadkill River. While Mark is up to other things, you can still get all you need from "Pints and Paddles."

Coworker Profile

"I wear a lot of hats" is a way of life for Mark Carter at Dogfish Head.

In his 10+ years, he has been Tour Guide, Tour Room Manager, Events Director, Merchandise Assistant, Beer and Benevolence Director, Community Relations Guy, and Donation Dude. Not a bad run for a career. Feels more like a lifetime of roles. When it comes to events that Mark has either put on or executed, the list only grows longer. Mark was key in executing WOCAAW (Weekend of Compelling Ales and Whatnot); Analog-A-Go-Go; and Intergalactic Bocce Ball Tournaments—annually in Milton, one on the roof of a Whole Foods in Chicago, one next to a swimming pool in Palm Springs, and one inside a ballroom in San Diego, to name a few. He also directs Benevolence Day, a day all coworkers unite to build homes for local families through Habitat for Humanity; Off-Centered Film Fest; the Delaware Restaurant Association's Bocce Tournament; the IPA aka I Pedal A-Lot bike tour; and the Dogfish Dash, which is now a serious beast of an event. The Dash will have raised over $1,000,000 for the Delaware Nature Conservancy Chapter in 2021. It will be the 16th annual running of the Dash and the 14th one Mark has directed. He has been written up in *Runner's World,* and somewhere in there, he finds time to raise his kids, tend his chickens, and ride some waves on Assateague Island—when the swell is right. The next time you think you don't have time to get involved in a community movement you feel strongly about, think of Mark Carter and get to work.

Mark's favorite Dogfish beer is Indian Brown Ale—American Brown Ale crossed with a scotch ale and continually hopped. What's the worst Dogfish beer? This one stumped him a bit, but he is not a big fan of 90 Minute. 60 has more sessionable qualities, 120 is a conversation beer, but 90 is no man's land.

When asked about his fondest memories at Dogfish Head, the nostalgic poet comes out in Mark. Mark's favorite memories are the moments of pause he has found with Sam and Mariah separately. He recalls eating an Indulgence Burger with Mariah after Dogfish Dash packet pick up in Rehoboth. They took some time to smell the hops. Time to reflect and feel grateful for all that was happening. He recalls bumming around Texas with Sam and riding bikes to hunt up some vinyl. Mark recalls many days going into the brewery when nobody else was there except Sam, and they would talk about their kids. These moments of connection can't be forced or created. It is up to us to pay attention to them when they appear. People are often too busy to notice them: Sam, Mariah, and Mark cultivate them. There is some serious value in it that will never be found in a PowerPoint deck.

Mark reminds all of us that we have more time than we think; we can do more than we think; we have more to give back to our community than we think; and that taking the time to pause in the moment is vital to seeing the big picture. He embodies a culture of giving at Dogfish Head that was instilled by Sam and Mariah from the very beginning. We are not defined by one beer or one event; we are defined by what we give back. Mark throws the karma boomerang with everything he has and it returns to him daily with gifts of gratitude. Mark makes an impact, and quietly he moves on to the next opportunity.

If you were on a deserted island and could have one album to listen to and an unlimited supply of one beer, what would it be?

Beer: Indian Brown Ale
Album: *The Endless Summer* original soundtrack

Chapter 10

Out with the Old, in with the New

For 22 years, the original Dogfish Head Brewings & Eats brewpub was a fixture in Rehoboth and a top tourist destination in Delaware. In 2017, after two decades of cranking out off-centered ales, we said goodbye to our very first location. Thousands of beers and countless memories later, it was time to build a brand-new Rehoboth brewpub.

Like every story worth telling, the creation of the brewpub was not without plot twists. The building had once been a crab house, followed by a bevy of failed restaurants. In April of 2015, we approached the city's Board of Adjustment for approval to renovate and expand the site and were initially turned down. We eventually got the green light to demolish the old brewpub and build a larger structure with an outdoor courtyard and indoor stage.

We wanted to create a one-of-a-kind environment for customers to enjoy Dogfish Head hospitality, beers, and food. The small parking lot next to the old brewpub became the site for the new and improved Dogfish Head Brewings & Eats, with updated furnishings, a state-of-the-art brewing system, and a bigger, better stage that better represented the influence music had on the beer, food, and culture of our community.

Demolition day was bitter-sweet on Rehoboth Ave.

Bar area from the OG Pub

"We couldn't abandon the spot where it all began, though. There were too many beers and memories to let it go quietly into the night."

So we knocked down the original brewpub and created a downright awesome patio that would connect the new brewpub with our other restaurant, Chesapeake & Maine.

The original brewpub remained open during the summer of 2017 for guests to pick up merch and fill their growlers. Then, before the old brewpub closed for good, we had a "Last Call at Dogfish Head Brewings & Eats." It gave locals a chance to grab their favorite brew and kick back in the old familiar space. While patrons enjoyed their final visit to the original brewpub, they also previewed the new brewpub with exclusive tours before it opened.

Dogfish Head tap handles, chairs up for auction

PATRICIA TALORICO
THE NEWS JOURNAL

Dogfish Head aficionados can bid on hand-carved, shark-shaped beer tap handles, tables, chairs, light fixtures and more during a silent auction being held on weekends throughout October at the Rehoboth Beach Fire Department on Rehoboth Avenue.

The items come from the original Dogfish Head Brewings & Eats, which opened in 1995 and closed this spring after the new $4 million brewpub opened next door to the flagship location.

The tap handles and other items will be on display at the fire department from 10 a.m. to 6 p.m. on Saturdays and Sundays.

"It's the end of one era for our original brewpub and the beginning of a new one," says Sam Calagione, founder and CEO of Dogfish Head Craft Brewery.

All proceeds raised from the Dogfish silent auction will benefit the local Rehoboth Beach Volunteer Fire Department.

For more information about Dogfish Head Craft Brewery, visit www.dogfish.com To view a full list of items available for auction, check out www.dogfish.com/blog

Twitter @pattytalorico

Tap handles are some of the items up for auction throughout October at the Rehoboth Beach Fire Department on Rehoboth Avenue. SUBMITTED IMAGE

The epic grand opening for the new brewpub featured live music by Richard Lloyd, a founding member of the punk rock band Television; brewpub exclusives; and a dramatic reveal of the new digs: a parking lot turned brewpub and restaurant.

For the inaugural brewpub exclusive, we teamed up with Joe Short, the owner of Short's Brewing Company, to make a Bloody Mary–inspired, imperial style beer: Bloody Beer. Brewers used 128 pounds of blanched, pureed Roma tomatoes and a combination of horseradish, dill, celery seed, and black pepper. The result? A golden, delicately spicy, lightly hopped beer with 7 percent ABV. We served Bloody Beer in the brewpub and sold a limited quantity of 32-ounce growlers.

The brewpub interior was inspired by the heart of Dogfish Head: beer. Booths in the restaurant are shaped like barrels and the windows like beer bubbles. Customers also enjoy live music while eating and drinking.

The brewpub interior was inspired by the heart of Dogfish Head: beer.

Jimmie Allen takes the stage.

Brewpub courtyard

The central feature of the new brewpub is a 220-square-foot stage with a professional sound and lighting system. Gone are the days of musicians falling off our small, makeshift stage. The new setup has hosted local and national artists, including Guided By Voices, Ron Gallo, Michaela Anne, BJ Barham of American Aquarium, Los Straightjackets, Marshall Crenshaw, and Steve Gunn.

We wanted the interior of the brewpub to feel open and airy and brought in architects from DIGSAU, a Philadelphia-based design firm. DIGSAU also designed the Milton brewery. The new brewpub has a tall exposed ceiling, large windows, and cozy wooden walls, with metal staircases that lead to a dining room overlooking the main room and stage. The walls feature photos of Patti Smith, the Ramones, Sonic Youth, Run DMC, and others.

Now, the food ... the old brewpub menu was all about comfort. When designing the new menu, we thought about how to elevate the options by sourcing unique ingredients and recipes, without losing the comfort. We focused on finding high-quality, regional ingredients for our chefs to use to create memorable dishes. Menu favorites include the reimagined Dogpile (previously an artichoke-spinach dip and now nachos), a Neapolitan-inspired pizza with house-made cheeses, and a wood-grilled grilled cheese with Palo Santo Marron onion jam. The revamped menu at Brewings & Eats matches the innovative

style of our brews that customers are accustomed to, and 24 taps pour patrons' favorite beers, along with a revolving list of brewpub exclusives.

The inspiration behind the Dogfish Head Brewings & Eats menu was simple: serve food that would pair well with our beers. That led us to wood-grilled pizzas, steaks, seafood, and sandwiches, each designed to complement our brewpub exclusives, small batch spirits, and our classic beers. The kitchen has a pasta machine from Italy, a custom-made open-flame pizza oven, and a wood grill with oak and hickory logs.

In 2017 Sam also happened to receive the James Beard Award for the most Outstanding Wine, Beer, or Spirits Professional. This elevated the profile of the new brewpub and placed a bigger spotlight on Dogfish Head's culinary adventures. Executive chef Zach Dick keeps the menu fresh so people keep coming back to see what's new, and there's always a brewpub exclusive to try.

Not only is the brewpub one of a kind, but it will also be the last of its kind in Rehoboth. The Rehoboth Beach commissioners voted to restrict restaurant sizes, limiting establishments that serve alcohol to 2,500 square feet of dining space and 500 square feet of bar area. Our original brewpub preceded this rule, and the new brewpub was in construction before it took effect. We lucked into building the right place at the right time, and now more than 1,000 customers enjoy all the brewpub has to offer on a busy day.

"Wooden... It Be Nice!"

Dogfish was among the first American craft brewers to specialize in wild or sour beers. We first started brewing sours nearly 20 years ago, beginning with Festina Lente. That peach wild ale won us a bronze medal at the World Beer Cup the year it was first produced. In 2016 we produced another popular sour, our SeaQuench Ale, which is now the top-selling sour in America. We quickly became the largest producer of sour beers in America as a result.

"The only war is the war against imagination."
—Diane Di Prima

When Dogfish Head produced that first sour ale, sours were really a very niche, marginalized style. As sours gained traction in the market, and excitement from today's beer drinkers grew, Dogfish decided to create a brewing process that would not only increase the volume of sour beer production, but would also expand the breadth of and creativity within sour beer production. We had been producing and perfecting sour ales for over two decades, and we got to thinking … wouldn't it be nice if beer lovers could get their hands on even more wild ales from Dogfish Head?

Our "Wooden … It Be Nice!" program doesn't take any singular set path during the brewing process.

And so, in 2018, our "Wooden ... It Be Nice!" program was born. Along with this new barrel-aged process, we dedicated a giant 2,000-square-foot space within our facility that we called the Sour Patch for the production of wild or Brettanomyces bacteria–fermented sour beers.

The "Wooden ... It Be Nice!" program was the foundation of our wild beer series, where we created all our wild bacteria and barrel-aged specialty beers. It was a playground for creativity and artistry. With all the different fermentation types, the Sour Patch provided a place where chemistry and a variety of ingredients played off each other to constantly evolve the "Wooden ... It Be Nice!" program.

There's no set of rules for brewing in the Sour Patch.

"Wooden ... It Be Nice!" was another step forward in our journey and evolution of goodness, incorporating everything from herbs and spices to local fruits and—of course—bringing it all together in wooden barrels.

So what makes a beer wild? It's different from traditional brewing in that it's fermented with other yeasts, beyond the yeast pitched during fermentation. It uses wild yeast variations like Brettanomyces, instead of the standard Saccharomyces. The yeast is carefully introduced to the wood-aged beer, which can develop a wide array of flavors, including degrees of sourness and fruitiness, and hop-level variations that occur during fermentation. Due to the untamable nature of the yeast and the longer length the fermentation process can take, the beer can sit in barrels for months or even years until brewers deem it ready for consumption. These wild yeasts also consume more of the sugar, resulting in more sour flavors in these beers. This uncontrollable process can sometimes delay the release of the beer, but when it's finally ready, it's truly remarkable. Isn't that wild?!

With our high-volume production beers, we truly have the process down to a science. We know those yeast strains and those ingredients so well that we can predict from the day we brew it how long it'll take—within 10 percent—before that beer is ready to be bottled or canned or kegged. This structure also allows us to achieve consistency, batch after batch.

Instead of having a similarly structured process down in the Sour Patch section of the brewery, we can brew a batch, lay it, add fruit, lay it again, add more fruit, mix it, blend it—and we're doing it across so many barrels that it's really up to the Sour Patch brewers to taste it and decide when the desired flavor is achieved.

Sometimes with those beers we can't tell what day we're going to bottle or package and sell them. The few intrepid brewers who work in that space oftentimes get outvoted by the millions of cells of bacteria and wild yeast that are also working in that space, and the bacteria and yeast tell the brewers when that beer is ready to be packaged, not the other way around. We never rush the process. We let the beer decide when it's ready. Because of that, these beers tend to be released in very small batches, which makes it really special and rewarding when beer lovers come to our facility. Even the packaging is very artisanal and hand done.

Our history of brewing sour beers goes back nearly as far as our history of using fresh local culinary ingredients.

Dogfish had a long tradition of sourcing ingredients locally even before the now widespread "locavore" food movement came in vogue. In the earliest days of Dogfish Head, I read a bunch about Alice Waters who, as a chef on the West Coast, was among the first to source the ingredients for her restaurant by forming relationships directly with local farmers. I really took that idea to heart, and when we began sourcing ingredients, always reached out to local businesses first. That is how the local coffee producers in Lewes became our first choice to roast the coffee beans for our Chicory Stout.

As Dogfish grew, producing our high-volume beers at the scale we do sometimes made it difficult for us to use local producers. We used to use local pumpkins in our Punkin Ale, but now that we're brewing hundreds of thousands of bottles of Punkin Ale we have to buy that pumpkin meat—yes, we still use real pumpkin meat—but we have to buy it in volume, already pureed.

The brewing coming out of our wild beer series program allowed us to return to the scale of brewing where we could again source and test with local ingredients. It reconnected us with this concept, rooted in our DNA as a brewery. The scale that we're brewing at today in the Sour Patch section of the brewery is more akin in scale to the way Dogfish started brewing its core beers 26 years ago, and that allows us to engage on a new level with local farmers and local makers of all sorts when it comes to sourcing herbs, spices, or fruits for our beers.

To launch the "Wooden ... It Be Nice!" program, we created three wild ales primed for a Milton-only release. Our brewers had to hand bottle and cork over two thousand cork-and-cage 375 ml bottles to prepare the beers for sale. I had the idea to emphasize just how artisanal these beers were by hand painting a special stripe on each bottle that would signify just how uniquely crafted each bottle was. The process was blissfully inefficient.

The maintenance and engineering team humored my request. When I suggested we hand paint a stripe on every single bottle, which obviously would be very time-consuming, our maintenance and engineering team created a small machine that would apply a different stripe of paint to each bottle. Every bottle was then like a snowflake—completely unique from the next bottle that came off the line because every stripe of paint was different. It reminded us just how complex and variable the beers are that come out of the "Wooden ... It Be Nice!" program.

ET HOP
AN SUMMER
KNOTTYBITS
EASTERN SEABOARD

KnottyBits
(8.2% ABV)

The first beer that came out of the Sour Patch as part of the "Wooden … It Be Nice!" program was KnottyBits—a wild ale, aged on both sweet and sour cherries and featuring local rhubarb.

To make this beer we teamed up with our friends at Fifer Orchards, a fourth generation, family owned orchard located in Camden-Wyoming, Delaware, to source the cherries and rhubarb. KnottyBits was first aged in wooden barrels for a year with Brettanomyces bruxellensis yeast. From there, we racked the beer onto several hundred pounds of sweet and sour cherries, as well as locally sourced rhubarb, at a rate of more than 2 pounds of fresh fruit per gallon! We juiced the rhubarb ourselves on a tiny little juicing machine owned by an entrepreneur in downtown Rehoboth, Twist Juice Bar.

The beer is then hand bottled and corked. Bottle conditioning provides an elevated carbonation that resembles a rose-colored sparkling wine of sorts. It is a perfect balance of funk and acidity.

KnottyBits rhubarb from Fifer Orchards

KNOTTYBITS

Wet Hop American Summer

(7.2% ABV)

Wet Hop American Summer also came from the Sour Patch. This was the second beer out of our "Wooden ... It Be Nice!" wild beer program. The name for this beer was a callback to a wonderful cult movie that my roommates and I were watching while I brewed that very first batch of cherry home brew in New York City. In fact, I think five of the cast members from *Wet Hot American Summer* were in the room with me when I first poured that beer. As a shout-out to them, because a bunch of them also came down and helped me build out the brewpub, I named this beer after their awesome movie—changing the hot to hop. Wet Hop American Summer is a wild ale, dry hopped with wet Citra hops.

To create the beer we started with a rustic farmhouse base ale. After aging the ale for more than a year in Chardonnay bottles, it was racked onto a selection of handpicked, unprocessed, whole flower, freshly harvested Citra hops that were still wet from the field we got them from.

Wet hop beers are more popular in the craft brewing community in the Northwest—northern California, Oregon, and Washington—because the process of making them necessitates quickly moving hops into the boil kettle from the moment they are clipped off the vines to make the beer. This is why you don't see a ton of wet hop beers made out of the high-volume hop growing regions in America. That said, there's more and more small-scale farmers in different geographies across the country who have figured out what varieties of hops grow well in their climate, and in our case we were able to find some mid-Atlantic farmers growing hops that we could make a wet hop beer with.

The beer finishes dry. It's highly carbonated, chock full of intensely earthy flavors, fragrances, and aromas of the Brettanomyces funk and hand painted with a special stripe signifying its uniquely crafted touch.

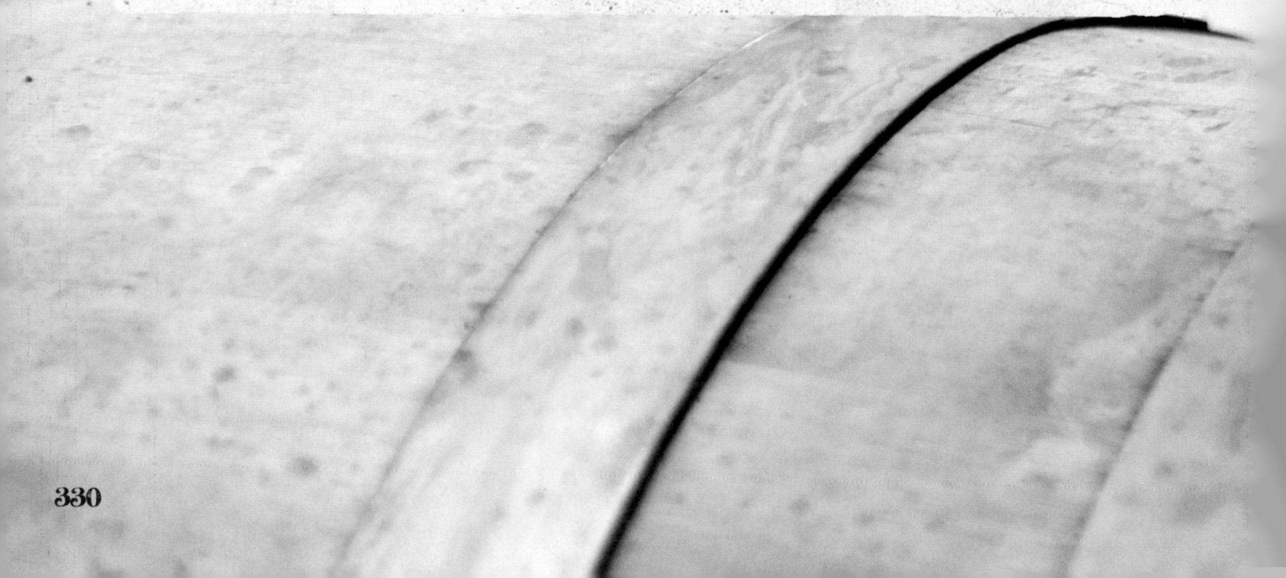

WET HOP
AMERICAN SUMMER

Eastern Seaboard

(7.2% ABV)

The third beer out of our "Wooden ... It Be Nice!" wild beer program was Eastern Seaboard. Eastern Seaboard is a jammy and tart wild ale made with handpicked blackberries and Eastern Shore beach plums.

For this we also started with the same rustic farmhouse base ale that we started with for Wet Hop American Summer. After spending nearly a year and a half in a mix of both red and white wine barrels, the beer was racked onto several hundred pounds of blackberries and locally sourced beach plums, which gives this beer a brilliant ruby red color.

Eastern Seaboard is deceptively dry and bottle conditioned to achieve a champagne-like carbonation.

EASTERN SEABOARD
WILD ALE AGED ON
BLACKBERRIES &
BEACH PLUMS

Bunyan's Lunchbox evolves to the full-fledged Tasting Room & Kitchen.

Experience Ambassador Kim Koot working the bar

Tap lineup in the tasting room

In our relentless pursuit of innovation at Dogfish Head, it became clear that with Bunyan's Lunchbox in Milton, our original food offerings of bratwurst, chowder, and pickles were not going to be enough. The Lunchbox menu had kept growing since we opened it in 2013, but we finally exhausted our capabilities in that small space. In 2018, under the leadership of our beer-geek and food Jedis, Matt Fetherston and Jon March, we opened a brand-new state-of-the-art kitchen offering beer-infused handcrafted pizzas, as well as calzones, burritos, sandwiches, fresh salads, and daily specials. Looking back to when we started in 1995 in Rehoboth, we would pull ingredients directly from the kitchen and use them to inspire us in the brewhouse. In Milton we pull beer directly from the brewhouse and use it to inspire menu items. Along with the addition of the kitchen, the tasting room is now equipped with 78 total taps pouring up to 34 different beers, eight different cocktails with spirits from the distillery, one beer flowing through Randall the Enamel Animal, and a growler and crowler bar.

When you visit us, do not forget to look up! With your head tipped back, you will notice the ceiling is covered in framed pictures. We populated it with images of other off-centered folks to keep you company.

Experience Ambassador Marge Eglen

With the expansion of the tasting room and the facilities up in Milton, we were also able to grow our tour programs, enhancing the guest experience on all fronts and providing multiple options. Just a sampling of some of the tours we offer includes a Quick Sip tour, which covers some key moments in our early years and takes a turn through our 200-barrel brewhouse (with samples); a Distillery tour, providing a deep dive into the spirits world at Dogfish Head; and then the Grain to Glass tour, which is a two-hour experience covering everything from cold storage and the R&D program to spirits and packaging. The best part about all these offerings from the beer to the food and the tours is it allows fans to spend more time with our amazing guides in Milton and really engage with multiple facets of our business and culture. On any given afternoon you might find a coworker from brewing or packaging having a pint at the bar, talking to a guest about 60 Minute or Hazy-O! The beer, food, and tours are phenomenal, but it is really the relationships built between our coworkers and our fans that stand the test of time and keep people coming back. Deeply connected to the local community, every month the tasting room selects a local nonprofit and donates all tips received in that space to that local nonprofit. Some months the tour team will raise up to $20,000 for a nonprofit. The Milton Tasting Room & Kitchen is a central hub for the town of Milton—a place where you can find our off-centered community alive and well.

"The best part about all these offerings from the beer to the food and the tours is it allows fans to spend more time with our amazing guides in Milton and really engage with multiple facets of our business and culture."

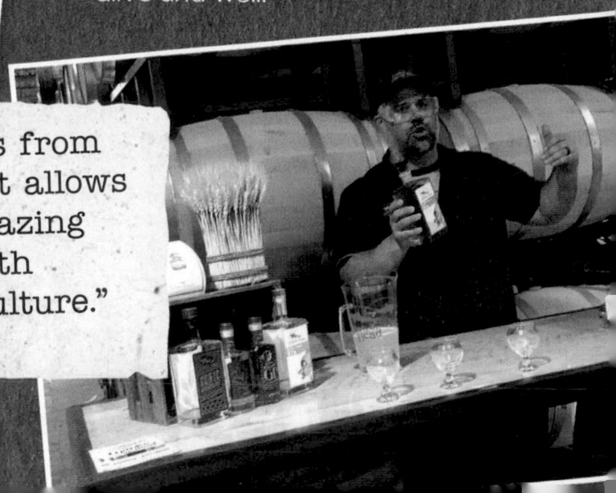

The tour team brewing up a small batch in Milton

Dogfish Head
Sea Quench Ale
90 MIN IPA
continually hopped for 90 minutes.
Namaste White
Hazy-O!
A hazy IPA w/ 4 types of oats.
Campfire Amplifier!
Sun-Day-Feels
DFH Kölsch
Cupricious & Cantankardous Mule-esque sour 7% ABV
This is Mrs. Ridiculous
Utopias Barrel Aged 120 MIN IPA
Pan De CoCo
Porter brewed w/ toasted coconut + cocoa
I Heard You Like Ella
Twist of Fate
Session India Pale Lager
Salacious IPA
Umeboshi
Because America
classic American lager
Liquid Amalgam
Straightforward Czech Pils
Sour Dream
I Remember My First Check In
Cuppa Cold Brew
Botania
gin-inspired farmhouse ale
Aequatorial Aether
My Friend Brecki
Pyrotechnic Space Lazerz
Mandarin • Mandarina Bavaria Hops Hard Seltzer
HAZY-O! IPA

American Beauty Hazy Ripple (7% ABV)

This beer is an evolution of our original recipe of American Beauty Pale Ale. For this one the inspiration actually came from Egypt. I was over in Egypt many years ago brewing a beer and doing a television show called *Brewmasters*. I talked to the head of agriculture for the city of Cairo, asked him about traditional grains that grew there, and he spoke about a grain from somewhere near that region called spelt. I did some research on it and it's considered to be an heirloom grain. We brewed a beer called Ta Henket with it in small batch, way back when. I remembered spelt when we decided to brew this beer. We did a test batch with it and found that it actually would be the perfect beer to do a hazy IPA with. Dogfish had already done a prototype version of the hazy IPA with Squall back in the mid-2000s in small batch, but after that we didn't really do much with that style. Then some wonderful New England breweries like the Alchemist and Lawson's Liquids in Vermont brought that style to the forefront. We figured out an off-centered way to do a hazy IPA that would differentiate it from those others that were already making a splash on the market. Our recipe had around 25 percent of the green build coming from this ancient grain, spelt, that cast a really predictable and deep haze naturally in the beer and created an earthy sort of trampoline that we bounced really juicy aromatic hops off of. This is the recipe that has become American Beauty Hazy Ripple IPA.

Ripple, of course, is probably the best-known song from the iconic *American Beauty* Grateful Dead album. We brewed American Beauty Hazy Ripple to commemorate the 50th anniversary of the *American Beauty* album being celebrated in 2020. We also finally had our collaboration with the *American Beauty*, including a new interpretation of its iconic dancing bear artwork into what is now the most popular package for a 12-ounce can, available year round coast to coast.

Sam shares some Hazy Ripple with David Lemieux, archivist and legacy manager of the Grateful Dead, at the Dogfish INN.

"There was nowhere to go but everywhere,
so just keep on rolling under the stars."
—Jack Kerouac, *On the Road*

Beer Exploration Journal

Suddenly Comfy

(8% ABV)

In 2019, we brewed the first batch of Suddenly Comfy. In the same way that Punkin Ale is probably our most celebrated autumnal beer, we wanted to create another beer that celebrated the flavors and harvests of the fall. Enter Suddenly Comfy. It's an Imperial Cream Ale brewed with fresh apple cider, Saigon cinnamon, and Madagascar vanilla beans—all the fixings that go into a great apple pie, just like your grandma used to make—only now in liquid form. When you drink this beer, you get notes of aromatic pie crusts and brûléed sugar with the fruity sweetness of the apples.

Suddenly Comfy is another great example of us crowdsourcing feedback that informs our R&D process through our Beer Exploration Journal. This program was designed to give our fans a peek into the world of R&D at Dogfish—allowing them to sample, evaluate, and rate new beers and the stories that surround those beers, on tap exclusively at our Milton Tasting Room and our Rehoboth brewpub.

The Perfect Disguise (8% ABV)

After the success of SeaQuench Ale—our mash-up of a Kölsch, a gose, and a Berliner Weiss—we thought we would do another mash-up—this time of a Kölsch and an IPA. For a long time beers brewed above the standard IPA level of hoppiness were unpopular, but now big IPAs and even bigger double or imperial IPAs are growing in popularity. Of course, we've been exploring increasingly intense IPAs while also making them more sessionable for a while. With IPAs now far and away the largest-selling style of craft beer, the variations of IPA-style beers continue to expand into various substyles of IPA, from session IPAs to sour IPAs to imperials to New Englands.

For this beer, we started with a unique German chit malt, fermented it with a Kölsch yeast, brewed it strong, and finished it with a blend of American IPA and German Kölsch hops. Unlike the hopping regimen for a traditionally English-style pale ale, which might add a half pound of hops per barrel and result in a nice hoppy, go-to pale ale—for Perfect Disguise we added over four pounds of hops per barrel, using a blend of both American and German hops. The result was a double IPA that brings forward these really intense tropical flavors of citrus, tangerine, mango, gooseberries, and peach.

> You don't know if it's an IPA disguised as a Kölsch or if it's a Kölsch disguised as an IPA—the perfect disguise.

With its golden appearance, the beer pours like a straightforward Kölsch, but the beer has a creamy mouthfeel and full body flavor thanks to the unique German chit malt—the first hint that this beer may be somewhat different. Deeper behind that German disguise is the rich citrus flavor of a dry-hopped American double IPA.

The term double IPA is fairly synonymous with imperial IPA. The terms indicate that the beers are stronger and hoppier than typical IPAs. Dogfish Head was the first craft brewery to brew, package, and distribute an imperial IPA coast to coast with our 90 Minute IPA, but 90 Minute fits more into the West Coast style of IPA, in that it's clear in color, it's filtered, and it has lots of bittering hops and aromatic hops. Compared to Perfect Disguise, 90 Minute has more of those earthy, leafy, herbaceous hops whereas Perfect Disguise is more of a New England-y style, tropical, hazy double IPA.

Artist Dan Stiles works on new art series label.

Illustration by Michael Hacker

Hazy-O! (7.1% ABV)

Hellooooo Hazy-O! Our latest off-centered innovation is now available coast to coast! Hazy-O! not only continues the legacy we've built for pioneering beers, brewed with high-quality culinary ingredients, but it also highlights the magic found at the intersection of two unexpectedly complementary trends: hazy IPAs, THE fastest growing beer style in America, and plant-based milks. Oat milk, specifically, is really having a zeitgeist moment, skyrocketing more than 220 percent in 2020 alone. After watching oat milk explode in coffee culture and chatting with some hardcore baristas about its ultra-creamy attributes, I got a crazy idea: oat milk would be the perfect ingredient upon which we could build a world-class hazy IPA recipe. Then, the experimenting began.

As the first ever nationally distributed oat milk–centric IPA, Hazy-O! took almost a year of R&D to perfect. To ensure we harnessed all the goodness of oat milk we called our friends and oat-milk scientists (yes, they exist) at Elmhurst 1925—a family owned, plant-based milk producer out of New York. Using Elmhurst's culinary prowess and its unsweetened Milked Oats, we finalized the recipe for Hazy-O! after more than a year of trials. At the end of the process, we were able to harness all the goodness of oat milk made with only three simple ingredients—oats, water, and a bit of salt.

The beer is brewed with truckloads of oats and wheat for a full body. We use four types of oats—yes, four!

Each does something a little different for your sipping experience ... malted oats for a delicate malty sweetness; rolled oats for a dense haze; naked oats for a subtle toasty and caramel character; and the pièce de résistance, real star, and our secret ingredient: oat milk, for a silky soft, creamy mouthfeel. Hazy-O! is then liberally dry-hopped to deliver juicy tropical notes of citrus, mango, and pineapple! But the ... oats!

You might be thinking, "Why so many oats?"

This beer drinks like a 5 percent ABV session sipper, even though it's a 7.1 percent ABV powerhouse. The foundation-of-four oats format is on point in the brewing process, allowing the beer's bright and juicy hops to hit the flavorful bull's-eye.

Playful and palate-pleasing, you'll find Hazy-O! in maroon and gold cans that feature intricate and storyful artwork with hand-drawn hops and wheat, the "Hazy-O!" sun setting over the water, and a four-ringed bullseye to represent the four oat varieties used in the brewing process.

It's been a labor of love to bring this one to life, but one sip and you'll find yourself saying, "Ooohhhh, that's good!"

OAT
HaZy-O!
1 2 3 4
HAZY IPA
ALE | 12 FL. OZ. | 7.1% ALC. BY VOL.

Lemon Quest

(Less than 0.5% ABV)

Today's craft beer drinkers, especially younger consumers, are actively seeking lighter, low, or no-alcohol options that are also lower in calories, but they aren't willing to sacrifice flavor. They want to "Have their beer and drink it too." Seeing this shift in drinkers' preferences, as well as watching the growth of the non-alc category, we developed the portfolio of active lifestyle offerings, which includes SeaQuench, Slightly Mighty, Namaste, Hazy-O! and now, our first-ever non-alcoholic offering, Lemon Quest. But no booze doesn't mean no taste! We have always been dedicated to creating flavorful products with high-quality culinary ingredients, and that includes Lemon Quest.

Lemon Quest is a fruited wheat brew with real lemon puree, blueberry juice, acai berries, monk fruit, sea salt, and special, polyphenol-rich Hopsteiner Hop Pellets™. The result is a refreshing drink with invigorating flavors of bright-citrusy lemon, slightly sweet berries, and just a bit of salt for a deliciously thirst-quenching, non-alcoholic alternative. Its active lifestyle-centric ingredients,

refreshing taste profile, and low calorie count (just 90 calories per can), make it the perfect pairing for any outdoor adventure ... and that's why we teamed up with our longtime pals at The Nature Conservancy (TNC), one of the world's leading environmental nonprofits, to celebrate the product launch.

In celebration of Lemon Quest's launch, we contributed more than $50,000 to TNC to support all the awesome work they do. We also feature TNC's logo on all our Lemon Quest packaging to help raise awareness for the organization and its initiatives.

Dogfish Head's relationship with TNC dates back to 2007, and since then we have contributed more than $1 million to the organization's Delaware chapter. For us, a partnership with The Nature Conservancy fits perfectly into our brand ethos. They work to protect and preserve the waters and land on which all life depends. Without the bounties of Mother Nature, the lands upon which our high-quality culinary ingredients are grown and where our coworkers go to play and find creative inspiration, our off-centered libations—including Lemon Quest—would not exist.

Canned Cocktails

The birth of the canned cocktail is all about quality and convenience. At Dogfish, our primary business, beer, is a product that people enjoy immediately straight out of the can. The limiting factor with cocktails is they are far less convenient. You need juices, you need equipment, you need mixers and so on. There's always been this tension and opportunity. We've been making cocktails and serving them but people can never take them home like the beer. You can get growler beers, cases of beer, bottles of beer, and kegs of beer. But what about the cocktails?! There was always this gap, which we started to close initially in 2017 with the introduction of Sonic Archaeology because it was really ready to serve out of the bottle. We were one step closer to home, but not home yet. You still needed a glass and ice! It was time to get home, so we started mixing up recipes we knew we liked. The bar at our Chesapeake & Maine, which earned us a 2017 James Beard nomination for best bar program, is also the proving ground for our canned offerings. As we angled on the canned cocktails, the bartenders at Chesapeake & Maine, the Distillers, and I started vetting ideas. And we vetted them just like we did the beers when we first opened ... right across the bar into the hands of the customer. From there, we leaned back into the amazing infrastructure that helps us make world-class beer. Between the folks enjoying the cocktails, the distillers and Sam making changes, and the quality team, we have all we need to dial in a great final product. The cocktails are really the culmination of twenty years of just constantly pushing the envelope.

The bar at Chesapeake & Maine, which earned us a 2017 James Beard nomination for best bar program, is also the proving ground for our canned offerings.

Our Latest

"Follow your inner moonlight, don't hide the madness."
—*Howl*, Allen Ginsberg

Exploration

We love bringing our brand to life in our retail spaces, which we primarily use as brand-building incubators and consumer-engagement hubs. In addition to our Delaware-based locations we have just opened Dogfish Miami in the Wynwood Arts District of this beautiful waterfront city. We believe this neighborhood and state offer the perfect location for our nautical-themed, East Coast–based brand to establish our southernmost roots—for a bunch of reasons. Florida has one of the most robust, year-round fruit- and vegetable-growing agricultural communities of any state in the country and any region in the world. Dogfish brews the best-selling fruited sour beer in America in SeaQuench Ale—and fruited session sour beers like SeaQuench are the ideal warm-weather drink—so they are perfect for the Miami climate. We will utilize Florida's broad array of local fresh fruits throughout the year in our brewing program in Miami and fresh vegetables in the seasonally rotating menu of small-plate food items available from our onsite kitchen.

Since Wynwood is the art district of Miami, and we love designing our beer labels and spaces with as much artful passion as we do our beer recipes, we will be creating a lot of beautiful off-centered mural art and can art designs, inspired by and in collaboration with local Miami artists. We have also designed a super-refreshing unique beer-cocktail hybrid we will make fresh onsite called MojitAle, which is a blend of light, refreshing wheat beer, predistilled rum, lime juice, fresh crushed mint, and fresh juiced sugar cane.

Dogfish Head
miami

Seth Limanek

Brewing Supervisor/Manager
Start Date: 2011

In the year 2011, Dogfish Head brewed 145,000 barrels. In 2011, Seth was at a company that brewed that in a week. Seth came to Dogfish Head from a background of big beer and a very structured brewing world for most of his life. It seemed odd to him to be throwing large chunks of bread into the mash tun, something that would have never happened in his old life. His wife, Jamie, was even part of the process and traveled to a bakery in Lewes to pick up some emmer farro bread specifically made for this beer: Ta Henket. Ta Henket is brewed with an ancient form of wheat and loaves of hearth-baked bread, and it's flavored with chamomile, doum-palm fruit, and Middle Eastern herbs. To ferment this earthy ancient ale, Sam and his friends traveled to Cairo, set out baited petri dishes, and captured a native Egyptian saccharomyces yeast strain. Looking back, loaves of bread were a pretty boring ingredient compared to all the outlandish items Seth has introduced into the beer-making process since he started at Dogfish Head. In his past life working for big beer, Seth spent two years in a quality lab as a production supervisor. Dogfish Head had been on his radar, and when his good friend and mentor Tim Hawn came over, Seth was soon to follow. Damn, we are sure glad he did. When Tim applied, Seth was his reference. When Seth applied, Tim was his reference. While this circular reference will not work in Excel, it does in some HR worlds. Yes ... we just made an Excel joke. Seth gets full marks on that one.

Thumbs up for Dogfish Head

The ASVAB test told Seth in the '90s that he should be a chemical engineer. The first full beer Seth had was after sneaking some Rolling Rocks from his buddy's father. He attended the University of Massachusetts, Lowell, which had a nuclear reactor on campus, a killer chemical engineering program, and some seriously zany professors. The homebrew scene emerged, and Seth got into it. He and his buddy had this wacky idea of opening a brewpub. In 2005, he packed up and left the eastern time zone for the first time in his life to attend UC Davis's brewing school. From there, he jumped into big beer, until eventually he found his way to Milton, Delaware.

With an old, tattered Boston Red Sox hat on his head, a Bad Religion T-shirt, an aggressive pair of prescription safety glasses, a dry sense of humor, and Excel jokes to boot, Seth thrives at Dogfish Head and helps push us to new heights. This pessimist-realist knows his stuff, and can problem solve with the best of them. During his time at Dogfish Head, he's built systems and teams from scratch.

Coworker Profile

Seth will not allow people to play favorites, and when having to pick out his all-time favorite Dogfish Head beer he says, "I love all my children." Well, we all know that all parents' love is unconditional, but ... even parents play favorites sometimes. Noble Rot and Urkontinent stand out for Seth. He still has some of the original brew sheets from these beers and the adjustments he made to dial them in. The more complex the beer, the more complex the data and variables. Seth and the whole brewing team in Milton are on point and don't miss a thing.

Beer for Breakfast is another child he is particularly fond of. He recalls going back and forth on the recipe to get it just right. Adjusting mash parameters was the cypher to get it right. Seth puts everything he has into dialing in the production beers, and this type of dedication is emulated all over the brewhouse.

As for the "child" that Seth would like to send off to summer camp forever, he doesn't miss a beat: "Rosabi." Sorry, Julianna Barwick. Seth loved your piece in the show *Room 104*, but the beer is still on his send-to-summer-camp-then-boarding-school list. Pretty much any brewer who ended up being involved in the making of this beer has echoed Seth's sentiments. For this beer, we used real, fresh wasabi. Seth recalls the brewers kept macing themselves when dealing with the wasabi, so they ended up having to use respirators to make this beer happen.

"Choc Lobster" is another one Seth doesn't reflect too fondly upon. Perhaps it was all his time working in seafood at a Whole Foods in New England before he got into brewing that put the bad taste in his mouth. He had killed copious amounts of lobsters and thought he had left it behind, but this beer triggered some flashbacks. The cocoa shells in the fermenters were another issue altogether. We had a good plan to get them in but getting them out was a whole other story. Seth found it at a bar in Pennsylvania after it hit the streets, and there was a bit of an ammonia smell that wafted off the glass.

When we build something from nothing, be it a beer or a brewhouse or a cellar, there are pitfalls along the way. This is the nature of the beast, and these are the moments that stand out for Seth. For him, the hard days are the best days. Moments like installing a new hot water system, with it not working properly and there being a tight timeline on it—having to adjust flow rates and building systems with consistency across the board. He lives for the days when there is a problem to solve like commissioning Brewhouse 2, our 200-barrel system. A day of getting hundreds of pounds of pine needles into a whirlpool. A day with the well pump dying in the middle of making Pennsylvania Tuxedo. Seth and Dan Weber, another brewing Jedi at Dogfish Head who oversees all our R&D in Milton, figured out a way to make hot water cold by using a glycol system and thus saved an entire run of Pennsylvania Tuxedo. Days of installing maturation cellars and adapting our processes to be more efficient. Days when it seems like the wheels are coming off and the brewing team doesn't quit until they figure it out are always the best for him. He lives for eureka moments. While many people work to avoid problems, his determination to stay in it and figure it out is a lesson for all of us. The hard days are when we become better at everything we do.

If you were on a deserted island and could have one album to listen to and an unlimited supply of one beer, what would it be?

Beer: SeaQuench Ale
Album: The Rolling Stones, *Exile on Main Street*

CJ Novack

Divisional Analyst
Start Date: 2017

Cindy Novack

Supplier Quality Professional
Start Date: 2016–2019

The Novacks have been rabid Dogfish Head fans since 2008. In those 11 years, they have visited the brewery and pub countless times, ran in three Dogfish Dashes (2010, 2012, and 2015), and attended any Dogfish events in Milton that they could. In 2015, Siege applied for an IT job at Dogfish. No callback and that was the end of it.

When 2016 rolled around, Cindy texted Siege with a screenshot of a job opening for a Production Buyer at the Milton Brewery. Three months of telephone and onsite interviews ensued, and Cindy was offered the job. In February 2017, they relocated to Milton, DE. Siege still needed work, though, and the rural nature of Coastal Delaware did not really lend itself to his prior career of 19 years. Cindy mentioned that Dogfish was hiring for Seasonal Packaging Coworkers, so he had some conversations, applied, and landed a seasonal job.

Siege and Cindy at the Inn

No longer fans, Dogfish Dashers, and Inn guests. They were in. They were coworkers. Siege worked as a Seasonal Packaging Operator from April until August 2017 when he was hired on as a full-time coworker. He went from a Seasonal Packaging Operator—primarily doing sanitation work and stacking cases—to a Packaging Technician running the bottle and can lines. In late September 2018, he interviewed and was hired as Inventory Coordinator.

These two have a long-standing love of the company. It is no surprise that our "Off-Centered Ales for Off-Centered People" slogan resonates with them. With a Stiff Little Fingers T-shirt and tattoo ink to match, these two get it. The evolution of Dogfish Head is not just the evolution of the company but the evolution of our people. Cindy and Siege are part of it. They knew Dogfish from its formative years in Rehoboth to its current merging of powers with the Boston Beer Company. The Shark and Shield continues to foster a feeling of pride for both of them.

Siege has had many beers in his time as a craft beer hunter. To this day, Squall IPA stands out to him as one of his DFH favorites, but 60 Minute was undeniably his entry point. However, Squall kicked off an insatiable thirst for what Dogfish could come up with next. Cindy has a taste for Punkin, a beer that Sam made in '94 and had its own following before we opened in '95.

When asked, "Are there any bad beers from Dogfish Head?" Cindy and Siege have some thoughts. "We have had people ask us this question of both Dogfish and other beers, and we honestly find it impossible to answer. Aside from a serious aversion to anything big beer, we cannot name a beer that we would call a 'total fail.' If at least one person in the world enjoys the beer, it cannot be deemed a total failure. So, we respectfully decline to name a Dogfish Head beer that stands out as a total fail. Granted, we have heard stories of Black and Red—but we never had it."

Good Dogfish Head memories are in strong supply with Siege and Cindy. Siege and

Coworker Profile

Cindy both lived by our Rules of Thumb and in particular, "Constructive Ideas and Solutions, Bring 'Em On!" Siege would daydream about different ideas and concepts that could fit into the craft beer world—particularly when it came to Dogfish Head. He was never shy about sending unsolicited ideas directly to Sam, and one of those ideas took off ... quickly. Sam reached out to the whole company about Siege's idea on March 30, 2018, at 1:05 pm:

Hello y'all and happy Friday. Today, we are announcing to the beer trade media and our distributors all the deets about our supercool, mixed 12-pack cooler coming out in time for summer that includes three cans each of 60, LUPU, NAMASTE, and SeaQuench and also includes a Koozie and the chance to win a trip to our brewery, and holy crap, the thing converts into a functional cooler you can add ice to! I want to give mad shouts to CJ Novack in Packaging who first shared his idea with me on January 12th for a tropical-leaning, mixed summertime pack that would double as an ice cooler. Here's a quote from CJ's email:

"With us putting Lupu Luau into cans, I was wondering if it would be feasible to have a mix 12 pack of Lupu Luau and SeaQuench. The tasting room had already come up with the blend of the two, calling it 'Lime in a Coconut.' I feel that this could be elevated from just a tasting room blend to a Summer time mix 12 pack of the same name." (Cool name for this blend, Tasting Room team!)

Hells yeah, CJ—we can make this happen—CONSTRUCTIVE IDEAS AND SOLUTIONS ... BRING 'EM ON!!! A few days after CJ first shared this idea, Justin Brunda, Mike Kompare, and I were chatting whilst drinking SeaQuench 19.2s at 70 MPH barreling up Route 1 on the way to a hockey tournament with Ryan and Corey riding shotgun ... hold up ... NONE OF US WERE DRIVING—Lars was driving and we were watching the movie Slapshot and drinking and chatting about this potential package. (Interesting fact—it is perfectly legal to be a passenger in a moving vehicle whilst drinking a beer in Delaware.) As we talked about this 12-pack concept, Mike and Justin chatted through production and considerations and we discussed the potential to add a Koozie into the mix. We looped in Cindy Novack and Brian Hollinger and we started exploring this idea in earnest. From there the idea blossomed and coworkers in sales, design, accounting, legal, marketing, merch, production et al added to the process and ...

Oh My GOSH ... We brought this puppy from CJ's initial idea to a finished product we planned, costed-out, forecasted orders for, designed, announced, and showed final artwork for in EXACTLY 79 DAYS!!!!!

To quote Morris Day and The Time ... "The Wright Brothers can't fuck with that."

Hope you guys are as proud of this massive communal achievement as I am ... STOP, COLLABORATE, AND LISTEN ... COMMUNICATE THOUGHTFULLY IN ALL DIRECTIONS ... TOGETHER WE ARE HEAVY!!! This project embodies pretty much everything I love about our creative, fearless culture. We are off-centered goodness for off-centered people. Here is the first major beer industry story to break the news of our cooler pack, which was just published a few minutes ago.

Namaste. Sam

(continued)

Coworker Profile
(continued)

CJ and Cindy Novack

If you were on a deserted island and could have one album to listen to and an unlimited supply of one beer, what would it be?

Beer: Liquid Truth Serum
Album: GBH, *City Baby Attacked by Rats*

CJ shows Sam and other coworkers how he earned his Eagle Scout "Dancing Badge" at an end-of-year Hootenanny.

At Dogfish Head, ideas come from everywhere. Siege knows this and offers up his thoughts freely. Oftentimes, when ideas don't stick, people stop sharing. This is not the case at DFH. This helps us be who we are. Everyone is invested in our success. Everyone is part of it.

Opportunity knocks, though, and on a difficult day, Cindy accepted a job in Maine and informed management of her ensuing departure. Siege reflects, "We had never worked as coworkers in the same company before, and for 2+ years we had done just that. It was hard to see that time come to an end. Even more so, because I thought that my time with Dogfish had expired. Imagine my surprise when I was told that I would be able to carry on as a coworker working remotely from Portland, Maine. While this was the most difficult day, I have to say that finding out that Dogfish was as invested in me as I was in Dogfish was an amazing personal revelation."

Siege and Cindy are currently in Maine and they are in constant contact. It is fitting that they landed in the state where our name comes from. While many companies would have seen this as a departure point, for us at DFH it was an opportunity to go deeper. Cindy doesn't officially work for Dogfish anymore, but she will always be a coworker to anyone at Dogfish Head. There is no leaving. These two know that the liquid is just the beginning. It is the experiences and the relationships built while sharing the liquid that is the real heart of a our community and culture at Dogfish Head.

A Fan's Perspective On 26 Years

My love affair with Dogfish Head started at an unlikely time. In an unlikely place. Which I suppose is very off-centered.

It was 1984. More than ten years before Dogfish was founded. Sam was in high school making trouble. And so was I. Something tells me that many of us who were attracted to craft beer—before it was trendy—were troublemakers. We enjoyed thumbing our noses at tradition. For Sam, that meant "giving the middle finger" to the Reinheitsgebot—the Bavarian Beer Purity Law of 1516.

But let's go back to high school for a moment. Ninth grade. English class. We read Ralph Waldo Emerson's essay "Self-Reliance." 1984 might have been the symbol of an Orwellian dystopia, but for me—with all the wisdom of a 14-year-old—it was the start of my journey to a life of principle and authenticity. That essay changed my life. And put me on a course that would intersect with Dogfish more than 15 years later.

It's hard to fully understand Dogfish without understanding the ideas conveyed in that essay. You'll find them all over Dogfish. Literally. They're on the wall outside the brewery in Milton and above the pizza kitchen in the brewpub.

> Whoso would be a man must be a nonconformist. He who would gather immortal palms must not be hindered by the name of goodness, but must explore if it be goodness. Nothing is at last sacred but the integrity of your own mind.
>
> **—Emerson**

If you don't have the time or inclination to read the essay, you can get pretty far with that one quote. Emerson is telling us that what makes us human is our soul. Our creative spirit. Our drive to explore. Our yearning to make a mark on the world. He's telling us that we shouldn't take, on faith, someone else's point of view about what "good" is. That we have to use our own mind, our own judgment, our own soul to determine what good means for us. Basically, he's telling us that it's fucking crazy to limit how you express yourself to what some dude thought was good more than 500 years ago (before they'd even discovered yeast!).

As soon as I could legally drink—yes, not one minute before—I was drawn to beer. I had a German phase. Then an English phase. Then Belgian. And then I discovered American craft beer.

Dogfish quickly became my favorite brewery. I loved the beer. I loved the stories. And I loved the fearlessness.

Nobody was doing the crazy shit they were doing. We take that for granted now—in no small part because of Sam's restless creativity and pioneering spirit. Back then, putting apricots in beer was laughable—until Dogfish launched Aprihop. Back then, a sour beer? Gross! But Dogfish launched Festina Pêche—and then had to take a bunch of it back because drinkers and retailers thought it had just gone bad.

At some point in my craft-beer journey, circa 2008, I saw an article in *The New Yorker* about Sam and Dogfish Head. The article mentioned that Dogfish had a quote from Emerson's essay emblazoned on the wall of their brewery.

Cue the romantic sound effects. The thunderclap. The blaze of lightning. All right, you get the point.

At that moment, the article I read as a teenage boy, the one that had guided me throughout my life (and still does), collided with another driving passion of my life: craft beer. This was my "you had me at hello" moment.

> Do not go where the path may lead, go instead where there is no path and leave a trail.
>
> **—Emerson**

Today, there are more than 7,000 breweries in the United States. If you want a fantastic craft beer, you don't have to look hard. You can find them in bottle shops, liquor stores, supermarkets, drug stores. Even at gas stations on highway rest stops!

It's easy to find great craft beer today.

And it would be easy for me to satisfy my desire for great beer without ever drinking Dogfish Head. But I never would.

Long ago, I fell in love with Dogfish Head. Not merely with their products, but with their brand: what they stand for. Products come and go. They are easily copied by competitors; but ideas, values, and character are harder to replicate. As someone who believes that human life, values, character, and soul matter—when I find someone taking a stand for the human spirit, I am going to stand with them.

I'm not just an Emerson fan and an aficionado of indie craft beer. I'm also a marketer. I've spent years helping some of the world's best-known brands—and some that are a bit more niche—identify, tell, and live their unique story. I love Dogfish Head as a human, and I profoundly respect them as a marketer.

Over the years, I've learned that brands are ideas. Great brands share their idea in the spirit of generosity—without elitism or judgment. They're happy to include anyone; but they aren't going to compromise what they stand for to win a popularity contest or make another buck. They live their idea purely and powerfully in everything they do—knowing that some will find it attractive and some will think it's crazy. Great brands understand that success depends on amazing some people, not simply pleasing everyone.

You don't get there through traditional marketing. Certainly not from focus groups or market research. Great brands start from a place of passion and deep conviction. Great brands come from the heart. You can't make this shit up just because you read a trend report. Dogfish is teenage Sam getting kicked out of prep school. It's who he was after college, homebrewing on the side while trying to make a go of a creative-writing career. And it's who he, Mariah, and every one of the hundreds of Dogfish coworkers are today.

Dogfish Head makes great beer, spirits, and food. They've got a fantastic inn. But Dogfish is so much more than that.

Which is why even with 7,000 breweries in the U.S., Dogfish Head stands out. It's not just what they sell, it's what they represent.

Dogfish Head is a testament to—and a beacon for—the human spirit.

We need that now more than ever. Big corporations in their drive to grow have made everything they do about scale. About the lowest common denominator. It's about what can appeal to a mass audience and how they can make it as cheaply as possible. They've pushed aside the human drive to explore, to experiment, to create. They've lost what it means to take pride in a craft. To care about a community. They've made it all about numbers and machines.

Dogfish Head, on the other hand, is about brewing beer with wood from a tree in Paraguay that can only be cut down with diamond-tipped blades because it's bulletproof! It's about a brewing technique that involves boiling rocks (hoping they don't explode), and tossing them into a kettle to caramelize the mash. It's about brewing a beer during the Iraq war, with an ingredient from every continent—a beer, as Sam put it, "that brings a fractured world together."

Can you imagine those beers getting made by a corporation with an army of lawyers requiring everyone to sign a waiver in case one of those rocks did explode—or with the finance team questioning why the hell they need bulletproof Paraguayan wood or water from Antarctica?

The ingredients in our recipes come
From the earth and the oven.
They come from interfering
And letting be.

We use organic and natural
Ingredients wherever possible
And our recipes are
Blissfully inefficient ...

For us, brewing is not a process
Of automation,
But of imagination and passion ...

We wrap our hands around our work
Because we are proud to make
Something with our own hands ...

(the bottom of a Dogfish four-pack)

"Blissfully inefficient!"

This isn't the sort of corporate blather you read on most product packaging. It's not a slogan or a tagline. It's an ode to human creativity: a love poem to art and possibility.

As a society, we need an antidote to mass corporatization. We need a reminder that there's much more to being human than numbers. That's what Dogfish is about.

I stay at the Dogfish Inn a lot. I've been going to their signature event, the Weekend of Compelling Ales & Whatnot, for eight years in a row. This year will be my ninth. I organize my schedule around it because that weekend is sacrosanct for me. Eight years ago we met a couple there while waiting in line for the bathroom. In no universe would you ever imagine we'd become friends with this couple. We live hours away from them, come from entirely different backgrounds and, on the surface, have little in common. Today, they are among our dearest friends; a few months ago, we were honored to have Charles and Melissa at our wedding. They came with Nate and Sherri—another couple we met through them at the same Dogfish event the next year. That's what a great brand does—it brings together a community of people who are different on the surface but the same in their souls.

To the frequent amusement of my kids and coworkers, half my wardrobe is comprised of Dogfish T-shirts. I have far too many Dogfish glasses and a collection of Dogfish beer that would be the envy of many a bottle shop. I took my three kids and my brother to Dogfish for my bachelor "non-party" and then went back a few weeks later for a brief honeymoon with my wife. Dogfish helped us design a custom cocktail for our wedding. They called it "Happily Ever After Lavender Lemonade"; we called it "Wedded Bliss."

Yeah. I know. I'm crazy. But here's the thing. I'm crazy about Dogfish Head, but I don't feel that way about any other brand. It's not the T-shirts, the beer glasses, or even the beer. It's the idea they stand for. And it's their people.

It's about showing up to the Extreme Beer Fest that Dogfish sponsors and getting a huge smile and big hug from Trish.

When I go to the Dogfish Inn, I'm not just excited about the new beers I'll try. Or about the Re-Indulgence burger. (But seriously, you have got to try that burger!) I'm excited that I'll get to see Jean when I check in. We'll talk about how my wife, Josette, and I are doing. She'll want to hear about the kids. We'll talk about how she's been doing and her vacation plans. I'm excited that I'll run into Andrew and we'll talk about ... whatever. Beer, life, what he did with that awesome beard.

I love heading to the tasting room in Milton and seeing Matt. If I'm lucky, I'll bump into James who can give me a heads-up about something new that's coming out of the distillery. Or I'll see Lars and ask him about his latest cocktail invention. Sometimes George will be around and we'll talk about life and love.

And once in a while, Sam will walk by. He'll be rushing to a meeting but will make the time to stop and say hi, buy me a beer, and high-five all the fans that came from far away to experience what makes Dogfish unique.

These people are the Dogfish brand. They are off-centered goodness. They came together not just to build a business. They came together from a place of passion and a belief that people, their humanity, their creativity, their differences, their dreams, their loves, their quirks, and their imagination—matter. They came together to declare that the human spirit is worth being lived, worth being loved, and worth being celebrated.

Happy anniversary Dogfish! Thanks for the great beers, the great times, and more than 25 years of non-conformity.

Here's to many more off-centered years.

—**Adam Schorr,** Founder of Rule No. 1
Rule No. 1 is a consultancy that helps organizations uncover their purpose and bring it to life in their culture and in the world.

Head

Dogfish Head

Cheers to the Next 26!

"Stories are for joining the past to the future. Stories are for those late hours in the night when you can't remember how you got from where you were to where you are. Stories are for eternity, when memory is erased, when there is nothing to remember except the story."

—Tim O'Brien, *The Things They Carried*, from the City Lights Library at the Dogfish Inn

With all the stories we have covered in this book, stories of the recipes we love to make; stories lived and told by us and our coworkers; it's astonishing to think of the multitude that didn't make it into these pages. The (Dog) fishes that got away: at least in the context of what we did and didn't capture within these pages. We hear them every day in our kitchens, across the bar, in the cottage at the Inn, and in the seats surrounding our tree house in Milton. We hear them on our packaging line and in the brewhouses from Milton to Miami. We make and share and live new stories, in concert with the customers and communities that sustain us every day. While they may not have all been captured on these pages, they live on every time they are told, so please keep sharing them over pints and in good company. They are the fabric from which we have collectively woven together this off-centered story.

Thanks to you: the readers, fans, coworkers, and supporters of Dogfish Head for being central participants in this amazing journey that we are continuing to construct and articulate today and into the future. As we venture forward on the next stretch of our exploratory path, we will keep daring to push the envelope in all we do and defy the status quo, because that is part of our DNA. Since 1995, it is what has always motivated us in our art with everything we put out there, from our liquids to brewpubs, restaurants, inns, and beyond. It is an unwritten future for all of us and that unknown drives us not only to hone our craft on all fronts but also to go beyond where we are today. Who knows what the next year may hold, much less the next 26+ years, but we do know that boundaries set before us are the ones we will incessantly keep pushing, redefining, and smashing as we go. Keep supporting independent craft breweries, distillers, artists, and creators of all stripes and sizes. Don't be satisfied. Be daring and dare us on. We wrote our past together and every day we begin a new chapter in the story of Dogfish Head. We start NOW.

Cheers!
Andrew, Mariah, and Sam

Index